Cataloger's Judgment

Cataloger's Judgment

Music Cataloging Questions and Answers from the Music OCLC Users Group Newsletter

JAY WEITZ

ARRANGED AND EDITED BY MATTHEW SHEEHY

WITH A FOREWORD BY H. STEPHEN WRIGHT

A Member of the Greenwood Publishing Group

Westport, Connecticut • London

Library of Congress Cataloging-in-Publication Data

Weitz, Jay, 1953–
    Cataloger's judgment : music cataloging questions and answers from the
  Music OCLC Users Group newsletter / Jay Weitz ; arranged and edited by
  Matthew Sheehy ; with a foreword by H. Stephen Wright.
      p. cm.
    Includes bibliographical references (p.) and index.
    ISBN 1–59158–052–8 (alk. paper)
    1. Cataloging of music.   2. Cataloging of sound recordings.   I. Sheehy, Matthew.
  II. Newsletter (Music OCLC Users Group)   III. Title.
  ML111.W34   2004
  025.3′48—dc22   2003058907

British Library Cataloguing in Publication Data is available.

Library of Congress Catalog Card Number: 2003058907
ISBN: 1–59158–052–8

First published in 2004

Libraries Unlimited, Inc., 88 Post Road West, Westport, CT 06881
A Member of the Greenwood Publishing Group
www.lu.com

Printed in the United States of America

The paper used in this book complies with the
Permanent Paper Standard issued by the National
Information Standards Organization (Z39.48–1984).

10 9 8 7 6 5 4 3 2 1

AUTHOR'S DEDICATION

This book is for all of the catalogers over the years who have challenged me with their questions and trusted my answers, in spite of my human fallibility. It is especially for H. Stephen Wright, who was this collection's main champion. And as always, it's for Esther.

EDITOR'S DEDICATION

I would like to dedicate my effort to my wife Rebecca Sheehy, who supported me through the late nights, and even gave birth to my third child, Owen Sheehy, one month before the deadline for this project. I would like to thank Owen for being such a great baby, and my daughters Frances and Ana who helped their mother with their new brother while I worked on the final stages of this project.

Contents

Foreword

When I embarked on my music library career almost 20 years ago by enrolling in Indiana University's School of Library and Information Science, I did not initially imagine myself becoming a cataloger. Of course, as the greenest of recruits I admittedly had amorphous notions of what librarians did, but cataloging certainly wasn't on my personal radar screen. It was only after mentors and colleagues apprised me of the realities of music librarianship and the dearth of job opportunities for music librarians without cataloging skills that I chose to begin my career by identifying myself as a music cataloger. Nevertheless, I did not feel particularly comfortable at first with this newly acquired professional persona. You see, there was something frightening that towered in my path, and that something was *Anglo-American Cataloging Rules*, second edition. In its power to awe and intimidate, it loomed like a slightly wider, burnt-orange version of the mysterious monolith from *2001: A Space Odyssey*.

A friend who was a couple of semesters ahead of me in the program assured me that I'd want to buy a copy of AACR2, and I dutifully did so. Leafing through it before starting my first cataloging course, I was instantly overwhelmed. The sheer quantity of the rules was dumbfounding, and they seemed to be written in a peculiar, almost Borgesian dialect, with familiar words and phrases like "title," "place of publication," and "edition" mixed with weirdly grandiose phrases like "statements of responsibility" and "title proper." At first I couldn't comprehend why so *many* rules were needed; then I slowly realized that the rules were supposed to cover every possible cataloging situation—an insight that made me wonder how catalogers got *anything* done. The rules formed an impenetrable, generalized thicket; each rule was presented with exactly the same emphasis, with no indication of which ones were important and which were rarely used.

To make matters worse, I had purchased a *used* copy from a classmate. How I envied the students who had bought pristine, untouched copies of AACR2 from the campus bookstore; they could bask in the transitory fantasy that cataloging rules were something historically static, like the Bible or the Rosetta stone. My copy contained dozens of odd little handwritten emendations and taped-in bits of photocopied information; I was distressed to learn that these were *revisions*—revisions of rules published only a few years earlier! I could understand the need to correct misspellings and other errata, but these revisions didn't seem to do that; they seemed willful and wholly arbitrary, as if some capricious god didn't like the idea of catalogers growing too complacent.

Fortunately, under the tutelage of my cataloging mentors at Indiana, particularly Ralph Papakhian and Sue Stancu, I slowly learned to navigate these rules—as well as the equally baffling MARC format. As I originally suspected, some rules were absolutely critical in music cataloging and others were far less essential. I also learned, to my delight, that there was a stylistic component to what catalogers did; although AACR2 presented a bland menu of equivalent options, I found that there were paths that skilled catalogers favored and artful turns of phrase that novices such as myself sought to emulate.

When I began my first professional music cataloging position, I soon discovered that more surprises awaited me despite my thorough training. I was continually encountering perplexing and confounding situations that defied the cold logic of AACR2: multiple dates that seemed impossible to reconcile, variant titles that contradicted each other, and bizarre terms like "duophonic." In those pre-Internet, pre-electronic mail days, I struggled alone with these oddities, devising my own sometimes-awkward solutions. Eventually, though, I discovered a font of astonishingly useful and practical information: Jay Weitz's "Questions and Answers" column in the *Music OCLC Users Group Newsletter*. Normally I pride myself on scrupulous avoidance of clichés, but this column was, quite simply, a gold mine.

The innocuous title of Jay's column belied its remarkable utility and accessibility. The premise of the column was simplicity itself: Ordinary, working-stiff catalogers such as myself sent their music cataloging and tagging problems to Jay . . . and he answered them. He responded not in the stilted, officious voice of AACR2 or Library of Congress rule interpretations, but in a friendly, casual tone that suggested that he was *one of us*. Furthermore, Jay's explanations were models of succinctness and clarity; there was never any trace of ambiguity in Jay's tone, even when the problems people submitted to him were profoundly ambiguous (which was frequently the case).

Not too many years later, as music librarian at Northern Illinois University, I found myself teaching a series of music tagging workshops offered through the Illinois OCLC Users Group. It was in the first of these workshops that I had another epiphany: I discovered that there was a vast, hidden strata of music catalogers who never appeared at the conferences I attended and didn't have the specialized training I had experienced. These were catalogers at suburban public libraries, community colleges, and small private universities who didn't set out to be music catalogers but were given the responsibility of doing it anyway. They were in the same position I had been in years earlier: they couldn't imagine where to begin. In order to help them develop the practical skills they needed, I directed them to Jay's column. I handed out photocopies of some of Jay's most perceptive answers (particularly those dealing with problematic dates of publication) and vigorously encouraged them to subscribe to the *MOUG Newsletter* so that they would have the benefit of Jay's wisdom delivered to them thrice yearly.

Eventually I became chair of the Music OCLC Users Group myself, and one of the goals I pursued during my term was the publication of a compilation of Jay's "Questions and Answers" column. I felt that the cumulative knowledge found in these years of columns would be of incredible value to music catalogers everywhere, and I was tormented by the thought that it would remain forever buried in something as evanescent as a newsletter. We considered publishing a compilation ourselves, but the cost was prohibitive; then we contemplated placing all the columns on a Web site. Alas, these things didn't happen during my term, but I am delighted that the idea outlasted my chairmanship and eventually found a home.

The book you now hold in your hands is a truly amazing resource—one that tackles *real* music cataloging situations, not examples contrived to illustrate rules. If you are a cataloger, keep it close at hand; you'll be consulting it often. And if you're *not* a cataloger, browse through this book anyway and enjoy Jay's effortless lucidity. You may find yourself disabused of the common perception that catalogers are humorless drones who care nothing for the needs of library users. More importantly, though, you'll gain a new appreciation of the problems catalogers face every day, and how they solve them with grace and style.

H. Stephen Wright
Associate Dean for Public Services
Northern Illinois University

Acknowledgments

AUTHOR'S ACKNOWLEDGMENTS

Thanks go first to the dozens, if not hundreds, of catalogers whose questions have formed the basis of the Q&A column and this book. Members of the Music OCLC Users Group, especially those on the MOUG Executive Board over the years, are to be thanked for their continuing encouragement. In particular, I have valued the succession of MOUG Secretary/Newsletter Editors who have kept their eyes on my column since 1989: Linda Barnhart, Karen Little, Sue Weiland, Judy Weidow, Lynn Gullickson, Mickey Koth, and Stephen Luttmann. Again, I must acknowledge H. Stephen Wright's tireless efforts to bring this collection into existence.

All of my many colleagues at OCLC, the Library of Congress, and throughout the library world who have helped me answer these questions and who caught and corrected my mistakes have my sincere appreciation.

Additional thanks to OCLC and to Glenn Patton, in particular, for giving me the opportunity to serve as OCLC liaison to MOUG and for allowing me the time to deal with our users' questions.

To Martin Dillon and Libraries Unlimited, I am indebted for their interest in bringing this compilation to print.

To Matthew Sheehy, thank you for being an eager and accomplished editor.

To my wife, Esther Silverman, my deepest appreciation for valuable editorial advice, patience, and support.

EDITOR'S ACKNOWLEDGMENTS

I would like to thank Dowling College for giving me the time and support to work on this project, and Jean Harden for the confidence in a young cataloger who raised his hand at a MOUG meeting and volunteered to create an index, and, of course, Jay Weitz for his continued support and advice.

Cataloger's Judgment: A Sort of Introduction

A BIT OF HISTORY

Exactly who first suggested that I start a question-and-answer column in the *MOUG Newsletter* is, unfortunately, lost to history—or at least to my memory. Clearly documented in the first of those columns, however, are the time and place of that suggestion—at the joint Music OCLC Users Group/ Music Library Association (MLA) meeting in Cleveland in March 1989. Perhaps it was sheer exhaustion that inspired the idea, because this was the only MOUG meeting in history that followed rather than preceded MLA. MOUG never tried that again.

Although the originator of the idea for the column may be lost, the person responsible for suggesting that those columns be collected and published in some form is easily identifiable. H. Stephen Wright, who was MOUG's continuing education coordinator (1990–1992), vice chair/chair elect (1997–1998), chair (1998–2000), and past chair (2000–2001), was the earliest and most vocal advocate for this collection. With Steve, who possesses one of music librarianship's driest wits, it's not always possible to know how serious he might be. When he talked about wanting such a collection at least partly for its entertainment value, I knew he wasn't being entirely serious. But he wasn't entirely kidding, either. Coming from him, that was a humbling and unexpected compliment.

In the late 1990s while he was on the MOUG board, Steve made several inquiries regarding the publication of this collection. Eventually, MOUG decided to self-publish and asked for volunteers to edit, organize, and index. Matthew Sheehy was chosen to work on the text.

Not long thereafter in August 2001, I was in Boston for the International Federation of Library Associations conference. I stopped by the Libraries Unlimited booth at IFLA to talk with my former division director at OCLC,

Martin Dillon. In his semi-retirement, Martin was serving as Libraries Unlimited's acquisitions director and somehow, our conversation wandered to the MOUG Q&A compilation. Martin was interested in having Libraries Unlimited publish the collection.

ORGANIZATION OF THE TEXT

Early in 2002, Matthew and I (to be perfectly honest, mostly Matthew) began to organize my columns, going all the way back to the first, published in *MOUG Newsletter* no. 39 dated May 1989. Back in those ancient days, questions came by phone or letter, in workshops and conference Q&A sessions, or as part of a bibliographic or authority record change request. In the library world, electronic mail was in its infancy, if memory serves, but over the years, that has become the dominant source of such questions.

During the years that MOUG had talked about this compilation, there had been debate over whether it should be comprehensive or selective, arranged topically or chronologically. Matthew and I continued the debate in phone calls, e-mails, and one visit that Matthew made to OCLC. We realized that there was no intuitively obvious logical organizing principle and that no matter what choices we made, there was no pleasing everyone. We finally decided to collect pretty much every Q&A, except for a few stray ones that were hopelessly misinformed. And we decided to arrange things in a roughly topical manner, generally starting from the most recent Q&A within each topic and working back through time. The idea was that the most current treatment of an issue would be first, with historical perspective provided by earlier Q&A, for those who wanted such perspective. We hoped that this would balance the needs of those who wanted a practical tool for answering cataloging questions with those who favored a historical document that would reflect the evolution of music cataloging during a tumultuous period.

As I had suspected, and as Matthew quickly discovered, there were several problems inherent in these attempts at organization. First, so many questions and answers tended to stray defiantly across categories. Second, as anyone who has read my column over any length of time will know, I am an unrepentant plagiarizer of my own work. Not to sound defensive, but there is a legitimate reason for this. Similar questions are asked all the time because the same problems arise all the time. When the answers haven't changed, I have shamelessly stolen text from earlier iterations. When the answers *have* changed because of rule revisions, MARC format changes, new technologies, or the like, I would often use an outdated answer as a springboard to its updating.

In the interest of preserving the historical record, we have minimized our tinkering with questions and answers. You should be aware, however, that as a result, there are countless references to outmoded technology; superseded documentation and page numbers; old forms of headings; dead URLs; bibliographic and authority records that have long since changed; ancient rules; and obsolete practices. You will notice LCCNs with suffixes and revision information that would no longer be included. You will see what we now know as MARC 21 referred to by its old shorthand moniker, USMARC. You will see references to task force reports and official guidelines that were promised but never delivered (a standard for "score order," rules for treating "enhanced" compact discs), the cataloging equivalent of vaporware.

There are a few places where I have added corrective or clarifying notes. And of course, in those cases where an erroneous answer was corrected in a subsequent issue of the *MOUG Newsletter*, the corrections have been situated directly following the error. In one particular instance, that of field 246 and its use for variants of the first title when there is no collective title, my misunderstanding persisted. Rather than perpetuating the error (which continues to plague both bibliographic records and me to this day), I have explained my original mistake in a note, then corrected each answer.

All of this is, in part, a measure of how dynamic our profession of music cataloging really is. In the period covered by these questions and answers, technology changed time and again, CDs swamped vinyl, format integration happened, electronic resources filtered into every aspect of knowledge. The cataloging rules and bibliographic formats struggle to keep up, and we in turn, struggle to keep up with the changes.

"CATALOGER'S JUDGMENT" AS IDEA AND TITLE

When MOUG was discussing the possibility of creating this compilation, the aforementioned Steve Wright came up with the playful title "The Jay Files," a clever play on the title of a then-popular television program. Much more a fan of cleverness than of television, I nonetheless could not countenance such an immodest title. Besides, for a tool of this sort, I felt a descriptive title was more appropriate. As Matthew and I worked on the text, I would reread the Q&A with an eye toward coming upon something catchy. The result was a list of maybe half a dozen awkward ideas.

Then in July 2002, the MOUG executive board met in Chicago. In the course of conversation during our Saturday evening dinner, Stephen Luttmann, the MOUG secretary/newsletter editor at that time, mentioned the familiar phrase "cataloger's judgment." I realized immediately that this was the title I'd been seeking. For a complex of reasons, I've always had a warm spot for the idea. It highlights the notion that cataloging is an art rather than a science. It emphasizes that real-world instances, in spite of our never-ending efforts to codify practices, will always defy those efforts. The world of stuff to catalog is so vast, so slippery, so surprising, that individual judgment will always enter into our decisions. And it suggests that catalogers are not the mindless drudges that many non-catalogers imagine, but instead are thoughtful judges concerning matters of description and access.

Like many of the catalogers I know, I tend to be a bit obsessive and have a great appreciation of the rules that govern our cataloging activities. At the same time, however, I revel in the opportunity to bend those rules, to adapt them to new or unexpected situations. Built into the structure of the rules are so many instances where cataloger's judgment is critical: "if in doubt" contingencies, "if appropriate" qualifiers, places where different options are presented. Cataloger's judgment is the wiggle room, the space between written rule and stubborn reality, where the dictates of AACR2 and MARC 21 intersect with the challenges and joys of cataloging. Likewise, I hope that *Cataloger's Judgment* will fill a need somewhere between the practical and the entertaining. No one is going to mistake this for beach reading, but when you're trying to crack the mystery of cataloging that especially pesky CD, perhaps an answer to your nagging question will also cause you to crack a smile.

Editor's Note

When Jean Harden, the then president of MOUG, was looking for someone to index Jay Weitz's "Questions and Answers" from the *MOUG Newsletter*, I thought it would be an interesting project, and raised my hand. Little did I realize how this project would grow from an online index to an arranged and edited collection. When I began, I was looking forward to doing a little bit of reading and I thought it would be a great way to learn more about the history of cataloging as well as hone my cataloging skills along the way.

The interdependent nature of cataloging often made it difficult to categorize a Q&A into a single topic. Rather than agonizing over topics, breaking Jay's first rule in the process, I decided to place the Q&As into broad categories. The Q&As have been kept in reverse chronological order so the most recent is first, except in cases where one Q&A refers directly to a previous one. I have also added references to questions that are referred to in the text of another Q&A.

The text has been largely unmodified from the original presentations, other than the removal of the names and institutions of those asking the questions and the addition of some transition language. In order to preserve the sense of a dialogue between Jay and others in the profession, initially incomplete answers were left in place, and were immediately followed with the corrections. In some places, these corrections were integrated directly into the text, such as the mini-lesson for title added entries where there were added notes. After each Q&A, there is a reference back to the newsletter in which it originally appeared.

Over the course of this project, I have come to realize that Jay's approach to the Q&As exemplifies all the characteristics of a great cataloger. He listens to the question, and even when he knows the answer, he verifies the answer against documentation just to be sure; he then makes a decision, and after presenting his answer, he is willing to be corrected. When he is unsure of an answer, he simply asks someone who is sure. I did become a better cataloger, not just from reading the answers, but also from learning *how* Jay answered the questions. Of course, the most important thing I learned was Jay's first rule: "Don't agonize."

Acronyms, Abbreviations, and Other Cryptic Designations

Cataloging, like every other profession, has its own vocabulary, one that is peppered with an alphabet soup of acronyms, abbreviations, and other cryptic designations for organizations, ideas, publications, things, and other stuff. This list is intended to identify most of those used in the text. Used in conjunction with the bibliography, it will also help the user of this book understand references to old documents.

AACR1	*Anglo-American Cataloguing Rules*, 1st edition (superseded by AACR2)
AACR2	*Anglo-American Cataloguing Rules*, 2nd edition (usually used interchangeably with AACR2R); see bibliography
AACR2R	*Anglo-American Cataloguing Rules*, 2nd edition, Revised (usually used interchangeably with AACR2); see bibliography
AccM	Accompanying Matter (OCLC fixed field element)
A/D	Audio/Digital
ALA	American Library Association
ALCTS	Association for Library Collections and Technical Services, a division of the American Library Association
ANSCR	Alpha-Numeric System for Classification of Recordings
ANSEL	American National Standard for Extended Latin
ANSI	American National Standards Institute
arr.	Arranged
ARSC	Association for Recorded Sound Collections
ASCII	American Standard Code for Information Interchange
Audn	Target Audience (OCLC fixed field element)

AUTOCAT AUTOmated CATaloging e-mail discussion list

AV   Audio-Visual

BCC   Bibliographic Control Committee of the Music Library Association

BF&S   *Bibliographic Formats and Standards* (OCLC documentation, used interchangeably with BFAS); see bibliography

BFAS   *Bibliographic Formats and Standards* (OCLC documentation, used interchangeably with BF&S); see bibliography

BIBCO   BIBliographic Cooperative, a component of the Program for Cooperative Cataloging

BIS   *Bibliographic Input Standards* (former OCLC documentation; superseded by BF&S)

BLvl   Bibliographic Level (OCLC fixed field element)

BMS   Bibliographic Maintenance Section (former name of OCLC's Quality Control Section)

BWV   Bach-Werk-Verzeichnis, the Johann Sebastian Bach thematic index

CatME   OCLC Cataloging Micro Enhancer for Windows (OCLC software)

CC:DA   Committee on Cataloging: Description and Access of the American Library Association

CD   Compact Disc

CD-ROM   Compact Disc—Read Only Memory

CF   Computer File

CIP   Cataloging In Publication

COM   OCLC Computer Files format

Comp   Form of Composition (OCLC fixed field element)

CONSER   Originally CONservation of SERials Project; since 1986, Cooperative ONline SERials, a component of the Program for Cooperative Cataloging

CPSO   Library of Congress Cataloging Policy and Support Office

CSB   *Cataloging Service Bulletin* (Library of Congress publication); see bibliography

Ctry   Country of Publication, etc. (OCLC fixed field element)

DAT   Digital Audio Tape

DDC   Dewey Decimal Classification

DDR   Duplicate Detection and Resolution, the OCLC automated duplicate merging program

Desc	Descriptive Cataloging Form (OCLC fixed field element)
DIDX	This prefix to certain numbers on sound recordings is some sort of recording industry designation of unknown meaning
DLC	MARC 21 and OCLC symbol for the Library of Congress
DOS	Disc Operating System
DtSt	Type of Date/Publication Status (OCLC fixed field element)
DVD	Digital Video Disc (or Digital Versatile Disc)
EAN	European Article Number (or International Article Number)
ELvl	Encoding Level (OCLC fixed field element)
FF	OCLC Fixed Field
FI	Format Integration
FMus	Format of Music (OCLC fixed field element)
GMD	General Material Designation
HTML	HyperText Markup Language, the language used for the display of Web resources
ILL	Inter-Library Loan
ISBD	International Standard Bibliographic Description
ISBN	International Standard Book Number
ISMN	International Standard Music Number
ISO	International Organization for Standardization
ISRC	International Standard Recording Code
Lang	Language Code (OCLC fixed field element)
LC	Library of Congress
LCCN	Library of Congress Control Number (or Library of Congress Card Number)
LCNAF	Library of Congress Name Authority File
LCRI	*Library of Congress Rule Interpretations* (Library of Congress publication); see bibliography
LCSH	Library of Congress Subject Headings
LP	Long Playing record (vinyl 33 1/3 rpm sound recording)
LTxt	Literary Text for Sound Recordings (OCLC fixed field element)
MARBI	Machine Readable Bibliographic Information Committee of the American Library Association
MARC	Machine Readable Cataloging
MARC 21	*MARC 21 Format for Bibliographic Data* (Library of Congress publication); see bibliography

MCAT	*Music Coding and Tagging* (book by Jay Weitz); see bibliography
MCB	*Music Cataloging Bulletin* (Music Library Association publication); see bibliography
MCD	*Music Cataloging Decisions* (Library of Congress publication); see bibliography
MFBD	*MARC Formats for Bibliographic Data* (superseded by MARC 21)
MIDI	Musical Instrument Digital Interface
MLA	Music Library Association
MOIM	*Music and Sound Recordings Online Manual* (Library of Congress internal document); see bibliography
MOUG	Music OCLC Users Group
MPN	Music Publisher Number
MUMS	Multiple Use MARC System, the former Library of Congress Online Catalog
NACO	Name Authority Cooperative, a component of the Program for Cooperative Cataloging
NAF	Library of Congress Name Authority File
NGDMI	New Grove Dictionary of Musical Instruments
NLM	National Library of Medicine
NMP	NACO Music Project
NOTIS	Northwestern Online Totally Integrated System
NUC	National Union Catalog
OCLC	Online Computer Library Center
ODQCS	Online Data Quality Control Section (former name of OCLC's Quality Control Section)
OLAC	Online Audiovisual Catalogers
OLUC	Online Union Catalog (former designation for OCLC's WorldCat)
OPAC	Online Public Access Catalog
PCC	Program for Cooperative Cataloging
PDF	Portable Document Format, a file format that preserves the fonts, images, graphics, and layout of its source
PRISM	Former designation for OCLC's WorldCat
REC	OCLC Sound Recordings format
RI	*Library of Congress Rule Interpretations* (Library of Congress publication); see bibliography

RISM	Répertoire International des Sources Musicales (International Inventory of Musical Sources)
RLG	Research Libraries Group
RLIN	Research Libraries Information Network
SACO	Subject Authority Cooperative, a component of the Program for Cooperative Cataloging
Schwann	Generically, any one of the many comprehensive catalogs of sound recordings published beginning in 1949 by William Schwann and his successors
SCM	*Subject Cataloging Manual* (Library of Congress publication); see bibliography
SCO	OCLC Scores format
SMD	Specific Material Designation
SOLINET	Southeastern Library Network, Inc.
SPARS	Society of Professional Audio Recording Services
TMat	Type of Material (OCLC fixed field element)
t.p.	Title page
UFBD	*USMARC Format for Bibliographic Data* (superseded by MARC 21)
UKMARC	British Library's former version of the MARC format
UPC	Universal Product Code
URL	Uniform Resource Locator
USMARC	*USMARC Format for Bibliographic Data* (superseded by MARC 21)
u.t.	Uniform title
VHS	Video Home System (video recording format)
VIS	OCLC Visual Materials format
WorldCat	OCLC's online cataloging system and union catalog

CHAPTER 1

When to Input a New Record

INTRODUCTION

One of the great joys of cooperative cataloging is finding exactly the record you need so that you don't have to catalog it yourself. But often, you come across a record that *almost* matches what you've got in hand, save for that nagging little difference. A never-ending source of questions is the issue of when a new record is justified and when it's not. Differences in dates, publishers and distributors, various sorts of numbers, series, titles, edition statements, and the like are considered.

NEW RECORDS

1.1 QUESTION: I am working on original cataloging for a boxed set of Vladimir Horowitz original jacket collection recordings on CD. There are a total of ten discs in this collection which means ten separate contents notes and approximately sixty 700 fields for uniform titles. Am I going to run into any problems if I attempt to enter that many fields in OCLC? Please advise.

Answer: Unfortunately, under current system limitations, you are likely to run up against either record size or field number restrictions. Rest assured that under the future platform to which we are currently planning to move, these restrictions would not be a factor. In the meantime, however, many users get around the system limits in cases such as these by, for instance, breaking up large sets bibliographically (not necessarily physically) into logically divided separate records (for each disc, for instance) joined by "With" notes. That might allow fuller description and analysis of each disc without hitting system limits. *Newsletter 81 (September 2002)*

1.2 QUESTION: I have a good 10–15 scores that have Hal Leonard added in the imprint as distributor of G. Schirmer editions that were first published many years ago. My supervisor wants me to enter new records, because she believes they are new editions. I believe these do not warrant new records, because, everything is the same except Hal Leonard is the distributor, there is a new publisher no. (ex. HL50336900), and New York as place is no longer present. As well, there is no new publishing or printing date. I notice some libraries are putting in new records and guessing a new publication/printing date (see OCLC#18030988 vs. 42219960 or 32418829). Could you provide some guidance on dealing with Hal Leonard as distributor of older imprints? (New or not? or sometimes?)

Answer: Since I don't have your specific item in hand, and since it's also likely that different instances may differ, it is hard to make any generalizations. Usually, a new or different distributor alone does not justify a new record. When there are other significant differences such as the absence of a place of publication where there had previously been one, or the presence of a new publisher number where there had previously been none, a new record may be justified. Under AACR2 1.4F4, 1.4F7, and related rules and LCRIs, you may give or supply a date of distribution when you deem it to be bibliographically significant and not the same as the date of publication. My guess is that this is what many catalogers are doing with the Hal Leonard items, and I think this is probably a legitimate approach in many cases. You *always* have the option of using an existing record when you are in doubt about what to do. *Newsletter 80 (May 2002)*

1.3 QUESTION: This may be a retread, but here goes. When *Bibliographic Formats and Standards* describes circumstances that justify a new bib record, the section on 028 says, "Specific differences in numbering, except for minor variations in completeness, justify a new record." Have you ever issued any opinions on what the nature of these "minor variations" might be? My own guideline would be to heed variants that affect searchability—in particular, added letters or numbers that would change the "mn:" search key. The particular item that triggers this question is an Acanta recording that appears to match OCLC #14584230 except that the OCLC 028 is 40.23543, while my item's label no. is 23 543 in all printed iterations (the number embossed into the vinyl is C-40.23 543, with a hyphenated alphabetical extension for side A and side B). Any guidance you are able/willing to venture is most welcome.

Answer: Your guideline on considering as significant any 028 differences that affect searching is generally sound, up to a point. Certainly, there are many cases where the difference in an alphabetic prefix, for instance, designates a different recording format (CD versus cassette versus LP). One also needs to be aware, as you suggest however, that different music publisher numbers may appear on different parts of the item (disc label, container, container spine, embossed in vinyl, etc.). The "minor variations in completeness" are meant to include the differences that might arise when catalogers don't notice that similar but not identical numbers appear in different places. If you have the first edition of *Music Coding and Tagging* handy, the "Claves" example on p. 70 would be one such instance where a variation that affects indexing does *not* justify a new record.

```
028 00    Cla D 907 $b Claves
028 00    D 907 $b Claves
500       Claves: Cla D 907 (on container: D 907).
```

"Minor variations" would also include those really long numbers that are strung together on, say, the container spine, but get broken into two or more separate numbers on the label. Catalogers can interpret such variations differently (as one long number or multiple separate numbers). It could also cover cases where there are both a set number and individual disc numbers, but catalogers have differed in what they included. LCRI and MCD 6.7B19 also give a few implied hints about what might count and what might not count as significant differences. Remember also that the 028 text in "When to Input a New Record" covers scores, too, where there can be similar variations in plate and publisher numbers. Several years ago, I answered a question (which might not have made it into the Q&A column) about dashed-on numbers in plate numbers, another example of a "minor variation" that doesn't count. The AACR2 definition of "plate number" says that the plate number itself "is sometimes followed by a number corresponding to the number of pages or plates." The implication here that these additional numbers are not to be considered part of the plate number proper was shored up by an old Music Cataloging Decision 5.7B19 (MCB 13:1:4, January 1982) that said this explicitly. Although the specific wording did not make it into AACR2, the current definition still implies the same thing, I believe. Both Richard Smiraglia in *Cataloging Music*, 2nd edition (1986, p. 30; Richard did not carry this over to the 3rd edition, *Describing Music Materials*) and I in MCAT, 1st edition (p. 71; this *has* been carried over to the upcoming 2nd edition) say not to transcribe those dashed-on numbers. In the specific case that you describe, it sounds like these are distinct numbers that would justify separate records. Hope that offers at least a little guidance. *Newsletter 78 (May 2001)*

1.4 QUESTION: Should we consider the following two publisher numbers to match one another?

```
028 02    289 445 185-2 $b Deutsche Grammophon
028 00    445 185-2 $b Deutsche Grammophon
```

In general terms, are there "numeric prefixes" (289 in the first publisher number above) that might be associated with a particular publisher, that some catalogers might record as part of the publisher number and others not? Is absence or presence of such a "numeric prefix" a "minor variation in completeness," not justifying a new record or a "Specific difference in numbering," justifying a new record?

Answer: You may generally consider such differences as these to be "minor variations in completeness." Often these numbers in differing degrees of completeness appear on different parts of an item (disc label, container, container spine, accompanying material, etc.) and the differences escape the cataloger's notice. In cases such as these, a new record is not usually justified, all other things being equal. *Newsletter 78 (May 2001)*

1.5 QUESTION: I'm puzzling over "When to Input a New Record" regarding the 028. My score has "UE 13641" (also an ISMN which I'll add in an 024). I find four likely matches on OCLC, all of which have "UE 13641" in the 028. But all four ALSO have a second 028, with "UE 7028." This second number is nowhere on my item. "When to Input . . ." has this marvelous phrase, "Absence or presence of field 028 alone does not justify a new record." I confess I've never been clear on exactly what "absence or presence" means in practical application. It would seem to be saying that I can use one of the records in OCLC even though there is an 028 "present" which is "absent" in my score. New record or not? The four existing records are all for the same thing already. I hate to further clutter the database, but. . . . Thanks.

Answer: That "absence or presence" phrase is intended to cover a whole range of possibilities and does it vaguely. The general point is supposed to be that you shouldn't assume that simply because an existing record does not have certain information that it does not appear on the actual item, at least in certain circumstances. Or that the presence of something on your item in hand may not make it different from an existing record that does not contain that piece of information. The idea is that you need to use your judgment regarding certain differences, and that in many cases, it makes more sense to edit an existing record than to (in your phrase) "clutter the database." A good example is the presence of the ISMN on your item, where it may not appear on any existing records. Since the ISMN is a fairly recent phenomenon, you're not likely to see it on a record for something published several decades ago, except that many newer printings of such older items may well include this new standard number. If the presence or absence of an ISMN is the only significant difference between a record online and an item in hand (and the item in hand with the ISMN does not otherwise appear to be a new edition or new publication under the definitions of AACR2), it's probably wise to simply edit the record and not add a new one. I'd lean toward the same solution in the case you describe. Hope that helps. *Newsletter 78* (*May 2001*)

1.6 QUESTION: If I have a score and parts for an item, and the bibliographic record in OCLC shows only the score or only the parts, am I required to input a new record? Likewise, if I have only the parts and I find a bibliographic record for only the score (or only the score and find a bibliographic record for only the parts). . . ? I seem to remember these situations discussed in the OLD *Bibliographic Input Standards,* but cannot find our copy (if it still exists). I see nothing about these situations spelled out in the new manual. I'm interested in documentation as well as the current/past policy.

   Answer: *Bibliographic Formats and Standards* doesn't refer explicitly to scores and parts, but states more generically: "Analytical vs. comprehensive entry. A record for a multi-part item or serial and records for their individual parts or issues may coexist. If a record for an item as a whole exists, you can create a record for a part and vice versa" (http://www.oclc.org/oclc/bib/ 4_1.htm or p. 46 in the paper BF&S). It is also implied in the statement for field 254, Musical Presentation Statement: "Absence or presence of 254 does not justify a new record. Specific differences in musical presentation statements (e.g., miniature score vs. playing score) justify a new record" (http://www.oclc.org/oclc/bib/4_2.htm or p. 53), as well as that for 300: "Specific differences in the extent of item . . . justify a new record" (p. 55). Separate records for the score, the part(s), and for the score and part(s) are all justified, though you always have the option of using an existing record and editing it for local use (understanding that this may misrepresent your holdings for resource sharing). These policies have always been the same. The only substantive difference between the current texts in BF&S and the text in the final (5th) edition of the old *Bibliographic Input Standards* before it and all the formats were combined into BF&S is, again, implicit. It is in the (now obsolete) "Format" fixed field (p. 33): "A difference in coding of 'Format' alone does *not* justify a new record. Compare 245, 250, 254, 300, etc. Specific differences in the format of a score justify a new record." That BIS is the only old version that I have at hand, but I don't recall anything more explicit than that in even older versions. I know that I've answered similar questions in my Q&A column over the past ten or more years and have always said the same thing. *Newsletter 77* (*November 2000*)

1.7 QUESTION: Something mentioned at the OLAC/MOUG scores workshop tugged at my brain and I thought I'd double-check with you. If in a piece of chamber music, a score and a set of parts are published together, is it legal to catalog the score and the parts separately, putting separate records in OCLC? I've always believed the best route to go is to catalog the *published item*; and to have a very good reason if you don't; and if you don't, to not put it in OCLC. Examples are some toys I got stuck doing: Thomas the train engine, Harriet the boxcar, and Annie(?) the caboose. Each was available only as separate items in a catalog. We decided to put together the three train cars and catalog them on one record. But we only did it locally, not in OCLC. Maybe I don't have to worry about that? If determining the published item is important, I've found it's difficult to tell with scores. They're available this, that, and some other way, sometimes the publisher tells you, but often not. Indeed, some publishers don't seem to care. We receive the score, for instance, but were under the impression there were parts, so we call the publisher, and they say "oh sure," and send us some parts, which turn out to be a different font, with numbers that bear no relation to the score, are in their own cover, have a date wildly different from the score, and a different version of the publisher's name. Sounds like the score is one thing and the parts are another thing, but the vendor hasn't noticed, just pulls from various piles according to what the library wants. I've puzzled several times trying to determine if I have one thing or two. Any light you can shed would be appreciated.

Answer: You are permitted to catalog multipart items together or separately. As you point out, it is not always easy to determine what the "published item" may have been, and in the case of scores and parts, they may appear in numerous permutations. You are also permitted to combine things into a single record, as you did with the trains. *Newsletter 77 (November 2000)*

1.8 QUESTION: I've been informed that the rules for cataloging double-sided sound recordings have changed. Under the new rules, one can catalog the sound recording using only a single record instead of the old one record per side rule. We would like to create new records for the work that we are doing on some jazz 78s using the new rules as opposed to simply attaching holdings to the old records that were created using the old rules. What do you suggest that we do?

Answer: AACR2 Rule 6.1G allows you to catalog such sound recordings either as a single unit without a collective title OR as separate records. That choice is up to you, and those records following either practice are not considered to be duplicates by OCLC. Although LCRI 6.1G1 stipulates that such items should be described as a single unit, that is LC policy and is not binding on OCLC users. OCLC, however, prefers that you NOT enter duplicate records to represent AACR2 cataloging when there is an existing record cataloged (using the practice that you prefer) under pre-AACR2 rules.

If I've understood your question correctly, if there are pre-AACR2 records following the separate-record practice and you want to create AACR2 records following the single-record practice (and no record for the single-record practice already exists), you *are* permitted to do so. *Newsletter 77 (November 2000)*

1.9 QUESTION: I have some questions about when to input a new bibliographic record. *Bibliographic Input Standards*, 2nd ed. says about field 245 subfield $b, "absence or presence does not justify a new record." Does this mean that if the item you are cataloging lacks a parallel title but a parallel title does appear on the record in WorldCat, you are required to use the existing record anyway? About field 300 subfield $a, BIS says, "variation in preliminary paging, post paging, or separate numbering do not justify a new record." Does this mean that if you are cataloging something with six preliminary pages and the record in WorldCat shows eight preliminary pages, you are required to use the existing record? The situation I have is a score that is published with title proper and accompanying material in German, vs. an OCLC record for this title with a parallel title in English and a different number of preliminary pages, presumably because the preface is in English as well as German. It seems as though BIS prevents a new record from being created in such cases. Is this true?

   Answer: That section of the old *Bibliographic Input Standards* was superseded by the introductory Chapter 4 (pp. 45–57; or http://www.oclc.org/oclc/bib/chap4.htm in the electronic version) of *Bibliographic Formats and Standards*, "When to Input a New Record." One of those differences alone might not justify a new record, but evidence in the existing record of the presence of a preface in both English and German, versus your own item in hand with only the German language preface, would certainly justify a new record. Optionally, if you want to be a real stickler, you could indicate in your record that another version is available with the additional English-language preface. *Newsletter 74 (November 1999)*

1.10 QUESTION: I really like the ability to make a new record from an existing record, and would like to use it in cases where the bibliographic information is useful, but the item I am cataloging is in a different physical format, so that the record Type needs to be changed. When I simply type over the existing code for "Type" and send the change, the system will not allow me to keep that change, even before I type "new" (to make a new record). Instead it gives the error message, "Not authorized to change record format." I'm pretty sure it can be done, but I don't know the right way to do it.

Answer: In 1998 OCLC installed a new capability that allows users to change the Type Code on all unlocked or locally edited bibliographic records to any other valid Type Code value, but this technique cannot be used on a workform (that is, a record that is not yet added to the database). The announcement of this is in OCLC System News as item "Type Code Editing Capability" (just type "news" and <send> in Passport and browse the list of news items). When you are doing a "new" command, you can change the Type simultaneously with that "new" command by entering "new wfXX" where "wfXX" is the workform command for the Type you want. So if you have a Books format record and want to do a "new" command to change it to a Sound Recording, for instance, type "new wfmj" and the information will transfer to a Sound Recording workform. This is documented in Technical Bulletin No. 209, section 2.1 (on the OCLC Web site at http://www.oclc.org/oclc/tb/9417pris/9417.htm#2.1), and is being incorporated into the new third edition of the *OCLC Cataloging Service User Guide*, which is currently in the works. *Newsletter 74 (November 1999)*

1.11 QUESTION: If my item says "with accompaniment for rehearsal only" and the WorldCat record does not, is this enough difference to justify a new record? This situation sometimes results in contradictions within the same record, for instance a 500 note that says "with piano accompaniment for rehearsal only" but a subject heading that includes the "Unaccompanied" qualifier.

Answer: Generally, works that are said to include piano accompaniment intended for rehearsal purposes only are still considered to be unaccompanied, since they should be performed without the piano. My guess is that some catalogers don't notice the presence of such accompaniment or simply fail to mention it. If everything else matches (plate and/or publisher numbers, pagination, etc.), I think you can consider them to be matches. *Newsletter 73 (August 1999)*

1.12 QUESTION: I have here a divertimento by Michael Haydn (OCLC #4312054, though it doesn't help this question much). It was published in 1960 by (and I quote the bottom of the title page) "VEB Friedrich Hofmeister Leipzig." The caption is a little different; it says, "VEB Friedrich Hofmeister, Musikverlag Leipzig." The cover shows a series title, too (*Studienwerke*). The plate number is 7299. Now, do I have a new edition, or a reprint, of this piece? The content and layout of the piece is exactly the same, the typeface has not changed except it is a touch smaller. This is published by (again I quote the title page) "Friedrich Hofmeister Musikverlag" and underneath it "Hofheim–Leipzig." Again the caption reads a little differently, [copyright symbol] by "Friedrich Hofmeister Musikverlag, Leipzig."

There is no series statement. The cover, near the bottom, says "Reprint" and right below that, "Friedrich Hofmeister." There is no plate number, but the first page of music has FH 2245. So the differences are a plate number, series versus no series, and if you believe the title page, a different place of publication, though it seems there has always been a presence in Leipzig. But the darn thing says "Reprint," there has been no change of publisher, and most importantly, the pages look exactly the same. The title and composer and even Spieldauer of the caption are even the same typeface, just a little smaller. It does seem that the plate number and form of the publisher's name at the bottom of the caption has been excised and replaced. I read fixed field DtSt in BF&S, which is fairly detailed on what is and is not a reprint, but here I'm just not sure. Can you help?

Answer: Given the absence of the series and the difference in numbering, I would say to input a new record. You didn't mention anything about a date on the new item, but that would also have a bearing on this question. Just to clarify the differences, you might want to include a note indicating that there was an earlier version of this item published in 1960(?) with plate number 7299 and in the series "Studienwerke." By the way, the difference in the name of the publisher seems to be a legacy of German reunification. As I recall, "VEB" (Volkseigener Betrieb, roughly "people's industry") was used in East Germany as a communist analog to the capitalist "incorporated," or something like that. (Given my luck in translating German lately, though, you might want to take this with a grain or two of salt.) *Newsletter 72 (May 1999)*

1.13 QUESTION: OCLC#37007224 is a recording of *Die Meistersinger*. It basically seems to match what we have, with three problems: (1) 246: There is no such title on my CD, on the label or anywhere else; (2) 260 $b: "London" is clearly the label on my CD; Decca does appear in tiny letters as the copyright (i.e., phonogram) holder; (3) 300 $a: The container of my CD has a clearly stated total time of 255 min., 26 sec., in pretty big letters; rounding up to 260 seems unusual. The 028s match, recorded date is same, and so forth. I guess most troubling is that "When to Input a New Record" guidelines don't consider variant titles—they used to be in a 500 note, after all. But a variant title that just *isn't there* seems like a good reason to make the record new.

Answer: My inclination would be to say that the label difference alone would justify a new record. The history is convoluted, as you can imagine (you can get a flavor/flavour from the "Decca" and "London" articles in the *New Grove Jazz*), but the (British) Decca Record Company seems to market its records in the United States and Japan under the London label, at least. Decca and London discs often use the same publisher number, just to confuse things further. (For some reason, I'm reminded of the old Hellmann's mayonnaise labels when I was growing up in New Jersey. In fine print there was a note that said something like, "West of the Rockies, Hellmann's is known as Best Foods Mayonnaise. It's the same fine product." Of course, when was the last time you had to catalog a jar of mayo?) Why the timing would be different, I can only guess. Your London disc has the total time prominently displayed on the container. One wonders if the Decca version didn't have the times totaled, and if rounding up over the course of four discs might not account for the difference. Then again, they do tend to take things more slowly on the other side of the pond. The presence or absence of a possibly title-like thing such as "Solti 50 golden jubilee" could be another corroborating factor in the decision. In short, I'd say a new record is justified. *Newsletter 71 (May 1998)*

1.14 QUESTION: In Japan, companies often release identical CDs with new music publisher numbers. Is a new record justified?

Answer: When you are uncertain about whether a new record is justified because of some minor differences, you always have the option of simply editing an existing record for local use and not inputting a new record. That is a perfectly respectable choice. When the music publisher number is the only difference, many libraries choose to use an existing record. When there are such differences, however, it is wise to be especially alert to other differences such as dates and minor variations in contents. All other things being equal, if the number on your item is only slightly different from the number in the existing record, I'd lean toward using that record. If the numbers were entirely different, I'd lean toward inputting a new record. *Newsletter 70 (September 1998)*

1.15 QUESTION: In cataloging a piece of nineteenth-century sheet music called *O Swiftly Glides the Bonny Boat*, I have discovered that I have two pieces of music with the same name, publisher, and so forth with no date of publication on either. The only differences are that added to the caption of one is the line, "For sale by E. Johns & Co., New Orleans," and that there are distinct differences in the typeface of the two pieces. According to the Bibliographic Standard for the 260 subfield $b, "The following differences do not justify a new record: . . . Absence or presence of multiple publishers, distributors, etc. as long as one on the item matches one on the record, and vice versa. . . ." Does this mean that the presence of a distributor on one, but not on the other, is not sufficient justification for a new record? Or, should I catalog them as two separate records?

Answer: For bibliographic purposes, these two items sound like they would have a single bibliographic record. The presence or absence of a distributor would not be justification for a separate record. Locally, you may want to note the differences between the copies. Of course, for archival purposes, the distinctions you've made could be very important in helping determine dates of publication and so forth. You might also want to take a look at MLA's *Sheet Music Information* page (http://www.lib.duke.edu/ music/sheetmusic/), which has a link to the draft *Guidelines for Sheet Music Cataloging* among other things. *Newsletter 70 (September 1998)*

1.16 QUESTION: During the workshop you gave at the recent SOLINET meeting, I was especially interested in your statement about catalogers always having the option to edit copy for our use, even if the guidelines indicate that we could input a new record. Is this still true if our holdings are accessible by ILL? Wouldn't that mean that our library's symbol would be attached to a bibliographic record that describes something slightly different from what we own? I currently have quite a few items here waiting for original input because the OCLC copy is just slightly off. But I'd be more than happy to use the existing copy if you say it's OK. The typical discrepancies involve dates, number of pages, size, and scores that may or may not have parts with them.

Answer: You have hit precisely on the chief drawback of editing existing copy in cases where a separate record is justified. Adding your symbol to a record that is almost, but not quite what you have, can be misleading, especially for purposes of ILL. Depending on the item(s) in question and the nature of the user's request, the differences may be trivial. But there are certainly instances when the differences are meaningful. You need to fall back on good old "cataloger's judgment." As I hope I made clear in the workshop (and as I'm sure you've seen in everyday cataloging), dates can be extremely problematical. If the item has more than one date in different places, consider the possibility that a previous cataloger may have overlooked something. Check the "Entered" date on the record to see if that gives you any help regarding differences between the record online and the item you have in hand. Differences in pagination and size can also be tricky. If paging is just one or two off, I usually don't worry about it, unless it's something with just a few pages to begin with. Same thing with size: A few centimeters here or there don't matter, especially considering different measuring practices, local binding, and so on. When differences are more than just a few pages or centimeters, they start to make a difference. When you're talking about scores with or without parts, remember that separate records for scores alone, parts alone, and scores with parts are all legitimate. Putting your symbol on the "wrong" record in these cases is a real impediment to successful ILL. These are, of course, only general comments; my reactions to more specific instances might be different. *Newsletter 70 (September 1998)*

1.17 QUESTION: I'm staring at a score (2 parts, actually) of violin duets by Haydn, published by International Music Co. The title page appears as follows:

HAYDN
THREE DUETS
(from three String Quartets)
For Two Violins

I have copy on OCLC that is a match except for the title, substituting "op. 99" for the parenthetical phase. The copy and my score have the same plate number, consist of two violin parts, and have no date (the copy has guessed at "[197–?]," which is as good as anything else). According to OCLC's guidelines, I guess I'm justified in putting in a new record. The question is larger than this one record, however. International has this type of problem a lot. A few weeks ago, I had a similar problem where the LC cataloging copy had the Fanna number of a Vivaldi piece as part of the title, and my score did not. Recently, I had a score where the name of the editor was given in full, while the OCLC copy had only his last name. I suspect that the publishing practices of International are such that slightly different title pages and covers are prepared whenever more copies are run. But that's just my suspicion, and chief sources are chief sources. So my overall question is: How should these situations be treated? Does OCLC prefer a "when in doubt, don't" or "if the title is different, the item is different, put in a new record" approach? Or is there no opinion?

Answer: Of course, it's not just International Music Inc., but you know that. First thing to do is make sure you're taking into account all possible titles (title page, caption, cover, spine, list, etc.). Next, consider how the titles differ. Are we talking substantive differences, or mere differences in fullness of transcription? As you suggest, publishers are careless about these things. Unfortunately, there are no hard rules about what sort of difference really makes a difference. If I am looking at two records, the only difference being the absence of an opus number or thematic index number on one and its presence on the other, I'm probably going to consider them the same. Differences that we might readily recognize if we could compare both items right in front of us become much more blurry when all you've got are bibliographic records cataloged by different people (or even the same person) over a period of time, or one record and one item. This is where the old standby/copout "cataloger's judgment" comes in. Comparing OCLC #3898584 with your item, yours has no opus number but does include the "(from three String Quartets)" designation. Those differences combined would probably justify separate records, but it's very difficult to generalize and I would urge you to use your good judgment. *Newsletter 69 (April 1998)*

1.18 QUESTION: This afternoon I was working on a Mozart CD and was almost through editing it for our local system when I discovered a real discrepancy between the item in hand and the OCLC record. I think I shall have to create a new record but wanted to ask your opinion about this first. The music number on the CD that we have is 417 395-2, and everything about our CD matches the OCLC record (well, the original cataloger used "c1986" in 260 $c instead of "p1982"—both appear on the back of the jewel box). Performers are the same: Te Kanawa, Popp, von Stade, etc., with Sir Georg Solti and the London Philharmonic. Selections are identical to the ones in the OCLC record. However, the OCLC record describes an accompanying booklet of 23 p., with notes and libretto (or synopsis) in English, French, and Italian. The CD that I have here has an insert of 7 p. with very brief program notes and synopsis in English only. So my question is, does this justify a new record in OCLC?

Answer: Accompanying material generally is not taken into consideration in the decision about when to input a new record. We'd prefer that the existing record be edited, in this case the 300 subfield $e, the 041, and the 500 note on the program notes. *Newsletter 67 (August 1997)*

1.19 QUESTION: Yesterday I cataloged a CD of Rimsky-Korsakov's *Scheherazade & Russian Easter Overture* issued by CBS Masterworks. On the container back, it says the pieces were recorded at Mann Auditorium in Tel Aviv in 1987; this is followed by copyright and phonogram (c and p) dates of 1988. At the top of the container back it says "Consists of previously released material." The only other date is on the label, "p1988". I found two records for the item in OCLC, an I-level and an M-level, and both ignored the previously released note, coding DtSt as "p" and recording 1988, 1987 in DATES. What's going on here? If it was recorded in 1987 and copyrighted in 1988 but still managed to be previously released, that was *fast!* More likely(?) it came out in 1988 on LP? (but CDs had been around for five years by that time . . .) and is now being reissued on CD but there is no date for the CD issue? I can't come up with a reasonable explanation; and no, I've not done any digging in OCLC to see if I can turn up the history of this recorded performance. Any ideas?

Answer: About the Rimsky-Korsakov CD, who knows? It's entirely possible that the copies cataloged didn't include the "previously released" notation that was on your container. Many such variations of printing show up all the time. I'd probably just edit one of the existing records for your own use, adding the "previously released" note and changing the Dates/DtSt as appropriate. *Newsletter 67 (August 1997)*

1.20 QUESTION: I'm cataloging a CD of Schumann lieder on the Hungaroton label. On the CD label is the date "p1994." On the container back and the insert is "p1989." Those are the only dates. There are two records in OCLC for this item (both I level—don't know how that happened) and both record the "p1989" date. Except for the date, the item I have is exactly the same as what is already in OCLC. (There is one possible small difference: The existing records have the label as "Hungaroton" and mine has "Hungaroton Classic" in a couple of places as well as just "Hungaroton"—but that's not enough of a difference to justify anything.) BF&S "When to Input a New Record" is no help; it says, for instance, that a variation in copyright dates does not justify a new record if the publication date is the same. In sound recordings, all we *ever* have is copyright dates. I considered the possibility that the catalogers of the other copies either didn't see the "p1994" or chose to ignore it; but both the records were input in 1990, so it's clear "p1994" does not appear on their items. I'm inclined to say Hungaroton made some more copies and through usual publisher paranoia, re-copyrighted the new copies. Should I invoke OCLC's dictum, "when in doubt, don't" and use one of the existing records, recording the new copyright date in 260 and mentioning "p1989" in a note in my local editing?

Answer: Given that your item has "p1994" on the CD label and that the existing records were both input in 1990 and have only the "p1989" date, I think you are fully justified in inputting a new record. The full BF&S reference on p. 54 says that "variation in copyright dates if the publication dates are the same" does not justify a new record. Remember, looking at the rules and RIs under 1.4F (particularly 1.4F5 and 1.4F6), that copyright (and phonogram copyright) dates are a second choice after a publication, distribution, etc., date. In this case, we're using the "p" date as an implied date of publication, lacking any other evidence. The "variation in copyright dates" provision would apply in cases where the real or implied publication dates are the same on two items but they have different copyright dates, for whatever reason.

260 . . . $c [1994], p1989.
260 . . . $c [1994], p1990.

We can only speculate on why your item has "p1994." Perhaps something was remixed or re-recorded, who knows? *Newsletter 67 (August 1997)*

1.21 QUESTION: Here's another one of those "Would this be considered a duplicate?" questions. I've got two albums (*Barry Manilow Greatest Hits*—yes, I get to catalog these things), both technically duplicates in that the Arista label number is the same, and the contents are the same, and *every-*

thing is the same, *except* that one indicates it is a "collector's item and sou-venir" on the container and the record itself is of the picture variety, display-ing Barry's poignant face through the grooves. I know the ARSC people are very interested in picture records, so I am loathe to consider this "collector's item" merely a second copy and put it on the same bibliographic record in OCLC. At the same time, well, it's all just packaging, like a copy of a book coming out with a blue cover and one with a red cover. Would/could this picture record be considered a candidate for new cataloging?

Answer: It may well be just packaging (some would say that Manilow's entire career amounts to little more than packaging), but sometimes that packaging has bibliographic (as opposed to artistic) significance. What might be the deciding factor is how the difference is presented on the item. You say that the container "indicates it is a 'collector's item and souvenir.'" If that information appears as something that can be construed as an edition statement, I'd say you can consider this a separate bibliographic entity. Since the container is a prescribed source of information for the edition statement (AACR2 6.0B2), it does not have to be bracketed, but I would probably include a note that says where the edition statement comes from. If there is nothing on the label, container, or accompanying textual material that can be taken as an edition statement, you could invoke rule 6.2B3 (and LCRI 6.2B3, which refers to LCRI 1.2B4: "If differences are *manifest*, however, but the catalog records would show exactly the same information in the ar-eas beginning with the title and statement of responsibility area and ending with the series area, apply the option") and supply a bracketed edition state-ment such as "[Picture disc ed.]" or something appropriate. Any other dif-ferences such as extra program notes, inserts, or accompanying material, should also be noted. If the differences that would make this another edi-tion are not obvious from the edition statement, you might also want to note what the differences are.

250 Special collector's ed.
500 Ed. statement from container.
500 Photographic image of Barry Manilow visible though yellow-tinted vinyl disc.

In cases where there isn't really anything bibliographically significant about the differences, you might want to seriously consider editing the existing record for your local use. *Newsletter 65 (November 1996)*

1.22 QUESTION: We are in the midst of cataloging the Columbia la-bel and have run into differing alphabetic codes in the manufacturer's num-ber. The numeric code is the same, the albums are both stereo, and so forth; everything is the same except the initial alphabetic character (e.g., CS 1234 and another "copy" of the LP under PC 1234). In speaking to the archivist, he said these alphabetic characters are merely pricing codes the manufacturer supplies, and for all intents and purposes are treated as duplicates in his collection. I have seen these treated differently in OCLC: sometimes both manufacturer numbers are included in 028 fields in the same record (with a 500 "Also issued as . . ." note); sometimes there are separate records for each differing number (perfectly allowable under "When to Input a New Record," true?); and of course, sometimes only one number appears. I myself am trying to decide how to treat these "duplicate" LP's when doing originals. To catalog them on the same record or not to catalog them on the same record?

Answer: Well, that is the question, isn't it? But you've both asked and answered it. Columbia LPs were notorious for changing the alphabetic prefix whenever the price changed. New records are certainly justified for each such change, but if you find it more useful to catalog these as copies (choosing one prefix as the "real" one and noting differences in a note, for instance, with 028s for all), you may do so. OCLC really has no preference. That doesn't help you decide, I know, but you might sleep better knowing that whichever choice you make, it's OK. *Newsletter 64 (August 1996)*

1.23 QUESTION: I read the transcription of your question-and-answer period at the most recent MOUG meeting and noticed that OCLC will be more restrictive in regard to duplicate records in light of the new 006 field capability. I am having a bit of trouble deciding what to choose for my type code for two titles. One is a tape of complete folk songs; it has an accompanying booklet with the printed music and words along with some historical background on the songs. Should it go on the scores or the sound recordings format? My other example might be a little more straightforward. It is a score of mariachi music with an accompanying tape of the songs in the score. I assume that the score is really meant for performance and that the tape is there just to give the uninitiated player an idea of what to shoot for. Both the mariachi and the folk song examples have some use as pedagogical items in addition to the performance possibilities. I can easily see that a music literature textbook with accompany sound medium would probably work best as a bibliographic record for the book and a 006 for the sound medium. What criteria do I apply in the examples above and would these examples be a place where OCLC might be a bit more lenient with duplicate records in the database?

Answer: As you have noticed, Format Integration has not solved all problems or simplified all questions. One category of materials that *is* cleared up is the nonprint serial, which is now to be input on the nonprint format with BLvl "s" and an optional serial 006. The cases you ask about are still ambiguous and in some cases you'll have to toss a coin. The folk song tape with booklet could go either way. Base your decision on how substantial the "accompanying booklet" is. Since it has the words, music, and historical notes, it sounds fairly substantial, sight unseen. If you can tell that it was intended merely to supplement the recording, though, I'd go with the Sound Recordings format. As a general guideline in cases of doubt, it might be best to follow the long-standing suggestion for read-along materials that consist of a book and recording: When in doubt, catalog as a recording with accompanying text. In your second case, since you can determine that the score seems to be the clearly dominant medium, I'd go with that. We might occasionally need to be a bit lenient on duplicates in these ambiguous cases, but I think we will try to make a reasonable choice whenever possible. We're all still finding our way here. *Newsletter 64 (August 1996)*

1.24 QUESTION: Given Format Integration Phase 2, will the rules concerning allowable duplicates need to be changed? Previously, it was OK to input a new record into OCLC when one disagreed with what was the predominant medium in an item. The example given in BF&S Chapter 4 (p. 39) is a set of slides with a book, or a book with a set of slides. If there is not a clearly predominant medium, it was OK to have two records, but "only if there is *not* a clear choice of predominant material. If in doubt, use the existing record." That's a pretty clear statement. And even under FI, catalogers still must decide what the predominant medium is, so won't there still be cases where it could easily go either way?

Answer: Yes, we will need to change the guidelines about allowable duplicates, though we're still contemplating all the details. Because all aspects of an item can be coded, we will be less willing to allow certain categories of duplicates. The second edition of BF&S is currently in the works; we hope to have it out during the summer of 1996. *Newsletter 63 (May 1996)*

1.25 QUESTION: I am wondering if I can justify inputting a series of Chopin CDs as new records. Arabesque Recordings issued four CDs in a series titled *The complete works of Frederic Chopin*; p1991 (e.g., #26864088, which is v. 2). It reissued these in 1995. The differences are: (1) the series now reads *The complete PIANO works of Frederic Chopin*; (2) the date is given as "pc1995, 1991." Using the OCLC input standards it appears that neither of these differences justifies a new record. Of course I can be conservative and use the records for the 1991 issues, editing them (or not) to match the 1995 manifestations. What do you think?

Answer: From your description of the Chopin CD, I'd say that a new record is certainly justified. The new date of publication (1995) and the new series name (it sounds as though it *could* be a new series rather than just a title change) together would justify a new record. Proceed with a clear conscience. *Newsletter 62* (*November 1995*)

1.26 QUESTION: We have noticed copy on OCLC consisting of two bibliographic records for one compact disc, with the first bib record saying "Tracks 1–16" in the 300 field, and the second, saying "Tracks 17–32." Our public service librarians are asking me to create another bib record for the same thing that would combine the two into one. Of course, the detailed contents notes and 7XX access points would be lost for all of the specific little titles, etc., but they don't particularly like two bib records for one CD. Is it OK with OCLC for me to create a third bib record that would combine the best of the other two? Or does OCLC prefer that multiple bib records for the same compact disc not be created in the first place?

Answer: Under AACR2 1.1G, multiple records linked by "With" notes are allowed. That rule covers items without a collective title (not necessarily the case with your example; you don't say), but OCLC recognizes that system limitations occasionally inspire users to do what you have described. It is legitimate. It is also permissible for you to add a record for the item as a unit. *Newsletter 61* (*August 1995*)

1.27 QUESTION: I am in the process of cataloging sound recordings that are problems in our bar-coding project. When different cuts on a sound recording have been cataloged on separate MARC bib records, I have deleted our holdings from these records and used instead a bib record for the "whole" sound recording. What do I do when there are not any "whole" bib records for these sound recordings? Do I (1) edit one of the bib records for part of the sound recording, so that the bib record reflects the "whole" sound recording, or (2) is it correct to create a new bib record for the "whole" sound recording?

Answer: A record for the entire sound recording and records for the individual works on a sound recording are both viable options under AACR2 (1.1G, 6.1G, and related rules). Hence, OCLC allows records following either method. If you find a record or records using one method and prefer to use the other method for which no record(s) exists, you are welcome to add a new record(s) in OCLC. *Newsletter 61* (*August 1995*)

1.28 QUESTION: If two scores otherwise match, but the number of parts differs (e.g., one has one score and four parts and the other has one score and eight parts), are we justified in inputting a new record? I read BF&S, p. 46, and find: "The following differences do not justify a new record: . . . . Variation in the number of parts for an incomplete multipart item (e.g., record indicates 5 v. and the library now has v. 6–7).” I take this to mean that variation in number of parts alone does not justify a new record. Do you agree?

Answer: The number of parts, and the instrumentation of the parts, may sometimes justify a new record. If the difference in the number is due to incompleteness (that is, the part for one or more instruments is not included), a new record is not justified. If the instrumentations are different (for instance, a work for cello and piano in a version for bassoon and piano, or a string octet arranged for string quartet) a new record is justified. *Newsletter 59 (November 1994)*

1.29 QUESTION: I’ve always understood that the presence or absence of parts does not justify a new record (i.e., if I have one score and find a record that describes that score and a number of parts, I cannot input a new record). I have looked for a rule that says this in *Bibliographic Formats and Standards*, but I cannot find it. Please let me know if I have merely invented this rule or that we cannot input a record if all else matches, but the item is “1 score” and the record describes “1 score + 15 parts.”

Answer: This must be one of your inventions, Edison. Separate records for scores, parts, and scores & parts have always been justified. The text in *Bibliographic Formats and Standards* is not as explicit as it used to be (as I recall), but it’s on p. 38 under “Analytical vs. comprehensive entry” where it says, “If a record for an item as a whole exists, you can create a record for a part and vice versa.” So if you have a score alone and the only record you find online is for the score and parts, you may indeed input a separate record and vice versa. Same goes for the part(s) alone. *Newsletter 58 (August 1994)*

1.30 QUESTION: According to “When to Input a New Record,” p. 45 of *Bibliographic Formats and Standards*, a new record is *not* justified by “Absence or presence of multiple publishers, distributors, etc. as long as one on the item matches one on the record, and vice versa.” OCLC #12999415 has a first 028 of R9-4 $b Charles Foley; the 260 states only one publisher, “New York : Charles Foley.” Our publication has no evidence of that first 028. The second 028 is identical to one we have, but “Charles Foley” appears only on the first page of our music. Our title page lists “Melville, N.Y. Belwin Mills Pub. Co.” The date is the same. Is a new record justified?

Answer: Though I’m hardly an expert on music publishing, from your description, it sounds like the “Charles Foley” on the first page of music may be the copyright holder (?) and no longer the publisher for this edition. I would say that a separate record is justified with Belwin Mills as the publisher. *Newsletter 57 (May 1994)*

1.31 QUESTION: Serial computer files, scores, audiovisual media, and sound recordings may be cataloged using either the specific format or the Serials format. It has been my understanding that the consensus of opinion of the Computer Files Discussion Group of ALCTS, for one, has been to prefer using the Computer Files format. CONSER, on the other hand, always uses the Serials format. (A serial is a serial is a serial!) I have read the "When to Input a New Record" guidelines very carefully and I still can't determine if it would be considered a duplicate to put in a record for the specific format if a Serials format record for the item existed (or vice versa). The term "allowable duplicate" comes to mind. What's the official word?

Answer: Records for the same serially issued item cataloged on the Serials format and on its corresponding non-Serials format (for instance, scores, sound recordings, computer files) are *not* considered duplicates. That information is, perhaps, not as prominent in the new *Bibliographic Formats and Standards* as it used to be. It appears at the top of p. 4 (the third bullet under "Serials"), on p. 61 (the fourth bullet under "Guidelines"), and most explicitly on p. 54 (the third bullet under "Permissible duplicate records" and at the very bottom of the page). OCLC has no preference, as either choice results in some gains and some losses. I should note that the effect of format integration on this question is yet to be fully determined. *Newsletter 56 (December 1993)*

[Note: Format Integration certainly did change this. With Bibliographic Level "s" now valid in conjunction with Type Codes other than "a", the formally permissible duplicates described here are no longer permitted.]

1.32 QUESTION: In hand is a compact disc that matches an OLUC record in every respect (including the publisher number) except that the UPC on the item differs from that in the record's 024 field. *Bibliographic Input Standards* does not list field 024, so should I use the existing record or input a new one?

Answer: The bibliographic significance of the Universal Product Code is still a topic of debate, especially in light of their inconsistent treatment by some music publishers. But as things stand now, a difference in UPC *does not* justify a new record. If all else is the same, use the existing record. Since the 024 field is repeatable, you could even add one for the number on your item.

Real differences in Music Publisher Numbers (028) *do* justify a new record, though. Those 028 differences are vexing. One always wonders if a change in MPN means anything more than a change in the recording's price. Is it a new mix? Are the contents different? Have different takes of a recording been substituted? Has some flaw in earlier pressings been corrected? Is it mere caprice? The same questions could probably be asked about differences in UPCs. If you've ever dealt with ISBNs, you know that publishers can be awfully capricious about *them* as well, even though they are *supposed* to be standard numbers. If we could only convince publishers to be more rational. Please remember that just because a new record *may* be justified by the input standards, you are not required to input a new record. If you have doubts about the justification or if you feel uncomfortable inputting a new record to reflect what you consider to be an insignificant difference, by all means use an existing record. *Newsletter 54 (May 1993)*

1.33 QUESTION: I have two Musical Heritage Society LPs that appear to be the same, except one has the publisher no. MHS 802 and the other, MHS 802S. According to the back of the containers, MHS 802 is in mono, but my MHS 802S has "stereo" printed on the label and container. Schumann's *Symphony no. 4* is on one side and Beethoven's *Symphony no. 8* is on the other. To complicate things, pre-AACR2 OLUC records exist for the mono MHS 802 Beethoven and the stereo MHS 802S Schumann, but not for the mono MHS 802 Schumann or the stereo MHS 802S Beethoven. The NUC has entries for both sides of the mono MHS 802 and both sides of the stereo MHS 802S. Should I enter pre-AACR2 records for the two "missing" sides? Or should I add two AACR2 records for the complete items rather than the sides? If I do the latter, what do I do with the 010s?

   Answer: Musical Heritage Society is notorious for mixing up labels and containers for stereo and mono, using the suffix "S" on a seemingly random basis. Strict application of OCLC *Bibliographic Input Standards* would dictate a separate record for the MHS 802 and for the MHS 802S, even if both happened to be stereo.

   But you might be able to hedge that if either item is inconsistent (on the label, the container, the spine, etc.) in its Music Publisher Number. In such a case, you could get away with one record and note the different numbers found in different places (of course, in any case, you have the option of inputting only one record and noting any differences as local information). You needn't feel obligated to "fill in" the "missing" pre-AACR2 records. If you want to follow the common AACR2 practice of cataloging the item as a unit, do that and don't worry about the existing records for individual works. Including or not including the LCCNs is up to you, especially if the numbers do not appear on the item. If you catalog the item as a unit and include the LCCNs, they both belong in subfields $z. *Newsletter 53 (November 1992)*

   1.34 QUESTION: Throughout the section "When to Input a New Record" in OCLC's *Bibliographic Input Standards*, one finds the phrase "Absence or presence of does not justify a new record." I take this to mean that we are to give the cataloger the benefit of the doubt and assume that perhaps information was simply left out of a record, not necessarily absent from the item itself. But what if I find a bib record that matches in every way what I have in hand, *except* that my item has no publisher or plate number anywhere but the bib record does. Is this a reason to input a new record, since that number must come from somewhere?

Answer: Logically speaking, a new record would be justified. The problem is that once both records are in the OLUC, there is no way for anyone looking at both to tell the difference between a record where the information is absolutely not present on the item itself and where the information has simply been left off the bibliographic record. The result is that there is no way to tell that these records are not duplicates, because according to the standards developed by OCLC and its various advisory groups over the years, these records appear bibliographically identical. *Newsletter 53 (November 1992)*

1.35 QUESTION: Should one catalog critical commentaries with the collected works or separately? Records are found on OCLC that treat the critical commentaries and their associated works both ways.

Answer: That's because either treatment is acceptable. Take your pick. *Newsletter 48 (August 1991)*

1.36 QUESTION: I have a compact disc that matches a record online in every respect but the publisher number. Do you suspect that this is an inputting error, or should I input a new record?

Answer: Difference in music publisher number certainly justifies a new record. However, in a case such as this, any of a number of inputting errors may have occurred. A record may have been created via a "new" command without making all the necessary subsequent corrections. The sound recording may have more than one music publisher number on it. It could be a simple typographical error. Or it could be a genuine difference; I've seen plenty of otherwise identical-looking things differ on just such minute details. If you suspect an error or other oversight, please send me a photocopy of the evidence from your item and I will ask the inputting library if their item agrees. *Newsletter 48 (August 1991)*

CHAPTER 2

Sound Recordings

INTRODUCTION

Humans have been recording sound for roughly a century and a quarter now, using a succession of storage media, from cylinders to compact discs. Each medium in its time was an innovation and most of them were improvements over what had come before (although eight-track tapes were probably an exception in that respect). The cataloging of a sound recording poses particular problems in several dimensions that are not factors in the cataloging of, say, printed music. A physical item is being cataloged, but consideration must also be given to such issues as dates of recording and publication; places of performance; intellectual responsibility both for composing and performing; multiple works on a single item; publisher and label names and numbers; and different recording media.

DATES

2.1 QUESTION: What's your take on the following imprint statement for a sound recording:

260   New York, N.Y.: $b London, $c c1991, p1972.

After reading 1.4F5 (and the associated LCRI) it looks like this is legitimate. (I can't find an MCD associated with this either.) It seems there is a WIDE opinion on the WorldCat database.

  Answer: Since this is a sound recording, you should look at 6.4F and ITS associated LCRIs first. Under LCRI 6.4F1, you'll find: "Do not regard as a copyright date *for the recording* a date preceded by the copyright symbol '[c in a circle]' that appears on the container or accompanying matter (cf. 1.4F5, 1.4F6). This symbol can apply only to the printed text. However, it can be used as evidence for supplying a date of publication according to 1.4F7 when neither a date of publication nor a 'p' date appears on the item." In other words, the 260 subfield $c in question should probably have been transcribed as "[1991], p1972." Depending on what other information is available in the record and/or on the item (does the "p1972" represent the date of original capture, or the date of previous release, for example) the fixed fields DtSt and Dates would be filled in according to the Type of Date hierarchy found in "Bibliographic Formats and Standards" and MARC 21. *Newsletter 80 (May 2002)*

2.2 QUESTION: I have a compact disc musical recording to catalog with a date of p1974. Since this was originally issued on an LP and CDs did not come into existence until the early to mid-1980s, what date would you recommend using in the Dates and 260 subfield $c? There is no other date on the disc, insert, or container. Does the "p" letter prior to the date indicate the copyright of the sound data? I am seeing many examples in OCLC that just use the one date for items originally recorded on LPs or sound cassettes and then reissued on CD. Do you know where in the literature I could find a discussion of this?

Answer: This is discussed briefly in my *Music Coding and Tagging*, 2nd ed. (Soldier Creek Press, 2001) on p. 216 (with further discussion of other date coding issues on pp. 39–43). But a more useful discussion for your purposes can be found in Richard Smiraglia's *Describing Music Materials*, 3rd ed. (Soldier Creek Press, 1997) on pp. 48–49. Dates on sound recordings that are preceded by the designation "p" are phonogram copyright dates, the copyright date of the recorded sound, corresponding to the date of the sound's first publication. In a case such as yours, where the latest (or only) date on the item predates the existence of the particular recording medium (audio compact discs were first made commercially available in Japan in 1982 and in the United States in 1983—no CD can have a legitimate publication date earlier than this), you must estimate a date of publication in accordance with AACR2 1.4F7. If there are no hints on the item itself, you may find help in discographies, sound recording catalogs, related bibliographic records, and the like. Making a guess at the decade may be the best one can do, in which case "[198–?], p1974" in the 260 subfield $c would be fine. The fixed field Dates would then be "198u,1974" with DtSt coded as "t" since you have an estimated publication date and a copyright date. *Newsletter 80 (May 2002)*

2.3 QUESTION: When I catalog a recording (e.g., a pop collection with 12 songs previously released from 1985 to 1990) that is a compilation of previously released material, do I code the DtSt as "r"? I'm having trouble because the compilation itself is a new issue, but the individual songs have been previously released. Does the DtSt apply to the whole entity (the new compilation, in which case DtSt=s) or the works contained within it (all individually reissued, DtSt=r)? I know Steven Yusko tried to clarify this at MLA, but I'm not sure I remember him correctly. The closest thing I see in any documentation is in the BF&S: "Use for items reproduced from two or more works, works that have first appeared in another country, and works that have first appeared under a different title, unless there is evidence it is a translation." Though this statement seems geared toward print resources, it leads me to believe that I should code such compilations as "r" with the earliest date of issue as Date 2. Anyway, I'd appreciate your advice on this admittedly minor point.

   Answer: Anthology recordings that collect material previously released from multiple sources qualify as reissues in this context. The date of the current release would be Date 1; the earliest date of previous release would be Date 2. I think you've got it right. *Newsletter 79 (November 2001)*

2.4 QUESTION: What's the latest on the sound recording copyright symbol?

260   [New York, N.Y.] : $b RCA Custom Records, $c [p1968]

Does one still use a "p" or should it be replaced or deleted?

   Answer: AACR2 6.4F1 allows you to use the phonogram copyright date (the "p" date) as a date of publication for a sound recording. You may transcribe it as it appears (for instance, "p2001"). There is the recent (May 2001) LCRI 6.4F1 that says a regular copyright ("c") date appearing on the container or accompanying matter cannot be used as a copyright date for the recording itself, as it applies *only* to the printed text. The LCRI concludes, ". . . it may be used as evidence for supplying a date of publication according to 1.4F7 when neither a date of publication nor a 'p' date appears on the item." Remember that for CDs, it is not possible to have a publication date earlier than 1982, which is when CDs were first made available. If your example is a CD, you would need to supply (as per 1.4F7) an approximate date of publication, such as [199–?]. *Newsletter 79 (November 2001)*

2.5 QUESTION: Please help. I cannot decipher the difference in code "p" and code "r" in OCLC's BF&S and the MARC 21 manual. When you have a sound recording of an item that originally was recorded in the sixties and released again in the 90s or whenever, do you use "p" or "r"? OCLC #39861877 uses a p; and #39750408 uses an r. Please differentiate these codes.

Answer: Which Type of Date code you use really depends on which dates you have available and how much evidence of a recording's pervious existence you have at hand. Remember that the rules do not generally require you to go beyond the item itself to determine such things as bibliographic history and previous manifestations. You also need to keep in mind the priority chart of Date Type codes (on p. FF:25 in the print BF&S, and http://www.oclc.org/bibformats/en/fixedfield/dtst.shtm online). If the item you have in hand says, for instance, something along the lines of "Previously released as an LP in 19XX," you would be justified in using Date Type "r" and the "19XX" date in Date 2 as the original release/publication date. If the item in hand says something like "Recorded in 19XX," but has no explicit mention of a previous release, you could use Date Type "p" and the "19XX" date as the Date 2 indication of the date of the original capture. In a case where you know that an item has been previously released in a different audio format but have no date for that previous release (say, a note that says "Previously released material") and no date for the original capture, you would use Date Type "r" and a blank Date 2. Obviously, there are many other possibilities, but I hope that gives you some idea. *Newsletter 76 (September 2000)*

2.6 QUESTION: In hand is a CD called *Music of the Ancient Greeks*, performed by an ensemble called De Organographia. The CD label has p1995. The back of the container has "c1995, 1997." My understanding is that I should infer 1997 as the date of publication, putting it in brackets in the 260. Then I'd put a comma, and record "p1995" after it. There are two records in OCLC that appear to be a match in every respect except the date. One is I-level and uses p1995 in the 260 *and* it was input in 1995. The other is M-level and uses just 1995 in the 260, but it was input in late March of 1997. The only possible difference is in the notes. Mine include explanatory notes, including a description of each of the instruments, information on each piece, including the source, the translation for vocal items, and sometimes more, plus a couple of sentences about each performer. The first OCLC record mentioned above (#32913801) says only that there are explanatory notes and translations. Maybe that's the same as mine, maybe not. The other OCLC record (#38260033) says there are program notes, translations, and details of the instruments and sources. That clearly is the same as mine; the biographical information is so brief that it might not have been mentioned. I'd say that my item has to be different, at least bibliographically, from the one input in 1995. But is the second record in OCLC, input in 1997, the same or different from the first? Seems my item matches that second record, especially considering the notes match, and they could have failed to see the 1997 on the container. So, the questions: 1) What's going on here? If the publisher did expand the notes when more copies were molded of the CD, he would definitely want to copyright them. That's the only thing I can think of. 2) How many records does OCLC want? Should I ask that the two existing ones be merged, then input a new record for my item? Or attach my holdings to the later record? I have run into this situation a fair number of times recently. It happens a lot on Hungaroton. The record in OCLC is a match except it has "p1996" and my copy has "p1997" or "p1996, 1997," or something similar. If I had some idea of why this is happening I could make a more informed decision.

Answer: It would be impossible to generalize about what might be going on here. In some cases, catalogers may have missed a later date, but it's just as likely that the later date was not there. In this case, since everything was the same in both records (I don't consider the 1997 input date on the ELvl "M" record to be a significant difference), I merged them. You are perfectly justified in adding a separate record with the bracketed "1997" date from the container. *Newsletter 74 (November 1999)*

2.7 QUESTION: This has probably been asked and answered before, but I have not encountered it anywhere and am not sure of the answer. When one is cataloging a recording (usually a CD) with multiple dates of earlier recordings (and, presumably, releases), and one can ascertain a "release" date of the item in hand, either from the "c" date on the notes or the latest "p" date on the disc, should the DtSt be "r", with the earliest "p" date as Date 2, or should it be "s", with only the release date of the "compilation" (presumably not previously made)? Or should it even be "p", with either the earliest actual recording (from 518) or "p" date from the disc or notes? (Or even "t"?) My inclination in these situations, since the item being cataloged is "new" as a whole, is most always to use "s" and the date of the compilation's release in Date 1 (with no Date 2, and with a 500 note stating the date of the compilation) but my cataloging supervisor and I do not see eye to eye on this. She favors the "r" DtSt with the earliest "p" date given. And, of course, many catalogers use the "p" DtSt, with the earliest date of recording from the 518 as Date 2, although one or more of the works on the disc have been previously released. Is there a "right" answer to this/these questions(s)? (And I know I have not mentioned all the possible combinations.) Any help will be appreciated.

Answer: The possibilities *do* seem endless, don't they? First, you need to determine what dates you actually have. For the collection you have in hand, you are correct in trying to discern the publication date from the latest date associated with the item, be it a copyright date on the notes or booklet or the latest phonogram copyright ("p") date. All of those other phonogram copyright dates can be slightly mysterious, even if we give publishers the benefit of the doubt and figure they are applying them correctly. I think these "p" dates are really supposed to signify original (previous) publication. Even an anthology recording that collects previously released material from multiple sources *does* qualify as a rerelease. Date 2 would contain the earliest of those original release dates and the DtSt would be coded "r". If, on the other hand, the other date information you have refers to the date(s) of original sound capture (the sorts of recording dates you would put in field 518) and you have no evidence of a previous publication in any form, then DtSt would be coded "p" and again the earliest recording date would be Date 2. The hierarchy of DtSt codes can be found in BF&S on p. FF:25 or at http://www.oclc.org/bibformats/en/fixedfield/dtst.shtm in the online version, or in USMARC under field 008/06-14. It would never be correct to use DtSt code "s" when you knew that the recordings had been published previously in any form or when you knew that the original date(s) of capture was not the same as the year of release in its present form. Even if you cannot determine the original date of capture or the date of previous release, you would code DtSt accordingly and code Date 2 as an unknown (or partially unknown) date. *Newsletter 73 (August 1999)*

2.8 QUESTION: I'm team-teaching a workshop in sound recording cataloging next month and was double-checking some things in BF&S. Something seems wrong with "DtSt", p. FF:25 in the precedence table at the top for single-part items. Value "s" for single date is *above* values "p" and "t" and "q". How can that be? I'll swear that the precedence order used to be "r", then "p", then "t", then "q", and if none of those applied, you were left with "s". With the current order in BF&S, if there were a single date in the 260, you'd never get to "p", having been stopped by "s". What I want to tell the folks—and how I've trained people here—is once you've finished the description and have all the dates lined up, look first for an "r" relationship and record it in DtSt. If the item is not a reissue, look then for a "p" relationship and record it in DtSt. If there's no 518, then look at the 260 for a "t" or a "q" relationship, and record them. (I'm not absolutely certain whether "t" has precedence over "q" or the other way around, from what I remember of the precedence order, and the "t"/"q" precedence is what sent me to BF&S to begin with.) No "t" or "q", then you have "s". Am I all wet?

Answer: That table of precedence comes straight from USMARC (008/06-14), but it is only superficially different than it used to be. The revisions were inspired by Format Integration's introduction of that beloved little "u" character (or more correctly, its expansion beyond the Serials format). The "u," you'll recall, substitutes for missing digits in a date. This meant that the single date code "s" would be used even more often than previously, especially when you encountered the run-of-the-publishing-mill uncertain date that used to be coded as Date Type "q" (for instance, our old favorites of the ilk "[199–?]"; doesn't the imminent prospect of "[200–?]" just give you chills of anticipation?). That's why code "q" had its rank busted; nowadays it's used mostly for those relatively infrequent dates explicitly expressed as uncertain ranges (in AACR2 1.4F7, "[between 1946 and 1955]") and those that are conjectural translations of non-Gregorian dates (in AACR2 1.4F1, "5730 [1969 or 1970]"). In fact, if you go back to an old OCLC format document, you'll notice that value "q" was divided: The top ranking was for "questionable date (when Date 1 lacks digits in imprint)" and the lower ranking, fifth in the list of seven, was for "questionable date (except when Date 1 lacks digits)." That first use of "q" would now be coded "s" and the second use is how "q" is mostly used now. When you remove that top "q" from the old table of precedence, it is almost exactly the same as the current table (except for a few new codes, the fact that the old "c" is now "t", and that "t" and "q" have switched places near the bottom). Setting aside the table itself, though, you would still determine the code to use the same way you always did (or should have), pretty much as you've described it. Consider all the pertinent dates associated with an item, determine their relationships to the others and their bibliographic significance, and only then look at the table of precedence to see which relationship of which dates is considered the most important. If you've got more than one bibliographically significant date associated with the item, you're probably not going to use "s" regardless of where that value ranks. *Newsletter 71* (*December 1998*)

2.9 QUESTION: Everything is coming out on CD, even obscure stuff. I have a new CD that makes no mention of the fact that it was an album issued/released in 1969, but I have the LP album so I know. Should I make a "reissue of" note, use an "r" code, and put both dates in the imprint, bracketing the old date?

   Answer: You are not required to go beyond the item itself for information such as this, but since you have the information anyway, you might as well include it in the record. A "reissue" note of some sort would be appropriate, as would an "r" Type of Date code. If the original issue date does not appear on the item you have in hand, it need not appear in the 260 subfield $c. If you do have that original issue date and have included it in your "reissue" note, it would go in the Date 2. *Newsletter 70* (*September 1998*)

2.10 QUESTION: Which date code should be used when there's a rerelease involved, clearly stated on the recording but without a date, and also a recording date clearly stated? I'm also a little confused by slight differences between *Music Coding and Tagging* and the 2nd edition of OCLC's BF&S, whether we can give an estimated date (especially the decade) for the first release. In other words, if a CD says "previously released material," followed by "c1973," and states "recorded Aug. 16, 1972," what should I do?

Answer: The Dates question is one that has changed somewhat because of Format Integration, particularly the post-FI use of the character "u" for missing digits in dates. The use of the "u" character in this way was restricted to serials before FI (and so was not in the first edition of MCAT). Now, when you know you have a rerelease but can only estimate a date, that estimate goes in Date 1 (for instance, 199u, from a 260 $c rerelease date estimate of [199–?]). The revised Type of Date precedence list (BF&S p. FF:25) would now call for DtSt "r", with the date of the original release in Date 2, if you knew that date. A copyright or phonogram copyright date isn't necessarily a date of original release, but could be used as one if corroborated by other evidence. If you can't be reasonably sure that the copyright date is the date of original release, consider it a copyright date and use DtSt "t" with the same dates ("199u, 1973" in your example). In this example, you'd use the date of the original recording capture (1972) only in a note. *Newsletter 68* (*November 1998*)

2.11 QUESTION: A follow-up question about sound recording dates. What if I knew the publication date but the date of previous release was uncertain? For instance, a CD had a date of p1997, and a note that the various works were previously released, and copyright dates c1973, c1974? And a definite recording date or dates (e.g., 1971–1973). Would I use DtSt "r" and "1997, 197u" rather than DtSt "p" and "1997, 1971"? This is pretty much the case on several jazz CDs we're looking at this week.

Answer: You'd use the DtSt value "r" if you could determine that the latest copyright date was actually the date of the original release (which is possibly, maybe even likely, but not necessarily, the case). A note on the recording ("Previously released as . . . in 1974"), an entry in Schwann, another bibliographic record, the previous release in your collection, could all be corroborating evidence. If you can't be reasonably sure, I guess DtSt value "p" is the next appropriate one in the precedence list. In that case you'd go with the earliest date of the original capture as Date 2. *Newsletter 68* (*November 1998*)

2.12 QUESTION: If a sound recording has a "p" or "c" date, can I assume this is a capture date for coding in field 033?

Answer: Neither a copyright (c) date nor a phonogram copyright date ("p") necessarily implies a date of capture. Unless you have other evidence to the contrary, don't consider those dates to be capture dates. *Newsletter 67 (August 1997)*

2.13 QUESTION: "The best of the Capitol masters" (OCLC #26907196) may never have been previously released, so would DtSt be "s"?

Answer: Both the 245 and the 500 notes say that these recordings are selections from the box set "Les Paul: the legend and the legacy," which the note says came out in 1991. Sounds like this CD *is* previously released material. If the notes give original recording dates, the DtSt should probably be "p" with the earliest original recording date as Date 2. If not, DtSt should probably be "r" with dates 1992, 1991. *Newsletter 64 (August 1996)*

2.14 QUESTION: In the process of editing a bunch of OCLC records for 10" sound recordings presumably from the1950s, I'm trying to understand the Date Type and Dates fields. These sound recordings mostly have copyright dates only (on the record jackets) and no dates of publication shown. Since BF&S does not have a code for situations where the copyright date is the only one known, what code best suits these recordings? I have seen a variety of codes in the records, both "q" with inclusive dates of the decade (e.g., 1950, 1959) and "s" with one date (sometimes the copyright date). What is correct? With format integration, the assumption may generally be that sound recordings have publication dates, but for many of the older sound recordings (I'd even say most of them) the publication date is not shown.

Answer: The situation you have described, a copyright date on the jacket with no other date available, could generally be handled as a single date (Date Type: s) in the fixed field. In the 260 $c, bracket the date with a question mark (for instance, " . . . $c [1956?]"); Date 1 would be "1956." This assumes you have no other date information either on the item or from any outside research you might do. Should there be no date of any kind on the item (or from research), you will have to try to guess a decade, year, etc., according to AACR2r 1.4F7, with the fixed fields coded accordingly. *Newsletter 61 (August 1995)*

2.15 QUESTION: As a follow-up, I understand that if we put something in brackets (like the date), that means it's a cataloger-supplied bit of info (i.e., not on the piece). Even if we want to be extremely careful and say that the copyright date applies to the information on the jacket and not to the recording itself, why should the date be in brackets? Is it because the only date shown in the 260 should definitely apply only to the recording? (I know, the recording *is* what we're cataloging.) My other question is, can we not safely assume that the copyright date on the jacket does also apply to the recording? Would it be incorrect to assume that the jacket date applies to the recording also? That would mean using an "s" in Date Type and the copyright date in Date 1. In the 260, we'd use no brackets or question marks and put a "c" in front of the date in the $c field. Do you think this is really bad and incorrect?

Answer: The (questionable) date that you take from the record jacket is placed in brackets in the 260 $c because it is an inferred publication date that does not appear on the chief source (the disc or its label, according to AACR2 6.0B1). Bracketed information may be cataloger-supplied, but it may instead be taken from somewhere other than the chief source. Most of the time, the copyright statement on a container will refer to package design or any text (program notes, lyrics, etc.) printed thereon, especially with older stuff like 78s. When we use that date as the assumed (that is, questionable) date of the recording's publication, as we are doing in this instance, we indicate that by the question mark and brackets in 260 $c. Omitting the "?" and brackets is not correct; Date Type "s" and that questioned date in Date 1 are quite correct. This is all so complicated partly because the copyright laws were vague and publishers were inconsistent. *Newsletter 61 (August 1995)*

2.16 QUESTION: We're cataloging a CD that consists entirely of previously released material. It shows a series of phonogram dates (e.g., p1968, p1972, p1973), which presumably correlate with when the various pieces on the CD were first copyrighted. There is also a c-date (copyright date) of 1988, which we have happily used to infer a publication date, using it in the 260 as [1988?].

In the midst of searching OCLC for copy for this CD, we happened across a record with exactly the same content, same series of p-dates, but it was for an LP. This record had [1975] in the 260, which seems a perfectly honest approximation of when the LP might have been released.

Dat tp will clearly be "r". Date 1 will be 1988. But what goes in Date 2? In your *Music Coding and Tagging* book (pp. 8–9) it says that the date of the original goes in Date 2, and when the original is a range of dates or consists of multiple dates, the earliest one goes in Date 2.

Given only the info on the CD, I would have put 1988 in Date 1 and 1968 in Date 2. However, because we are such super-duper searchers, I also know that the whole set was issued, as a set, at least once before, probably in 1975. The *ONLY* reason I know this is because we *happened* to run across a record for that LP in OCLC which some kind soul *happened* to catalog. Do I put 1975 in Date 2?

Sometimes the CD actually tells you the issue number and label of the previous release (e.g., "previously released on Harmony LS-2566"). It's easy enough to go to OCLC and pull up that record (if it was cataloged) to see when it was released. But I doubt OCLC expects us to do that kind of research! I guess the basic question is: Do we want to record when the compilation was first released or when the earliest item was copyrighted?

Of course if it were up to me I'd get rid of Dat tp and Dates altogether. The relationships of all the dates can be explained in English in the 260 and notes, and then we spend time learning the intricacies of Dat tp so we can code it in a much less clear fashion, where it goes on to be of no use to anyone! While we're at it, I'd get rid of 80–90 percent of the 007 and 008 as well, since most is a coded version of what has already been stated in the notes or the 300. (Sorry—those fixed fields are my current soapbox. Am I the only voice crying in the wilderness?)

Answer: Let's not forget that things like 007 and 008 were designed to be used by machines, which tend to be dumb and so need things spelled out as simply as possible. Were we designing the MARC format today, we would doubtlessly do it differently, but we haven't that luxury. Ah, the bane of technology that never stands still.

The Dates/Date Type question really isn't that hard, especially when you know as much about the history of the item as you have found out (if inadvertently) about this one. You know the presumed CD publication date, which is obviously Date 1. As candidates for Date 2, you know the phonogram dates of the various pieces of the whole, plus the date of the release of the whole as an LP. No one expected you to go beyond the item itself to find out that latter date, but since you *do* know it, it *is* more information.

With all this information, just go to the table of precedence for Date Type (BF&S p. FF:30; *Music Coding and Tagging* p. 6) and stop once you get to the first one that fits. In this case, you have the "reprint" date and the original date (1988 and 1975, Dates 1 and 2 respectively), Date Type "r". That's it. Of course, be sure you explain the 1975 date in a note about the LP release.

Had you been less diligent and not found the date of the LP release, but still mentioned the fact that it originally appeared on LP, the Date 2 would be blank, though Date Type could still be "r". If you knew only the phonogram dates but not about the item's previous release as an LP, you would code Date Type "p" (assuming the phonogram dates are the dates of the original recordings), with Date 2 as 1968. Proving once again that virtue is its own punishment. *Newsletter 59 (November 1994)*

2.17 QUESTION: How should libraries submit change requests for compact discs or videos that have been remastered from the original medium (LP, film, etc.) but without a publication date reflecting the new medium?

Answer: There is no special procedure for submitting change requests for CDs or videos released in the new format but still identified by the date of release in the original medium. AACR2r 1.4F2, 1.4F7, 1.7B7, 1.7B9, and related rules in Chapters 6 and 7, as well as RIs and Music Cataloging Decisions are all the justification needed. If there is evidence for a "better" date of publication (in accompanying material, a catalog, publisher's material, etc.), that can help, but at the very least, an approximate date of publication (1.4F7) can be supplied.

Compact disc sound recordings became commercially available in Japan in October 1982, in Europe in February 1983, and in the United States in March 1983. Hence, dates prior to these cannot be considered legitimate dates of publication for CDs. Videos are more problematic, but my research suggests that Beta format became commercially available in May 1975 and VHS format sometime in mid-1977.

This problem with dates is a perennial one, but we are eager to change or correct any record that appears to be coded incorrectly and to merge records that appear to be describing the same item despite such date discrepancies. *Newsletter 57 (May 1994)*

2.18 QUESTION: Looking at a set of LPs from Italy, I have been able to find neither a phonogram date nor a copyright date on the labels or containers. However, these recordings do have a date engraved in the vinyl outside the label: a "p" in a circle, then a date such as "20/4/82." Do you think this is actually a phonogram date? Can I use it in the 260? Do I need to do anything special with it, such as put it in brackets and/or use a question mark, use some kind of 500 note?

Answer: It sure sounds like a phonogram date. When I originally answered this question, I suggested using the date "[1982?]." However, going back to 6.0B1, the chief source of information for a disc is the disc itself as well as the label, so the brackets and the question mark actually are unnecessary: p1982. Just to avoid any confusion, I might want to add a 500 note about where the date came from. *Newsletter 51 (August 1992)*

2.19 QUESTION: The compact disc in question has no date on the label; on the back cover, it has the dates "p1986", as well as "c1979" and "c1987". I'm pretty sure the "c1979" has to do with the recording date (February 26, 1979) and perhaps a release at that time. I also know that the "c1987" refers to the printed material. What I'm not sure of are the dates for the fixed field and the imprint. Would an imprint of "[1987?], p1986" be correct?

Answer: "[1987?, p1986]" is a possibility (with both dates in brackets, as neither is from the label), but I'd opt for simply "[1987?]" in the 260 $c since there is no date on the label itself and a multiplicity of other dates of uncertain meaning on the container. With 1979 identified as the date of capture, what the "p1986" actually represents is something of a mystery. Any or all of the dates on the item not mentioned in the 260 $c can always be cited in notes. Barring any explicit evidence of a previous release, I'd give it a Date Type "p" with "1987, 1979" in the FF Dates, "[1987?]" in 260 $c, and a 518 note on the capture date. *Newsletter 49 (November 1991)*

2.20 QUESTION: How would you describe, in field 260 $c, a compact disc that has:

1. A "p1962" copyright date on the disc itself,
2. A "c1982" copyright date on the back of the container, and
3. "Consists of previously released material" on the back of the container?

Bearing in mind that no compact discs were published in the United States prior to 1983, my answer would be: "[between 1983 and 1990], p1962." I considered "[1983?], p1962" but was reluctant to infer a publication date from the "c1982." Using "[1982]" would clearly be incorrect. I am inclined to use something that is obviously not wrong rather than something that might or might not be exactly right.

Answer: Your solution of "[between 1983 and 1990], p1962" (Date type: q; Dates: 1983, 1990) seems reasonable, assuming that the CD in question was published in the United States (CDs were available in Japan in October 1982, if my information is correct). The "[1983?], p1962" (Date type: r; Dates: 1983,1962) idea is also acceptable, given what we know of CD history. Both that AACR2 question mark and the "between X and Y" construction indicate uncertainty; choosing between the two is choosing the degree of uncertainty you feel comfortable with. But let's not turn AACR2 into a pop psychology book. Either is OK, though you may want to include some kind of note that details the available dates and their sources (6.7B9) to prevent confusion. Plus, "Consists of previously released material" makes for a dandy quoted note. *Newsletter 48 (August 1991)*

2.21 QUESTION: I often find Date Type/Dates Fixed Field errors in the OLUC. Is there any way to encourage people to code them correctly, especially since incorrect dates can hinder access to items?

Answer: Those fixed field elements are among the most confusing in the MARC format. The situation is not helped by compact discs that carry only the date of their original recording or release while giving no hint of the date of release in the CD format. I wish there were some rule of thumb that could apply to every situation, but I haven't found one yet. Since CDs seem to cause the most trouble these days, you might want to try and see if this helps.

Consider all the dates found on the item, whether on the CD itself, the container, or the accompanying material, keeping in mind that the disc and label are the chief source of information. Remember also that CDs became commercially available in Japan in October 1982, in Europe in February 1983, and in the United States in March 1983. Use AACR2R 1.4F and 6.4F and their rule interpretations to determine the most reasonable date or set of dates. For CDs, it's useful to recall that "c" copyright dates will usually refer to the printed material or artwork accompanying the disc; this date may be used to help *estimate* a publication or release date. A phonogram or "p" date is the copyright date of the recorded sound; if it predates the commercial availability dates of CDs, it obviously cannot be the publication or release date of the CD. In such cases, an approximate release date must be formulated using one of the various options outlined in 1.4F. *Newsletter 47* (*April 1991*)

2.22 QUESTION: Compact discs sometimes carry only a date that is clearly too early to be the publication date of the CD. What should we do?

Answer: CDs became commercially available in Japan in October 1982, in Europe in February 1983, and in the United States in March 1983. If you suspect that the date on a CD does not correspond to the actual date of issue, formulate a more accurate set of dates by applying AACR2 1.4F2, 1.4F5, 1.4F6, 1.4F7, and their respective LC Rule Interpretations. *Newsletter 39* (*May 1989*)

006 FIELD

2.23 QUESTION: Say I'm cataloging a book that is accompanied by a clearly subordinate sound recording with musical examples. When I create field 006 for the accompanying sound recording, do I code the REC006 "AccM" for the book it accompanies?

Answer: Just a bit circular, no? Please, don't make me dizzy. I'd suggest reserving the REC006 "AccM" for material that actually accompanies the recording itself: the program notes or booklet in the CD jewel box, for instance. Coding for the book would be redundant and strictly speaking, inaccurate, since the accompanying relationship is really the other way around. *Newsletter 64* (*August 1996*)

007 FIELD

2.24 QUESTION: Could you please settle a debate for us? In field 007 for Sound Recordings, subfield $m would appear to not apply to many recordings due to the instruction, "Use only if a special process applied during recording must also be supplied during reproduction." Would, say, a Dolby-processed audiobook cassette get a value of "c" if the item states "Dolby"? Would a CD recording always get a value of "e"? Or is the field truly used only for special recording and playback situations? For subfield $n would the value be tied to the presence of DDD/ADD/AAD notations on the item?

Answer: As the recording industry has evolved in recent years, many things that were once "special" have become commonplace, so the choice of that term has grown to be unfortunate. The point is that subfield $m (Sound Recording 007/12) should be coded whenever it is necessary to indicate a relevant playback characteristic. You have noted the two most common instances. Subfield $m should nearly always be coded "c" for commercial sound cassettes (and other tape formats) that have a Dolby insignia. (The rare exceptions are those tapes that specifically require specialized Dolby-A or Dolby-C playback equipment, but those will be clearly marked as such. Code "c" is for the commercial standard Dolby-B.) All audio compact discs should have subfield $m coded "e" for digital recording, as they all require digital playback equipment (that is, a CD player). Regarding the coding of subfield $n (Sound Recording 007/13), those so-called "SPARS codes" can be of assistance. More specifically, the first position can give an indication of the correct subfield $n code. Remember that subfield $n indicates the *original* sound storage technique, not any subsequent manipulation of the sound (such as mixing or remastering). Where the first position of the SPARS code is "D" (for digital), the subfield $n should be coded "d" for digital storage. When the first SPARS position is "A" (for analog), you also need to pay attention to the era of the original sound capture. If the date of the original capture predates the 1927/1929 period when electrical recording techniques were being developed, the correct code would be "a" for "acoustical capture, direct storage." Recordings captured between then and the late 1940s (as well as more recent recordings touted as "direct-to-disc" and the like) are most likely coded "b" for "direct storage, not acoustical." From the development of magnetic recording in the late 1940s to the dawn of the digital age in the early 1980s, most recordings should be coded "e" for "analog electrical storage." The SPARS organization withdrew its endorsement of the codes in 1991, by which time the simple A/D dichotomy had become (in their own description) "cluttered." As a result, SPARS codes are far less common today than they had been in the past. If there is no SPARS code on an item, there may be some other sort of indication of the original sound capture technique in notes or credits on the item. In the absence of any definite evidence, and if you cannot make a reasonably good guess, code it "u" for unknown. *Newsletter 80 (May 2002)*

2.25 QUESTION: In the Sound Recording 007 field, subfield $c (REC 007/02, Original versus reproduction aspect), how do I figure this out? Are all mass-produced items reproductions, or what? Is it important to code this element? Moving on to the Sound Recording 007 field, subfield $m (REC 007/12, Special playback characteristics), often a tape will say Dolby (or have the Dolby double D sign) but the choices for coding seem to be Dolby-A, Dolby-B, or Dolby-C. Do I assume one of these choices, or mark unknown, or other?

Answer: The subfields $c (007/02) of all the 007 fields have been made obsolete in the newly published MARC 21. OCLC has long recommended omitting this subfield when you formulate any 007 field. Eventually, we hope to do a scan to delete all instances of the subfield from WorldCat. In the Sound Recording 007 field, subfield $m, code "c" (Dolby-B encoded) is used for the standard Dolby noise reduction found on most commercial audiotapes (often indicated by the "double D" insignia). Dolby-A and Dolby-C are techniques used in special circumstances and would be explicitly indicated as such on the item. *Newsletter 74 (November 1999)*

2.26 QUESTION: How should we describe the upcoming "DVD-Audio" and "Super Audio CD" formats? Would the 007 field remain the same as for regular CDs?

Answer: In terms of physical description, both DVD-Audio and Super Audio CDs would have the same 300 fields as those of standard audio compact discs, since they all look identical.

300   1 sound disc : $b digital, stereo. ; $c 4 3/4 in.

The designation of playback channels (stereo, mono, etc.) would depend on the individual item, of course. To distinguish either of these new formats, I would suggest using the 538 "System Details Note" to indicate which format is represented. Transcribe the format as it appears on the item.

538   DVD-Audio.
538   Super Audio CD.

Seeing that these formats are technically different and at least currently incompatible, they feel like the audio equivalent of the VHS/Beta difference in videos, so I think this treatment makes sense. The information I've seen on these formats has not said anything about the speed of these discs; if the speed is other than the standard for current audio CDs (1.4 meters per second), then you'd have to code 007 subfield $d with "z" for "other" or "u" for "unknown." If these discs are truly able to play back with multichannel capabilities (that is, as many as six speakers, according to some of the advance hype), subfield $e would have to be coded "z" for "other."

As far as I can tell from the available information, the remaining elements would not change. *Newsletter 74 (November 1999)*

2.27 QUESTION: I'm cataloging a CD of Marian Anderson singing. All the recordings were made between 1928 and 1939. The copy I have put "mono." in the 300, though that info is not on the item anywhere. AACR2 says to "give the number of sound channels if the information is readily available." I guess if you happen to know that stereo was not used until the late 1950s that info is readily available to you. But if you hadn't happened across that fact, putting no info about sound channels in the 300 would also be correct. Right? Same business with $n of 007. BF&S gives a nice little history of sound recording techniques in the instructions for when to use the various codes. Considering the dates of recording on this CD, it seems likely that "b", "direct storage, not acoustical" was the method used. (The earliest recording, from 1928, might even be "a", acoustical.) The item has a SPARS code of ADD (also says the sound was transferred from the original 78s and digitally remastered). Usually ADD is my cue to code $n as "e". But BF&S, in its little history, says analog electrical storage didn't exist until the late 1940s. So would $n "b" be best here? By the way, I listened to a couple of the tracks. You do hear music through both channels but as far as I can tell it is the same music (i.e., not more bass on one and more treble on the other). That is, mono sound manipulated to come out both speakers on your stereo system so it sounds a little more balanced in your living room. Sound reasonable? (Pardon the unintentional pun.)

Answer: Since you are not supposed to be required to go beyond the item itself for such information, if the item does not say either "mono." or "stereo." you may leave out the information all together in the 300. Since you know what you know about recording history and can confirm it with your ears and maybe a set of headphones, you may supply the correct designation. But you don't have to. That first "A" in the SPARS code signifies that analog technology was used in the original recording session. One suspects that in the SPARS definition, "analog" covers everything pre-digital (or even non-digital), so you may need your knowledge of the history to correctly code 007 subfield $n (if you choose not to use "u"). Chances are "b" is correct. Even monaural sound will come out of both speakers/channels. It's just that both will sound exactly the same, without any of the "channel separation" that creates the illusion of stereophonic sound. *Newsletter 69 (April 1998)*

2.28 QUESTION: What exactly is the "SPARS" code?

Answer: "SPARS" stands for the Society of Professional Audio Recording Services, the organization that created what we know informally as the

"SPARS code" in the early 1980s. You can read more about the organization on their Web site at http://www.spars.com/. Here is what the Web site has to say about the SPARS code: "[I]t was designed for use with CD releases to delineate exactly which parts of the recording process were digital and which were analog. This program consisted of a series of guidelines set down by SPARS and given to CD manufacturers so that they might mark their product honestly and precisely. This program flourished until the early 1990's when the digital/analog technical scene became so cluttered with conversions and algorithms for interface as to resemble rocket science. The simple code was no longer able to carry enough information to be meaningful. SPARS withdrew endorsement of the code in 1991, although some labels still use it today." The three-character code appears on many CDs, usually on the packaging or on the disc label itself. I am told that the code also appears occasionally on audiocassettes. "D" stands for "digital" and "A" for "analog." The three positions correspond to the technology used in the original sound capture, in subsequent mixing and editing, and in the mastering, respectively. The most common codes are: DDD, indicating that digital technology was used in the original recording session, in subsequent mixing and editing, and in the mastering; ADD, indicating that analog technology was used in the original recording session, but digital technology was used in subsequent mixing and editing, and in the mastering; and AAD, indicating that analog technology was used in the original recording session and in subsequent mixing and editing, but digital technology was used in the mastering. The first position of the code may be useful in determining the correct value for field 007 subfield $n ("Capture and storage technique"). The remaining two positions of the code are not useful for cataloging. *Newsletter 69 (April 1998)*

2.29 QUESTION: I'm cataloging a CD that says in little letters on the back of the container:

"(Recorded 1951–1958, in concert *1955, **1958) Mono except track 12."

Where and how is the "mono" information recorded, and how does it affect the 007? The copy in OCLC added the phrase, "principally in mono." to the 518 and said nothing in the 300, coding subfield $e of the 007 as "u" for unknown. I've considered a few options: (1) leave it the way it is on the copy; (2) leave the phrase in the 518 with nothing in the 300, but code the 007 $e as "m"; (3) put "mono., <stereo.>" in the 300 and use two 007s, one with $e as "m" and the other as "s". Since track 12 is the very latest of the recording dates, it's certainly in stereo, but the item doesn't *say* it's in stereo except by implication. Can I assume? Also, must one have information in the 300 specifically in order to code the 007 when it comes to mono/stereo? (Information for $n is not recorded anywhere at all in the bib record—you just figure it out and code it.)

Answer: Your third option sounds closest to what I would suggest. Just for your peace of mind, you might confirm with a set of earphones that track 12 is indeed stereo. You don't need to bracket the "stereo." since the 300 field does not purport to be transcribed data. Both "mono." and "stereo." do belong in the 300, as per AACR2 6.5C7. That would mean two 007 fields, one with subfield $e coded "m", the other coded "s". How you want to present the 518 note is really up to you, but you may note which tracks were recorded in concert and when, for instance (obviously, I'm making up the tracks):

518   Recorded 1951–1958; tracks 2 and 9 recorded in concert, 1955 and 1958, respectively.

A quoted 500 note, "Mono. except track 12" would also be appropriate. That could remain combined with the 518, but I think it can stand alone. I've always liked to think that the playback configuration should be stated in the 300 for it to be coded in the 007, but that's only my little compulsion. In fact, LC's stated policy in its "Music Files Input-Update Manual" is: "For CDs, LC practice is to code s unless the item is known to be other than stereo." *Newsletter 68 (November 1997)*

2.30 QUESTION: I'm cataloging an audiocassette where people are reading love poetry and love letters from across the ages (excerpts from the Song of Solomon to something Thomas Mann wrote to his wife). It's in German. Everything about it is relatively normal except the SPARS code, which is "DDA". No doubt that's possible, but hardly likely. The Germans don't do them backwards, do they? What should I record in 007 $n?

Answer: If you're absolutely sure that this is a SPARS code (I'm not sure I've ever seen one on an audiocassette), here is my guess. The original recording technology (first "D") was digital as was the subsequent mixing and editing (second "D"). As this is an analog audiocassette, the master tape ("A tape containing the final production version of a sound recording [after studio editing, special processing, etc.], and used to make . . . a tape duplication master for the manufacture of recordings in a tape format"—Thorin & Vidali *The Acquisition and Cataloging of Music and Sound Recordings: A Glossary*, 1984) could be analog. In any case, only the first code is important in determining the 007 subfield $n, and if that code is "D", the $n should be "d". *Newsletter 66 (May 1997)*

2.31 QUESTION: To follow up, I don't believe I've ever seen a SPARS code on a cassette or vinyl disc either, just CDs. On this cassette, the "DDA" is the right size, in the kind of typography you often see, in the sort of place you'd expect to see it. It just looks and smells and quacks like a SPARS code. The letters are enclosed in a rectangle with lines between the letters (which is not as typical) but that doesn't ruin the overall effect of looking like a SPARS code. And yes, if the Germans don't do them backwards (and surely a SPARS code is international?) then 007 $n is "d". I wonder if the master tape is often analog when the final playback format is going to be analog (cassette or vinyl disc). If the decision is ever made to reissue as a CD, you're stuck with the analog master and would have to remaster to digital. As this is spoken recording, however, a high-end sound is not so important. Maybe that's why.

Answer: The Germans wouldn't do it backwards. Now, if the cassette were in Arabic or Hebrew. . . . Seriously though, your speculation about analog masters for a final analog product corresponds with mine, but I don't really know enough about the recording process to be sure. In this case, since the original recording was digital, one supposes a digital master could later be created from it for the manufacture of CDs. *Newsletter 66 (May 1997)*

2.32 QUESTION: Is "Digalog" on audiocassettes another way of saying that it is a digital recording? Can I put a "d" in subfield $n of the 007?

Answer: The "digalog" designation, judging from the little blurb that accompanies the logo on the accompanying insert, seems to be marketing hype for a "new cassette manufacturing process [that] links state of the art digital mastering and duplication directly to the finished analog cassette." If this description is accurate, it says nothing directly about how the sound was originally captured (the basis for 007 subfield $n coding), only about mastering and duplication. Unless there is other evidence elsewhere on the item, we know nothing about the original capture and storage. Strictly speaking, 007 $n should be "u" for unknown in this case. Nowadays, however, unless there is specific evidence to the contrary (a SPARS code, something that says "analog recording" or something to that effect, a pre-digital era recording date, etc.), most recently captured recordings tend to be digitally captured and stored. Given that, code 007 $n according to how far out on a limb you are willing to go. *Newsletter 65 (November 1996)*

2.33 QUESTION: For the Sound Recording 007 field, what must the SPARS code be for the subfield $n to be coded "d"?

Answer: The only SPARS code that really counts for 007 $n is the first and it must be "D". *Newsletter 63 (May 1996)*

2.34 QUESTION: Very recently, I've been seeing compact discs that have the words "Digital Master" enclosed in a little rectangle somewhere on the item. I'm wondering if this should affect coding in 007 subfield $n. I know that digital remasters are considered analog recordings, but if the words are "Digital Master," I'm not sure. I was tending toward yes, those words would make it a digital recording. Then I was looking at a CD entitled *16 Most Requested Television Themes* (OCLC #31198359). There is no little rectangle, but in the little booklet it states, "Mixed and Digitally Mastered by: Chris Herles, Sony Music Studios, New York City" (not REmastered. Just "mastered"). Well, these are themes from *I Love Lucy, Green Acres, Hogan's Heroes,* etc. Some of them are marked as being in mono. These things *can't* be original digital masters. The booklet also gives the original recording dates for all these items, ranging from 1951 through 1966, with the theme from *Hill Street Blues* tossed in, from 1981.

As SPARS codes become less common, I depend on what other indications there are. Occasionally I see "Original Digital Recording!" splashed on the label or container and take that as sufficient evidence. But if the language is changing . . . well, in short, do you have any ideas on this?

Answer: These publishers just don't know how to behave in civilized company, do they? I'm doing some guessing here, but let's recall what a "master" is: "an original positive recording with pits etched on a blank disc by a laser activated by a digitally recorded master tape, and used to make the matrices from which compact discs are produced in multiple copies" (Thorin & Vidali *The Acquisition and Cataloging of Music and Sound Recordings,* 1984). In 007 $n, we're talking about the original capture and storage of the sound, not about any subsequent manifestation (such as mastering). As you've figured out, recordings predating the early 1980s (or maybe the very late 1970s, if we stretch it) cannot possibly be digital capture and storage. Unless you want to include a quoted note of some kind, I think you can pretty much ignore indications of both mastering and remastering. In SPARS coding, 007 $n is concerned only with the first character; the other two can be ignored. *Newsletter 62 (November 1995)*

2.35 QUESTION: Here's a follow-up as to what constitutes a digital recording. I'm never quite sure where the lines are drawn in the SPARS codes. The last one is the playback; the first one is capture; the middle one is mixing and editing; and I don't know where storage fits, the first or middle code. The 007 $n is for capture *and* storage. A digital master sounded like storage to me, but that didn't necessarily imply digital capture since there are remasters. But if $n is for both capture and storage, could one be analog and the other digital?

Answer: If you look at the codes in USMARC, you'll notice that the definitions already account for the distinction you're making. Code "d" (digital storage) indicates electrical capture and digital storage; "a" acoustical (nonelectric) capture and direct storage; "b" electrical capture and direct storage; "e" electrical capture and analog electrical storage. Other combinations (unlikely, I imagine) would be coded "z". I think the only "capture" options are acoustical/nonelectric or electric. The first SPARS code would actually be for "storage." From an old CD, I have explanations as follows for the SPARS first character: "D" is "digital tape recorder used during session recording"; "A" is "analog tape recorder used during session recording." "Capture" must be understood as electrical, I guess, via microphone. *Newsletter 62 (November 1995)*

2.36 QUESTION: Can you give me a year (either definite or approximate) when CDs started to be manufactured and sold? Sometimes we have trouble assigning a value to the 007 subfield $n, and knowing that such and such a date is before CDs existed would help.

Answer: Audio compact discs first became available commercially in Japan in October 1982, in Europe in February 1983, and in the United States in March 1983. Not until 1984 were they actually manufactured in North America. These facts are extremely useful when trying to determine the publication date of a CD, but are not directly related to the coding of 007 subfield $n. Subfield $n records "capture and storage," that is, the original recording method. Digital recording methods were around before CDs, certainly in the early 1980s and (according to my research) possibly as early as 1978. Code $n as "digital storage" only when the recording in question says so (many later LPs were digitally recorded, just as many CDs derive from pre-digital recordings, usually "analog electrical storage" [code "e"]. Those three-letter codes (DDD, ADD, and AAD) found on many CDs are a help, as the first character indicates either digital or analog technology used for the original recording. *Newsletter 61 (August 1995)*

2.37 QUESTION: To follow up regarding those CDs that were recorded say around 1990, am I wrong to assume that these would be digital storage, thus code "d" in 007 subfield $n? And if there is no evidence of recording date or reissue, and the CD issue date is say 1989, should I use "u" instead of "d" in 007 subfield $n?

Answer: If the CD contains no evidence of a recording date or any suggestion that it may be a reissue, and if you have no other reason to suspect that the original sound may predate the digital era, it is probably safe to assume that the capture was digital. It often seems that the earlier the CD, the more likely it is to be explicit about its recording technique. In cases where you have any doubt, coding subfield $n as "unknown" is certainly safe; no one will hold it against you. Above all, try to remember Weitz's First Law: Don't agonize. *Newsletter 61 (August 1995)*

2.38 QUESTION: In the 007 field, subfields $j, $k, and $l are for "archival use only." What does this mean? When cataloging your average, run-of-the-mill compact disc, can I assume subfield $j (kind of disc, cylinder, or tape) should be coded "m" for "mass produced, commercially produced"? Similarly, can I assume that subfield $k (kind of material) for a CD is "m", metal and plastic? Is subfield $l (kind of cutting) coded "n" (i.e., not applicable for a compact disc)? Perhaps I should simply ignore these fields?

Answer: Your 007 coding is right on the mark. The "archival use only" means that the positions are optional for most commercially available stuff. So unless you are a perfectionist, you can safely omit them in your usual work. You may want to make sure that leaving out these values does not cause a problem for your local system. *Newsletter 61 (August 1995)*

2.39 QUESTION: I have an LP that says DUOPHONIC on the label where the MONO or STEREO designation would normally appear. On the slipcase it says, "This recording should be played only with a stereo cartridge & stylus." In the past, I've given LPs that included such a warning a "u" code in the 007 $e, provided, of course, they were labeled neither mono nor stereo. Does that sound like a reasonable plan with this LP? I've never seen "DUOPHONIC."

Answer: This is a guess, but I seem to recall at least one record label (RCA?) using the "duophonic" designation as a fancy way of saying "stereo" early in the stereo era. It was probably marketing/advertising puffery and I'd say it's OK to consider this just plain stereo in the 007 and the 300. You might want to add a quoted note with the "duophonic" information to prevent any confusion. *Newsletter 55 (August 1993)*

2.40 QUESTION: As a related follow-up, I was always under the impression that when coding the subfield $e of the 007 (configuration of playback channels) and completing the "Other physical details" portion of Area 5 of the description, that I should describe the playback characteristics of the piece in hand, not the original recording or any subsequent/intermediate mixes, rechanneling, etc. If there are two channels on a "duophonic" LP and different parts of the mix come out of each of two speakers used in playback, I would be inclined to describe it as "stereo." Isn't that correct?

Answer: You are correct. All of those reprocessed "fake" stereo monstrosities of the past are to be coded as stereo, both in the 007 and in the 300. Of course, one could also include a quoted note about the nature of the particular "stereo-ness," such as it is ("Reprocessed to simulate stereo" or whatever the label/container says). What's important here for cataloging purposes is the playback equipment needed (stereo stylus, two speakers, etc.) for this particular manifestation of the recording, not how good or bad it sounds. That the original recording may have been mono is good to know, but it's irrelevant for playback purposes. *Newsletter 55 (August 1993)*

2.41 QUESTION: For sound recording cataloging, should we be using the 007 subfields $j, $k, and $l on new records for non-archival cataloging, that is, filling in all positions in field 007, even those that are not applicable?

Answer: Subfields $j, $k, and $l have always been optional in field 007 (see *Bibliographic Input Standards*, 5th ed., p. 50). You are welcome to include them if you wish, but you needn't feel obligated. No doubt, you have noticed that LC codes all the positions (at least all of the positions that they have so far validated in their version of the USMARC format). In LC's MARC format, the 007 is a simple string of characters; each one must be coded (or contain a fill character) in order for all the others to keep their respective positions and meanings. OCLC displays this string broken up into subfields, which allows users to omit certain optional positions. *Newsletter 54 (May 1993)*

2.42 QUESTION: If the SPARS code on a compact disc is DAD, is the capture and storage technique (field 007 $n) considered to be digital or analog? We have a difference of opinion about whether a tape digitally recorded but analog mixed and edited constitutes digital capture (yes) and storage (maybe not).

Answer: Frankly, I'd never seen or heard of a recording coded DAD or anything other than the three standard combinations that are sometimes listed on CDs: DDD, ADD, and AAD. The three letters refer to the equipment used during session (original) recording, mixing and/or editing, and mastering (transcription), respectively. In coding 007 $n, only the first letter of the code need be regarded, as it is the only one to indicate the original capture and storage technique. Any recording enhancements involving subsequent mixing or editing (the second letter of the code) or mastering (the third letter) can be ignored here. The apparent illogic of using analog equipment for mixing and editing but digital equipment for everything else makes me wonder if the "DAD" is simply an abbreviation for "digital audio disc," as is (sort of) suggested by Carole Franklin Vidali on p. 28 of *The Acquisition and Cataloging of Music and Sound Recordings: A Glossary* by

Suzanne E. Thorin and Vidali (MLA Technical Report no. 11). *Newsletter 44* (*August 1990*)

2.43 QUESTION: In the 007 field for sound recordings, both subfields $d and $g have special codes to use when cataloging compact discs. Subfield $d (speed) indicates that "f" is used for CDs (1.4 m. per sec.) and subfield $g (dimensions) uses "g" for CDs (4 3/4 in.). However, in our experience, we are finding that many institutions are using "z" for both of these subfields when cataloging CDs. Why is this?

Answer: Before the MARC format was revised to accommodate coding for CDs, there was no proper value for either the speed or the dimensions of compact discs. Until those values were assigned and revision pages to the OCLC Sound Recordings Format were issued in early 1987, "z" was the correct value in each case. Now, however, the specific values for each should be used for all current input. *Newsletter 43* (*May 1990*)

033 FIELD

2.44 QUESTION: In field 033 for sound recordings, how would one apply the section on time differential from Greenwich Mean Time? Would this always be standard time or does it also adjust for daylight savings time? Since daylight savings times vary, I would think that it would always need to be adjusted to standard time.

Answer (courtesy of Glenn Patton): According to ANSI X3.51-1986 (the ANSI standard on which this technique of representing local times by recording a combination of Greenwich Mean Time and a time differential), the time differential varies according to whether daylight savings was in effect. Thus, for example, the time differential for Eastern Standard Time is "–500," while the time differential for Eastern Daylight Savings Time is "–400." The standard contains two handy tables listing the time differentials for the nine time zones used in North America. There is a similar ISO standard (ISO 3307-1975) that may have a similar chart for the world as a whole, but I've never seen a copy of the ISO standard. *Newsletter 48* (*August 1991*)

041 FIELD

2.45 QUESTION: If only one language is associated with a score or sound recording, so that the fixed field Language and all relevant subfields of any 041 field would contain the same, single three-letter code, is it necessary to include field 041?

Answer: When only one language is involved and the Language fixed field covers it, no 041 field is needed. *Newsletter 54* (*May 1993*)

EDITION

2.46 QUESTION: Does the use of "abridged" and "unabridged" as edition statements for audiobooks appear in print anywhere?

Answer: The closest example that I find in print is in AACR2 Rule 21.12A1, the final example on p. 334. It's not an audiobook, but the edition statement reads: "Abridged popular ed. of the three vols. of Capital edited by Julian Borchardt ; translated by Stephen L. Trask." In OCLC's *Bibliographic Formats and Standards* (p. 2:40 in print; http://www.oclc.org/bibformats/en/2xx/250.shtm online), the section on the definition of "edition statement" includes several categories of different editions that might otherwise have identical titles; the final category is "General editions (e.g., editions that contain complete contents, whereas their special editions have only portions of the contents)," which seems to cover abridgements exactly. Audiobooks are so often issued in both complete and condensed versions that an "abridged" or "unabridged" edition statement taken from the item is the simplest way to distinguish them bibliographically. *Newsletter 79 (November 2001)*

PUBLISHER

2.47 QUESTION: The label says "Ruffhouse Records" at the top, "Columbia" at the bottom, and the jewel box spine reads "Ruffhouse/ Columbia." Which name do you use in 028 $b and 260 $b?

Answer: AACR2R rule 6.4D2 says that if the recording has both the name of the publisher and the name of a subdivision of the company or a trade name or brand name used by the company, to use the name of the subdivision, the trade name, or the brand name. *Newsletter 67 (August 1997)*

300 FIELD

2.48 QUESTION: On the compact disc I'm cataloging, there is no information about the type of recording speed, etc. The insert, which is in German and English, states only the dates and locations of the recordings. Because of this lack of specific data, I'm not sure what should go in the subfield $b of the 300 field.

Answer: Sound recording compact discs are of standard speed (1.4 meters per second, although that oversimplifies the technology involved, from what I understand), just as they are of standard size (4 3/4 in.). AACR2 6.5C3 stipulates that the playing speed is not included if it is the standard, so for CDs, it is left out. The "digital" in the 300 $b and the "4 3/4 in." size in the subfield $c define the item as a CD. Every compact disc will have "digital" in subfield $b. If the item lacks any indication about stereo/mono, do not supply that information (AACR2 6.5C7). *Newsletter 54 (May 1993)*

2.49 QUESTION: The container for this quadraphonic LP states "CD-4 channel discrete" and goes on to say that it may be played on stereo equipment. Do I need to mention this "CD-4" business in the 300 field?

Answer: Only the designation for "quad." needs to go in the 300. The rest sounds like marketing hype, though you may want to put it (and the stereo-compatible information) in a quoted 500 note. *Newsletter 53 (November 1992)*

2.50 QUESTION: An LP that I'm cataloging indicates that one side is a stereo recording, the other side mono. How do I indicate this?

Answer: AACR2R 6.5C7 says to include as many of the appropriate terms (mono., stereo., quad.) as needed in the physical description (300 $b).

1 sound disc : $b analog, 33 1/3 rpm, mono., stereo. ; $c 12 in.

Code a separate 007 field for each "number of sound channels" designation; in this case you would have two, the difference being the coding in subfield $e ("s" for stereo, "m" for mono). If deemed important, which works were stereo and which mono could be indicated in a note. *Newsletter 49 (November 1991)*

DURATIONS

2.51 QUESTION: Please help me understand the format of durations for sound recordings when they are entered in field 500. AACR2 6.7B10 has an example: "Durations: 17 min. ; 23 min. ; 9 min." Your workshop on the University of Buffalo Web site has an example: "Durations: 1:17:00; 22:40." Should we be using the min. and sec. approach, or the 00:00:00 approach?

Answer: Music Cataloging Decision 6.7B10 stipulates that durations appearing in the notes area (either in a 500 duration note or in a 505 contents note) are to be expressed in the HH:MM:SS format, with hours, minutes, and seconds separated by colons. When an item contains only one musical work (as defined by AACR2), the total duration is given in the physical description (300) field and is stated in the form "XX hr., XX min., XX sec." according to LCRI and MCD 6.5B2. *Newsletter 76 (September 2000)*

2.52 QUESTION: At the grade school where I'm volunteering, I'm currently working on "sound-books"—paperback books accompanied by a tape cassette, which has the uninterrupted story on Side A, and on Side B the story with turn-the-page signals. On Side A the time is given as, for instance, 9:25, and on Side B the time is 10:15. Which duration should be given in $300 after "1 sound cassette"?

Answer: It might be best in an instance such as this to leave the duration out of the 300 subfield $a and to put both durations in a contents note, instead. As a schematic example:

505 0   Side A. Story title [without turn-the-page signals] (9:25) -- Side B. Story
        title [with turn-the-page signals] (10:15).

Newsletter 67 (August 1997)

2.53 QUESTION: Why do you sometimes find a 306 field in a sound recording record without a corresponding note listing the timings?

Answer: When you see a 306 field, you'd generally expect to find the timings to appear also in a 500 field or in a 505 contents note. If you could cite specific records, I might be able to pinpoint why that's not always the case (aside from cataloger oversight). If records have been merged, for instance, a 306 from a deleted record would have transferred automatically, but general 500 notes do not transfer automatically; or even if the retained record's 505 did not include times, the corresponding 505 on the deleted record might have. *Newsletter 67 (August 1997)*

2.54 QUESTION: Does anyone know where we could get, via FTP or disk, a little utility program that can add and subtract time periods expressed in hours and minutes? I would be inclined to provide the total duration in the collation of sound recordings made up of a number of pieces, if I had a handy little program that could perform the calculations quickly.

Answer (of sorts): You should note that according to Music Cataloging Decision 6.5B2 (MCB 21:3 [March 1990] p. 2) the total duration goes in the physical description area *only* when the item contains one work (as defined in AACR2). *Newsletter 57 (May 1994)*

NOTES

2.55 QUESTION: Why do I often see "Compact disc" notes coded as 538s in OCLC records?

Answer: Sometimes the simplest questions have the most involved answers. This one is a long story. In March 1996, an example was added to the then-USMARC Bibliographic Format with the text "Compact disc" as a 538 field (System details note). Apparently, the addition of this example had bypassed certain of the usual review processes. At the 1998 Music Library Association meeting in Boston, the Bibliographic Control Committee discussed the issue and decided that the "Compact disc" note referred only to physical description (AACR2 6.7B10), and so should be coded as a general 500 note. LC practice had always reflected this. The misleading 538 example no longer appears in the print version of the MARC 21 Bibliographic Format or in the concise version on the Web, although it may not have been corrected yet in all print documentation. The 1999 edition of LC's "Music and Sound Recordings Online Manual" includes the "Compact disc" note among the examples in the 500 field. The BCC has issued an announcement that encourages "all sound-recording catalogers to return to the previous practice of coding 'Compact disc(s)' notes in the 500 field." *Newsletter 76 (September 2000)*

2.56 QUESTION: I recently purchased a "shaped" CD, the shape of which isn't the standard 4 3/4 in. circle, and it got me to thinking about how these things should be described. How do you reflect its dimensions in the 300 $c? Would you still give its diameter in inches (as for any other sound recording), or would you use centimeters? The container mentions that this type of disc is "Not playable in CD changer or car CD player." Would you put this information in a 538 note, or just a standard 500? The disc is (very) roughly triangular in shape. At its widest, the CD's diameter is about 4 1/2 in. The disc (for want of a better term) is an interview CD featuring the British heavy metal group Iron Maiden. It was published in 1997 by Sonotec for their Private Talks line, manufactured by Cuba GmbH, Berlin (in fact, they've trademarked the term "Shape CD"), and distributed by DA Music, Germany. The disc itself features a lineup picture of the band with their cadaverous mascot "Eddie" looming over them. The CD is shaped so that it's broad at the bottom and tapers off towards the top. For fans of *Star Trek: Deep Space 9*, it looks very much like a top-down silhouette of the USS Reliant. (How do you like that for an analogy?) The digital information itself is still in circular rings, but takes up only 1/2 to 3/4 of the disc's surface. For an actual picture of this "disc" (as well as others), take a look at the following Web site: http://members.xoom.com/shapecdclub/shapecat9.htm (mine is in the upper left corner of Seite 9).

Answer: Presumably, even though the shape is a bit odd, the CD is still designed to play in most standard CD players (with the exceptions noted). That means that its widest diameter should still be considered the standard 4 3/4 in. and should be so described in the 300 subfield $c (not that 6.5D2 gives us much choice in the matter). I am guessing that the actual playing surface (with the pits and spaces to be read by the laser) remains circular within the odd shape. In accordance with 6.7B10, try to describe the physical shape, perhaps something like:

500   Disc is roughly triangular in shape.

Optionally, as you describe the shape, you could also describe the illustration and how it defines the shape of the CD, for example:

500   Disc is roughly triangular in shape, with portrait of the band across the base and its mascot Eddie at the apex.

If the term "Shape CD" appears on the item, it would be a logical quoted note (500). Additionally, include the statement about the disc not being playable in certain types of machines, either in quoted form or in paraphrase, whichever is appropriate. I think this note fits into the definition of, and could properly be coded as, 538. One also wonders if this is some sort of limited or otherwise special edition, with a standard round disc also being available. If there is some indication of that on the item, you can transcribe an edition statement or optionally formulate one as per 6.2B3. *Newsletter 74 (November 1999)*

2.57 QUESTION: Reading the June 1997 *OLAC Newsletter* I see that computer files catalogers can now put "Compact disc" in the 538 field. Are we sound recordings catalogers still to put "Compact disc" in a 500?

   Answer: That "Compact disc" in 538 has turned out to be somewhat controversial in certain quarters. I think if the decision finally comes down on the side of putting that note in 538, it would apply to Sound Recordings as well as Computer Files. I don't imagine many Sound Recording catalogers are still using that note since CDs became the predominant medium for recorded sound. *Newsletter 67 (August 1997)*

2.58 QUESTION: Does OCLC have an opinion on where to record producers of sound recordings? AACR2R Amendments 1993 says that "producers having artistic and/or intellectual responsibility" can go in the statement of responsibility. But almost no one is doing that; mostly, one finds producers' names given in a vanilla 500 field, when they are mentioned at all. I suspect this is because it's usually very hard to tell whether the producer on a given recording has significant artistic and/or intellectual responsibility. There are a few obvious cases, one of which is the example in the Amendments. Some bands and pop singers apparently come to record with virtually everything decided; for others, the producer is practically part of the composing process. Apart from some folks who are really up on the pop scene, most of us catalogers don't know. So catalogers are hedging and putting them in a 500. Here we'd like to put them in the 508. Vanilla 500s aren't indexed in our keyword system and we don't want to trace them unless we're absolutely sure of their responsibility (in which case we'd put them in the 245 $c). Using a 508 would make them at least keyword accessible. No one else is using 508 (of course, until FI Phase I, it wasn't possible), but it seems a logical place given the definition of the field.

Answer: Field 508 is a fine place for record producers when you believe they need to be recorded. The decision to put them there (and the separate decision to trace them) will depend on individual case judgments, as you have so accurately pointed out the varying intellectual responsibility they may have. By the way, according to the *Guide to Searching the OLUC* (p. 5:32), 500 notes are indexed in PRISM keyword searches of Notes (nt). Here's an idea for a guideline about deciding between 245 $c and 508, but it's based on thin air: If the producer is credited on the disc label, put the credit in 245 $c; if it's only on the container, put it in 508. Does that make any sense? That might also help in deciding about an added entry, though that decision should be even more flexible. *Newsletter 62 (November 1995)*

HEADINGS

2.59 QUESTION: I'm on a music CD cataloging rampage, and I would like to know how others treat musical groups that have a lead performer backed up by other musicians. The item in hand is "Imagination" by Gladys Knight and the Pips. I have done it this way:

```
110 2   Gladys Knight and the Pips (Musical group)
700 1   Knight, Gladys.
```

I intentionally did not make an added entry for "Pips" since to my knowledge this combination of performers has never been known that way. Whereas, I would do an added entry, "Supremes" for a work by Diana Ross and the Supremes, in addition to a main and added entry as shown above. My reasoning here is that at one time the latter was known only as "Supremes." Is this practice correct?

Answer: First of all, I hope you are checking the LC Authority File before you start creating added entries for either personal or corporate names. You'll find that there are established headings for both "Pips (Musical group)" (n82063181) and for "Knight, Gladys, $d 1944–" (n82063180), and coincidentally none for the two together.

This situation of named individual with group is covered by LC Music Cataloging Decision 24.1A: "When the name of an individual performer appears in conjunction with the name of a performing group, ordinarily do not consider the person's name to be a part of the name of the group, in the absence of evidence to the contrary." There is also a reference to this MCD from MCD 21.23D. Since issuing these MCDs (in June 1990; they were published in the September 1990 *Music Cataloging Bulletin*), LC has tried to be consistent, but I bet one can find exceptions.

From what I've been able to gather about LC practices, when the individual's full name is stated, MCD 24.1A is followed, as in the separate headings for Gladys Knight and for the Pips. When only a first name (or a fanciful name) is stated, the established heading for the group tends to include that individual name (with the conjunction depending on predominance in the published works, presumably).

n94116228: Freddie & the Dreamers (Musical group)
n91058379: Echo and the Bunnymen (Musical group)
n91120888: Siouxsie & the Banshees (Musical group)
n91053842: Mike + the Mechanics (Musical group)
nr89012007: Derek and the Dominos (Musical group)

Considering full personal names and the group name to be separate headings also alleviates the identity problem when careers diverge or when the group's name included the individual's name (in varying degrees of fullness) at different times in their careers.

no92002593: Reeves, Martha.
no92002595: Vandellas (Musical group)

n88626491: Robinson, Smokey, $d 1940–
n88034850: Miracles (Musical group)

n88619772: Valli, Frankie, $d 1937–
n88619775: Four Seasons (Musical group)

n82063191: Young, Neil.
n91121880: Crazy Horse (Musical group)

n82089447: Ross, Diana, $d 1944–
n85269719: Supremes (Musical group)

n85235764: Burdon, Eric, $d 1941–
nr89011896: Animals (Musical group)

So if you've checked the authority file and found nothing helpful, you should keep MCD 24.1A in mind when establishing headings for musical performers. *Newsletter 73 (August 1999)*

2.60 QUESTION: I'm working on some more vinyl, mostly 45s and have one by Dave Kennedy (he is the performer; doing 32 instruments himself).

I have him as main entry, but he also cowrote the "A" side, "Pizza pie." The flip side is "Wait 'til the sun shines, Nelly." Should the cowriter and Kennedy get author/title entries? I would think the Kennedy 100 would be enough. I traced the wrong spelled "Wait . . ." in a 740 and did an author/title for "Wait . . ." author. As a general rule, all authors on these 45s receive author/titles tracing, right? It's the songwriter/performer deal I'm wondering about.

Answer: LCRI 21.29D for Sound Recordings says, in part, "If a performer for whom an added entry would be made . . . is also the composer of one or more works on the recording, make an added entry to represent the performing function in addition to any name/title access points (main entry or analytical added entries) made for his or her works." The rules, RIs, and MCDs about added entries are seriously convoluted, but as far as I have been able to disentangle, I think the cocomposer (assuming shared responsibility as defined in the AACR2 glossary and enumerated in Rule 21.6 and that Kennedy is named first) would get a simple name added entry (21.6B2 and 21.30B1). The author/title added entry for "Wait . . ." sounds fine. *Newsletter 69 (April 1998)*

2.61 QUESTION: In constructing headings, would something like "Tony and the Tygers" be considered a musical group itself, or is "Tygers" the musical group and "Tony Dancy" a 700?

Answer: This question is addressed in MCDs 21.29D and 24.1A: "When the name of an individual performer appears in conjunction with the name of a performing group, ordinarily do not consider the person's name to be part of the name of the group, in the absence of evidence to the contrary." Unfortunately, LC doesn't spell out what such evidence might be. Here's a bit of what I've been able to piece together on LC's choices, though one can find occasional exceptions in the authority file.

When the personal name is an integral part of the group name, it usually remains part of the heading:

Mary Lou Williams Trio (n 83045052)
Alan Parsons Project (n 88638380)
Wynton Marsalis Septet (no 96052071)
Paul Butterfield Blues Band (n 86855892)

When the personal name is either fanciful or incomplete (for instance, just a first name), it usually remains part of the heading:

Echo and the Bunnymen (Musical group) (n 91058379)
Mike + the Mechanics (Musical group) (n 91053842)
Sly & the Family Stone (Musical group) (nr 89011868)
Siouxsie & the Banshees (Musical group) (n 91120888)

The personal name may, of course, also have its own heading (as composer or solo artist, etc.):

Williams, Mary Lou, $d 1910– (n 82025133)
Rutherford, Mike (n 86025757)
Stone, Sly (n 91076127)

When the personal name is complete and the group has an identifiable name (as opposed to " . . . and her orchestra"), the personal name and the group name usually take separate headings:

Monroe, Bill, $d 1911– (n 82090832)
Blue Grass Boys (n 82091536)

Haley, Bill (n 82162699)
Comets (Musical group) (n 83046568)

Reeves, Martha (no 92002593)
Vandellas (Musical group) (no 92002595)

You should, of course, search the authority file for different variations before you go creating a heading on your own, as these rough empirical guidelines are not set in stone. *Newsletter 67 (August 1997)*

2.62 QUESTION: In Sound Recordings, should we include a separate added entry for a performer who also happens to be the composer, and therefore the main entry for the item?

Answer: LCRI 21.29D reads, in part: "If a performer for whom an added entry would be made according to the guidelines [outlined in the RI] is also the composer of one or more of the works on the recording, make an added entry to represent the performing function in addition to any name/title access points (main entry or analytical added entries) made for his or her works." Some systems may be able to distinguish performer from composer entries through the use of codes in subfield $4, which is both repeatable and optional. *Newsletter 59 (November 1994)*

2.63 QUESTION: Help me determine the correct form of names for musical groups. The record label reads "Gladys Knight & the Pips." There is an authority record for Knight, Gladys, $d 1944– (n82063180) and a separate record for Pips (Musical group) (n82063181), but no record for them together. On the other hand, the record label reads "Smokey Robinson and the Miracles." There is an authority record for the group together, Smokey Robinson and the Miracles (n88034850), and for Robinson, Smokey, $d

1940– (n88626491), but no record for the Miracles alone. As Marvin Gaye might have asked, What's going on? Why are they done differently and how should I handle other groups that can't be found in the authority file?

Answer: In September 1990, LC issued Music Cataloging Decision 24.1A: "When the name of an individual performer appears in conjunction with the name of a performing group, ordinarily do not consider the person's name to be part of the name of the group, in the absence of evidence to the contrary." It gives the example:

J.D. Crowe and the New South [on item]
Heading: New South (Musical group) (n83073203)

with (presumably, though it does not explicitly say so) a personal name entry for Crowe, J. D. (n82022727). LC probably did not go back to fix those group names already established before the MCD. If you don't find the group name, the individual name, or the combined name in the authority file, follow this MCD in tracing both a personal and a corporate name. Of course, if names are already established in the authority file, follow those. LC seems to be at least marginally more consistent when the personal name is a forename only:

Siouxsie & the Banshees (Musical group) (n91120888)
Mike + the Mechanics (Musical group) (n91053842)

Newsletter 51 (August 1992)

2.64 QUESTION: As a follow-up, in Rule Interpretation 24.4B, "Names not conveying the idea of a corporate body," under "Performing Groups," when does one add the qualifier "(Musical group)"? Paragraph 1 says not to qualify "Boys," but what about Boys (Musical group) (n92005114)?

Answer: Boys (Musical group) actually falls under paragraph 2 of that section of the RI, "If the name is extremely vague, consisting primarily of single, common words . . . add a designation to the name." However, no one will accuse LC of consistency in applying paragraph 1, either. There are authority file examples that both follow—Clay City Ramblers (n81149795)— and defy—Nash Ramblers (Musical group) (n92032662)—RI 24.4B. Oak Ridge Boys (Musical group) (n86116638) appears not to need the qualifier, though it has one. Some of these may (again) be explained because they predate the RI, but I think LC tends to err on the side of qualifying when there is doubt (the Nash Rambler was a car long before it was a musical ensemble). That's probably a good idea for us, too, when we don't find such ambiguous names in the authority file. *Newsletter 51 (August 1992)*

ACETATE RECORDINGS

2.65 QUESTION: I am taking some first trembling steps in cataloging on OCLC a few acetate discs we have in our sound archive, and was wondering if I could get you to hold my hand through some of this. I am not finding much help in the manuals. Acetate discs, as we know, are instantaneous recordings, and the one I have in hand is made of metal, coated with a lacquer compound. Check my logic, the only areas in the MARC record that would indicate the LP's "acetateness" are:

007   archival fields ($j = i and $k = a, and I threw in $l = l, because this was cut in 1967)
260   wherein I would only have a $c (because the thing isn't published)?
500   saying "Acetate disc" or something?

I don't know if you've run into the cataloging of sound recording formats other than the biggies (CD, LP, tape, even 78), but wondered if you had some ideas.

Answer: You seem to have figured out most of what the rules have to say (the AACR2 index under "Nonprocessed sound recordings" collects the major references together). You would use the archival subfields in 007. Only the date of the recording goes in the 260 subfield $c (AACR2 6.4C2, 6.4D4, 6.4F3). If there's anything out of the ordinary about the size, speed, and so on, you'd note that in the 300 field. Give details about the recorded event in 518 (AACR2 6.7B7), if appropriate. Definitely include a note that indicates it's an acetate disc (AACR2 6.7B10). Check for matrix numbers, especially etched into the acetate. There's an old LC record (#13760403, 86-750452/R/r91) that might be worth looking at, by way of example. Oh, and don't drop them. *Newsletter 72 (May 1999)*

COMPACT DISCS

2.66 QUESTION: How do you include a 006 in CatME? I did original cataloging of a bunch of CDs that are also serials. I cataloged them on a sound recording workform, then added various variable fields and an 006 for the seriality aspect. Come to put the record in OCLC through CatME, and you can't call up the prompt screen to fill in the 006. I checked TB 212 again, and all the "how to input the 006" refers to input on PRISM. There have been no update pages to our CatME documentation that I know of.

Answer (courtesy of David Whitehair, CatME Plus Product Manager): First, you must install CatMEPlus Version 1.30. Then, you enter the 006 as a variable field, being careful to get the spacing correct since this tag is position-dependent. CatME Plus does not offer a prompt to help you. However, that will be included in the Windows version of CatME, which is currently in development. *Newsletter 65 (November 1996)*

[Note: The current version of CatME does have the capacity of adding and editing field 006 with prompts using the "Edit" menu's "Field 006" submenu.]

ENHANCED COMPACT DISCS

2.67 QUESTION: I am trying to catalog the new Jesse Cook music CD *Free Fall*. This is a normal music CD for the most part with, if you listen to it on a CD player, 11 songs. However, like they're starting to do these days, if you put it into your CD-ROM drive on your computer, it plays two songs with videos that are not on it if played on the CD player. It states on the cover that "This is an enhanced CD including videos of 'Mario Takes a Walk' and 'Rattle and Burn.'" Is there an example of how to put in the "Mario takes a Walk" and "Rattle and Burn" so that it is easy for the patron to know just what this CD is all about? I looked at the Ricky Martin "Ricky Martin" OCLC #41417091, because it has a screen saver with it but all it said was "enhanced compact disc," which says almost nothing. Do you have any suggestions or are there any current rules you can hook me up with? Here is what I've done so far.

```
024 1    724384929008
028 00   72438-49290-0-8 $b Narada World
100 1    Cook, Jesse.
245 10   Free fall $h [sound recording] / $c Jesse Cook.
260      Milwaukee : $b Narada World, $c p2000.
300      1 sound disc : $b digital ; $c 4 3/4 in.
500      New Age guitar music ; all songs written by Jesse Cook.
500      "This is an Enhanced CD including videos of Mario Takes a Walk and Rattle
         and Burn."
511 0    Jesse Cook, guitars ; with additional musicians.
518      Recorded at Coach House Music, Toronto.
505 00   $t Switchback $g (4:04) -- $t Air $g (3:26) -- $t Virtue $g (4:07) -- $t Free
         fall $g (4:22) -- $t Paloma $g (4:10) -- $t Incantation $g (4:50) -- $t All
         that remains $g (3:15) -- $t On walks the night $g (6:36) -- $t Querido
         amigo $g (3:29) -- $t Viva $g (4:20) -- $t Fall at your feet $g (3:38).
505 00   $t Mario takes a walk -- $t Rattle and burn.
650 0    New Age music.
650 0    Guitar music.
650 0    Guitar music (Flamenco).
```

I did separate the two "hidden" songs.

Answer: The record you have created is a good start. Because you have already included the "Enhanced CD" quoted note with the video titles, you don't really need the second 505. What you do need is a 538 stating the system requirements for the two video tracks and a CF 006 field and CF 007 field for the computer file aspects of the disc. Although I've not examined these records closely enough to endorse all of the cataloging choices, here are a few samples of cataloging for "enhanced CDs": #45020530, #44625338, #44685581. *Newsletter 78 (May 2001)*

2.68 QUESTION: Is there any differentiation in the MARC record for enhanced CDs?

Answer: At MLA in 1999, LC promised it would issue some sort of guidelines on so-called "enhanced CDs," but I never heard anything about it after that. What I've been telling people is to include a quoted note, if appropriate, that indicates what the CD calls itself (or just a note that says "Enhanced compact disc"). A 538 field will be needed for the system requirements for the computer file aspects. A computer file 006 field will also be needed for those aspects. Whatever special features are included can be outlined either in a general note or as part of the contents, whichever makes more sense. Otherwise, the cataloging is pretty much the same as any other sound recording. There is currently no special coding for such enhanced CDs. *Newsletter 78 (May 2001)*

2.69 QUESTION: Here's a question for you about order of notes. When you have one of these "enhanced" CDs, which can be played on a regular CD player or on a computer, where do you place the system requirements note? For computer software, it's one of the first notes, but that does not seem appropriate in this case. Would it be considered as another format available, 6.7B16?

Answer: There doesn't seem to be a really obvious place to put the 538 for an "enhanced" CD. My inclination would be to include it somewhere after the various statement of responsibility notes such as 511 (corresponding to AACR2 6.7B6) but before any notes on accompanying material (6.7B11) and certainly before a formal 505 contents note (6.7B18). I guess it might be thought of as a sort of combination edition/history (6.7B7), physical description (6.7B10), and accompanying material note, depending on what information it provides. I wouldn't agonize over its exact placement as long as it's snuggled in there somewhere between the 511 and 505. By the way, the Library of Congress announced at the 1999 MOUG/MLA meetings in Los Angeles that the Cataloging Policy and Support Office was soon going to distribute its guidelines on cataloging "enhanced" CDs, so that's something to keep your eyes open for. *Newsletter 72 (May 1999)*

2.70 QUESTION: About your answer to the question on the Smithsonian/Microsoft "Crossroad" CD in the *MOUG Newsletter* no. 67

(p. 12, first question), it is my understanding that we are supposed to (and would want to) add a field 007 whenever possible. In the case of this audio CD/CD-ROM I would want to catalog it as a sound recording, add the 538 and 006 for computer files, in addition to any other informational 500 note describing the enhanced status, and also add field 007 for computer files. Do you see this last step as somehow redundant or unnecessary or not valuable? It was my understanding that 007s could (perhaps not should?) be added for every format possible. In other words if the 006 could have a corresponding 007 (not always possible), add it. Clarification?

Answer: Once again, bibliographic realities have overtaken the bibliographic format. To be honest, I've wondered the same question and have tried to avoid it. Historically, the 007 field has been a coded extension of the physical description field. There were cases where multiple 007s would be appropriate: for kits, when multiple physical items are being described; when multiple aspects of an item (most commonly, the presence of both mono. and stereo. tracks on the same sound recording or color and black-and-white sequences in the same film or video) required multiple 007s for each aspect to be coded; and when the same item is issued in more than one format and all are cataloged or mentioned in the same record (we generally don't do this much any longer). My first inclination was to say that, since this is one physical item, only one 007 would be needed. But as I think it through, this seems analogous to the second instance I mentioned, where multiple aspects of a single physical item could be brought out by multiple 007s. There is a fair amount of overlap between the Sound Recording 007 and the Computer File 007 (here, the information on dimensions corresponds, the SMDs tell us essentially the same thing). The only substantive information the CF 007 tells us that the REC 007 doesn't is the color characteristics. But I guess that's enough to justify multiple 007s. *Newsletter 69* (*April 1998*)

2.71 QUESTION: We are grappling with an issue that was apparently discussed at MOUG. The Smithsonian has produced in cooperation with Microsoft Corp. a CD with 16 folk songs that, if used in a compatible CD-ROM drive, is complemented by "hundreds of photos, texts, maps, audio and video clips and artist interviews" (*Crossroads—Southern Routes : Music of the American South*/Smithsonian Folkways). There is a record in OCLC for the sound recording aspect of this work. What does OCLC recommend? Shall we represent the fullest aspect of this work? Can we use additional 006s and 007s for something that is not "accompanying material"? Any comments would be much appreciated, since this item has been passed from cataloger to cataloger to decide what it is.

Answer: Here is a paraphrase of my answer to a similar question in the *MOUG Newsletter* no. 63 (May 1996). Your question concerns an interactive computer file that can also be played as an audio compact disc; or maybe it's an audio compact disc that can also be played interactively as a CD-ROM. You would first have to decide which aspect (computer file or sound recording) was dominant. If you chose computer file, you could add a field 006 for the sound recording aspect. (If it is interactive and you want to catalog it as such, please be sure you use the *ALA Guidelines for Bibliographic Description of Interactive Multimedia*.) If you catalog it as a sound recording, you could add field 006 for the computer file/interactive aspects. You'll also want to note the system requirements in a 538 field. As usual, we'd prefer duplicates that disagree over the predominant aspect of an item *not* be input. If you think an incorrect decision about format has been made, please report it as a potential Type Code change (with corroborating evidence if needed). From your description, it sounds like *Crossroads* would certainly be appropriate as a computer file with 006 for the sound recording aspects. Since the 007 field is supposed to be a representation/extension of the physical description, and this is one physical item, I think you'd have only one 007, for computer files. *Newsletter 67 (August 1997)*

2.72 QUESTION: I'd like to know if I may create a field 006 for an audio CD that can be played in a CD-ROM player if the user chooses to do so. The CD-ROM and audio properties are more aspects of the item rather than accompanying material. The title in question is the soundtrack to the movie *Nixon*.

Answer: If I'm understanding your question correctly, you are asking about an interactive computer file that can also be played as an audio compact disc; or maybe it's an audio compact disc that can also be played interactively as a CD-ROM. You would first have to decide which aspect (computer file or sound recording) was dominant. If you chose computer file, you could add a field 006 for the sound recording aspect. (If it is interactive and you want to catalog it as such, please be sure you use the ALA *Guidelines for Bibliographic Description of Interactive Multimedia*.) If you catalog it as a sound recording, you could add field 006 for the computer file/interactive aspects. You'll also want to note the system requirements in a 538 field. As usual, we'd prefer duplicates that disagree over the predominant aspect of an item *not* be input. If you think an incorrect decision about format has been made, please report it as a potential Type Code change (with corroborating evidence if needed). Of course, since the item in question is Oliver Stone's *Nixon*, maybe the whole thing is a conspiracy. *Newsletter 63 (May 1996)*.

2.73 QUESTION: Interactive compact discs are appearing more and more frequently now. Typically, they include a complete musical performance, pictures, commentaries, musical analysis, notes, and further audio examples. How should we catalog these?

Answer: The Online Audiovisual Catalogers (OLAC) addressed the same question recently. Such Hypermedia should be cataloged as computer files (AACR2R Chapter 9; Type code "m") with any appropriate accompanying material. You might want to stay tuned in the *OLAC Newsletter*, as well, for further ideas on handling these materials. *Newsletter 47 (April 1991)*

DIGITAL AUDIO TAPES

2.74 QUESTION: For a Digital Audio Tape (DAT), what would the physical description and 007 field look like?

Answer: It might be too early in DAT history to tell what the "standard" may be, but as far as I can tell, the standard DAT would be described as such in the 300 field:

1 sound cassette : $b digital ; $c 2 7/8 x 2 1/8 in., 3/16 in. tape.

If I knew the tape speed, I would probably include it in subfield $b. As far as the 007 is concerned, until codes are defined for the DAT's specifications, it would look something like this (with question marks in the positions that are likely to vary with the individual item—$e and $n—or on which I am uncertain—$i):

007   s $b s $d z $e ? $f n $g z $h z $i ? $j m $k n $l n $m e $n ?

Of course, subfields $j, $k, and $l are optional. You might also want to include a 500 note that indicates "Digital Audio Tape" or some such quoted equivalent from the item itself. *Newsletter 55 (August 1995)*

CHAPTER 3

Main and Added Entries

INTRODUCTION

When catalogs went electronic and catalog cards went the way of the dinosaur, many expected the differentiation between main and added entries to follow cards into oblivion. So far, that hasn't happened. Determining the correct entries for works both in the so-called "serious" idiom and in the so-called "popular" idiom remains a challenge. Practices regarding both the first and second indicators in 7XX fields changed over the years (the discontinuation of the first indicator value for multiple surnames; the simplification of second indicator usage in Format Integration) and led to lots of confusion.

MAIN ENTRIES

3.1 QUESTION: I'm planning a workshop on cataloging scores and part of my presentation concerns access points. I've been reading through AACR2, LCRI, and the MOUG newsletters but I can find nothing that addresses this question, which probably only requires a simple answer. It concerns the score or printed music version of popular rock sound recordings. I can justify putting the score of a rock band under the main entry point for the band because the performers usually write their music. When it comes to individual artists who don't write every song they perform on their sound recordings, that is what I have a problem with. Back when I was cataloging full-time I understood 21.19A to mean that the composer of songs gets the main entry and the performer an added entry status. When there was more than one composer listed it became title main entry. Now I've come to learn that many of these popular rock scores are now being placed under the singer

by some catalogers while others are following what I've always considered
to be correct. This is one question I know that will be raised especially by
public library catalogers because their collections are usually heavily popular
music. I'd like to tell my workshop people the right answer. What rule, if
there is one, would justify putting a score under the performer?

Answer: The LCRIs and MCDs refer to these printed music versions of
rock sound recordings as "popular music folios" and address them in LCRI
21.23C and LCRI 21.23D and MCD 21.23C. The essence is that you are
to follow the rules for sound recordings, but only when a sound recording
exists with basically the same title and contents as the printed folio being
cataloged. Of course, this applies only when the recording, and so the printed
folio, contains works composed by different persons or bodies. LCRI 21.23C
also explains how to determine whether you have a principal performer.
When two or more performers are named in the chief source, consider as
principal performers those given the greatest prominence; when only one
performer is named, that is the principal performer. Relative prominence is
based on the wording, layout, and typeface style and size. The principal performer may be an individual or a musical group. When there are determined
to be two or three principal performers, enter under the heading for the first
named. When there are determined to be four or more principal performers, or when there is no principal performer, enter under title. *Newsletter 80*
(*May 2002*)

3.2 QUESTION: Is it ever appropriate to make a main or added entry for
the Catholic Church, when you have recordings of Gregorian chant?

Answer: AACR2 Rule 21.22 states: "Enter an edition of music that is
officially prescribed as part of a liturgy as instructed in 21.39." It gives two
examples:

> The liber usualis : with introduction and rubrics in English / edited by the
> Benedictines of Solesmes
>   *Main entry under the heading for the Catholic Church*
>   The restored Holy Week liturgy : practical arrangement of the prescribed mu-
> sic for the average church choir / by Carlo Rossini
>   *Main entry under the heading for the Catholic Church*

At Rule 21.39, footnote 11 explains, "Liturgical work" includes officially
sanctioned or traditionally accepted texts of religious observance, books of
obligatory prayers to be offered at stated times, calendars and manuals of
performance of religious observances, and prayer books known as 'books of
hours.'" Rule 21.39A1 says in part "Enter a liturgical work under the heading
for the church or denominational body to which it pertains. When appropriate, add a uniform title as instructed in 25.19–25.23 to the main entry

heading." So it appears that, if the recording is presented as a service or as a liturgical ceremony, it would be entered under the heading for the appropriate religious entity. As examples, you might look at OCLC #17584857 (87-753198), #20632184 (89-751752), #21167516 (89-755593), #23837110 (91-751914), #30946620 (94-771275/R/r972), #33160942 (95-704488/R). *Newsletter 75 (May 2000)*

3.3 QUESTION: At some session at MOUG/MLA you reminded us that indicator "2" for multiple surnames was no longer valid. Were you saying that we should stop using X00 first indicator value "2"? This seems to contradict what it says in BF&S online currently, so I guess I'm a little confused about what OCLC wants us to do.

Answer: The X00 second indicator value "2" was made obsolete in USMARC/MARC 21 in 1996, but LC delayed implementation of this until January 2000. The policy in the online BF&S (as of this writing) still reflects the interim policy suggested by LC, but will be fixed along with many other changes in MARC updates to be implemented later in 2000. The second indicator "2" should no longer be used at all. Here is a statement from my colleague Susan Westberg about it that went out to many e-mail lists around the time of LC's announcement. The LC URL has additional details.

First Indicator Changes in Authority and Bibliographic Records

January 1, 2000 LC implemented a change to the first indicator value for personal name headings (fields 100, 400, 600, 700, 790, 800 in bibliographic records and fields 100, 400, 500 in authority records). Value 1 (Surname) was redefined to be used for headings with either single or multiple surnames. Value 2 is now obsolete. OCLC PCC participants should follow Library of Congress guidelines at <http://lcweb.loc.gov/catdir/cpso/multsur.html> when entering data. Authority records requiring changes have been identified by OCLC and will be corrected over the next few months and redistributed through LC. Changes to bibliographic records are not yet implemented. OCLC members should use 1st indicator value 1 for multiple surnames on all new bibliographic records. Headings on existing bibliographic records should be replaced as encountered and only if the record is already being worked on. Authority and bibliographic records may be out-of-sync for some time; however, users should not report first indicator changes to OCLC. Bibliographic records will be corrected through database scans.

Newsletter 75 (May 2000)

3.4 QUESTION: We sometimes get videos or audiocassettes of sessions from conferences. Usually a single lecturer, sometimes two, with or without a question-and-answer session. Never is it the complete proceedings of

the conference. Heck, MLA used to do this, audiotaping sessions and allowing you to order the tape from whatever company MLA contracted to do
the taping. As I revise the work of our rather new AV cataloger here, I find
a video situation like this and discover I cannot explain to her why the name
of the conference would not be the main entry. I guess I have always made
the conference an added entry. But the video, to me, seems to "emanate"
from the conference: though not actually publishing the video, the conference appears to have caused the video to be issued (I actually reread 21.1B2).
Does it depend on the relationship of the publisher of the video to the conference, assuming one could determine that? In this case, the publisher seems
to have repackaged the material, making some of the sessions into a Distinguished Lecture Series, but it also appears this company—with the useless
name University Video Communications—does sessions of other conferences,
too. I think I'm missing something; I don't really want to make the conference the main entry, but can't say why. Can you help?

Answer: The operative phrase related to your question in 21.1B2d (and
LCRI 21.1B2, Category D) is "collective activity." That is (as the RI states),
"It must deal with the activities of many persons involved in a corporate body
covered by the category, not with the activities of a single person." So a video,
sound recording, or print version of just one or two lectures or papers from
a conference would likely have the personal author as the main entry with
an added entry for the conference (see part 3 under the RI's "Applicabil-
ity" section), though you'd have to go through the usual intellectual process to determine that. *Newsletter 73 (August 1999)*

3.5 QUESTION: I want to make sure what "those given prominence (by
wording or layout) in the chief source of information of the item being catalogued" actually means. I have a CD with a title *The Art of Furtwängler*.
The names of performers are listed on the chief source with equal prominence
and in the orders of 1. Berliner Philharmoniker, 2. Wiener Philharmoniker,
3. Furtwängler. I consider Furtwängler to be given prominence since his
name is in the title. A colleague insists that considering names of performers, he is given equal prominence with the other two names, so these three
are all to be considered as principal performers.

Answer: The definition you cite is that for "principal performers," which
constitutes Footnote 5 in AACR2 Rule 21.23 (p. 344). The issue is further
discussed, if not exactly further clarified, in RI 21.23C, where the possibility of confusion is admitted. The relevant passages from the rule interpretation reads:

> When two or more performers are named in the chief source of information,
> consider to be principal performers those given the greatest prominence there.

If all the performers named in the chief source of information are given equal prominence there, consider all of them to be principal performers. . . . In judging relative prominence on the basis of wording, layout, and typography, consider names printed in the same size and style of lettering and in association with one another to have equal prominence. When names appear in the same size and style of lettering but in different areas of the same source of information, consider those in a location implying superiority (e.g., a higher position) to have greater prominence. Do not consider names near the beginning of a list or sequence to have greater prominence than those near the end.

Not having the item in hand, I can only speculate about wording, layout, and typography, of course. But in general, I would consider mention of a name in the collective title/title proper to constitute greater prominence on the basis of wording (certainly), layout (probably), and typography (possibly). As I read them, neither the rule nor the RI excludes the title from consideration of "prominence." Rule 0.8 states: "The word *prominently* (used in such phrases as *prominently named* and *stated prominently*) means that a statement to which it applies must be a formal statement found in one of the prescribed sources on information (see 1.0A) for areas 1 and 2 for the class of material to which the item being catalogued belongs." I would interpret that to include the title and so consider Furtwängler to be the principal performer. *Newsletter 69 (April 1998)*

3.6 QUESTION: If there are two or three principal performers, the rules say to enter under the first named. Usually the first named is a solo instrumentalist or vocalist, and it's OK. But in the case of orchestral music, the conductor's name sometimes comes first, and sometimes follows the orchestra's. In our library we prefer to enter under the conductor's name even if the orchestra is named first. As I find on p. 346 of AACR2R, a main entry under the heading for the orchestra, our practice may not be legal. Is it seriously illegal?

Answer: Since you ask about conductor and orchestra, you must be referring to AACR2 Rule 21.23C1 ("Works by different persons or bodies. Collective title") rather than Rule 21.23D1a ("Works by different persons or bodies. No collective title" [for works in the popular idiom]). Both of these rules include the identical text: "If there are two or three persons or bodies represented as principal performers, enter under the heading for the first named and make added entries under the heading(s) for the other(s)." Remember that you must take into consideration much of what was discussed in the previous question about determining prominence: wording, layout, and typography. So if either the conductor or the orchestra appears more prominently, the decision about principal performer would have to go with the more prominent of the two. If they are equally prominent according to the RI and definitions, the first named would be the proper choice, strictly speaking. But it's probably not a terribly serious violation of AACR2 to arbitrarily choose the conductor in all such circumstances, all other things being equal. In this era of computerization, the concept of the "main entry" is often considered something of an anachronism, anyway. As long as all the necessary access points are present, I wouldn't lose any sleep over it. *Newsletter 69 (April 1998)*

3.7 QUESTION: To follow up. Choice of entry rules are complicated. Today access points can are more or less equal in OPACs and we don't have to file cards anymore, so is it still necessary to agonize on which is the main entry? What is the point in making and maintaining such complicated rules on the choice of entry?

Answer: In most systems, the choice of main entry still has some impact on how entries look in full displays as well as how they sort in all kinds of ordered (brief, truncated, group) displays. The whole concept of "main entry" came up for discussion at the International Conference on the Principles and Future Development of AACR, which took place in Toronto in late October 1997. The Web site for the conference, the papers presented, and the electronic discussions that took place before the conference is at http://www.nlc-bnc.ca/jsc/intlconf.html. As the results of the conference continue to filter out, I'm sure there will be even more information at the Web site as well as discussion papers and possible rule changes. In the meantime, be aware that the question is getting serious discussion and that change is likely on the way. *Newsletter 69 (April 1998)*

3.8 QUESTION: LC often changes headings, seemingly in midstream. Should we always change with them or follow local practice?

Answer: As far as master records in the OLUC are concerned, names, uniform titles, series, and subject headings should *always* agree with the form found in the authority file or, lacking an authority record, be constructed using the most current rules for formulating such a heading (AACR2R, LCSH, *Subject Cataloging Manual: Subject Headings*, etc.). Conforming to agreed-upon standards is one of the obligations of contributing to a shared database. What you do in your local catalog is up to you, but if authority control means anything to you, the sooner you deal with changes the better. *Newsletter 48 (August 1991)*

3.9 QUESTION: Do you treat transcriptions of recorded jazz solos as compositions by the recorded performer or as arranged by the transcriber?

Answer: If we're talking about the transcribed solos of a particular jazz player, the item would likely be entered under his or her name; look at 88-754207/M, where Oscar Pettiford is given the main entry and the transcriber is an added entry. Here the primary intellectual responsibility belongs to the soloist. Where a jazz soloist has taken the work of another composer and significantly altered it (say Miles Davis's interpretations of George Gershwin's *Porgy and Bess*), the work probably would fall under 21.18C1, "a distinct alteration of another work." Here, Davis would be the main entry as the "adapter" of Gershwin's music, with an added entry for Gershwin. In cases of doubt about whether a work is an arrangement or an adaptation, 21.18C1 says to treat it as an arrangement (see 21.18B). *Newsletter 48 (August 1991)*

ADDED ENTRIES

3.10 QUESTION: I've got a question about relator codes. If you look at the code list (http://www.loc.gov/marc/relators/relacode.html), you'll notice that some definitions indicate "for a person" while others say "for a person or corporate body." I'm assuming that if the definition does not include corporate body, then I shouldn't apply the code to one. Would you agree with this interpretation? The reason I'm wondering is that I can't seem to decide on the best code to use for production companies on videos and DVDs. (Not a big deal in the grand scheme of things, I know, but I can't seem to let it go until I reach a decision.) Seems to me the most logical code would be Producer ("Use for a person who is responsible for the making of a motion picture, including business aspects, management of the productions, and the commercial success of the work."), except the definition does not include corporate bodies. Options that *do* allow for corporate bodies are Creator ("Use for a person or corporate body responsible for the intellectual or artistic content of a work.") and Originator ("Use for the author or agency performing the work, i.e., the name of a person or organization associated with the intellectual content of the work. . . ."). These may allow for corporate bodies but are much less descriptive of the actual role played by these companies. What do you think?

Answer: What an interesting question, and one that suggests you *really* read the documentation. My first reaction was confirmed in conversation with our MARBI representative, Rich Greene. We agreed that the limitation of some of the definitions to "persons" was most likely unintentional. In fact, the more we looked at the list, the more such anomalies we found. Some relator terms would logically be limited to persons (singer, host, lyricist), but many others would seem to have equal application to both persons and corporate entities, regardless of whether the definitions explicitly include both. (Aside from "Producer," another particularly egregious example was

"performer," the definition of which mentions only "person." Music catalogers routinely use "prf" for choruses, orchestras, and other performing ensembles, as well.) Rich and I figured that these apparent inconsistencies are
a result of the list's checkered history. The codes and their definitions tend
to come from a large variety of communities with their own special needs,
and the results do not get adequately coordinated. You may use code "pro"
for a production company in good conscience. *Newsletter 80 (May 2002)*

3.11 QUESTION: Want to give me a "rule of thumb" when to use $e (re-
lator term) and when to use $4 (relator code)? I am not able to locate any
guidelines on their use. Most of what I know about these has been from
"instinct" and from examples seen with LC. But I'm drawing a blank on a
few items for which I have to create original records.

Answer: AACR2 allows the optional use of relator terms (officially "Designations of function") in only four cases according to 21.0D1: compiler
(comp.), editor (ed.), illustrator (ill.), and translator (tr.), with occasional
other terms that may be called for in specific rules. It also allows other terms
derived from standard lists in specialist and archival cataloging. LCRI 21.0D1
further limits the use of these abbreviations to "ill." alone, for illustrators
of children's materials. So in general, unless you're cataloging children's
materials, you should not be using subfield $e or these terms in headings.
These relator terms should not be confused with additions to personal name
headings that serve as points of differentiation (such as terms of honor, terms
of address, designations of sainthood or royalty, etc.), as are called for in rules
22.12 through 22.16 and elsewhere (and which usually go in subfield $c).
On the other hand, relator codes (subfield $4) may optionally be used wher-
ever appropriate. If your own local system cannot use them to differentiate
the different roles of a particular individual (for instance, Leonard Bernstein
as composer [$4 cmp] versus pianist [$4 prf or $4 itr] versus conductor
[$4 cnd] versus speaker [$4 spk]), you needn't feel obligated to create them.
Newsletter 78 (May 2001)

3.12 QUESTION: I have been studying about field 711 and have a question about the use of "2" as a second indicator indicating that the item
contains the item represented by the added entry. I have a sound recording
of the music from a benefit concert (War Child (Concerts)) (see record
#40137390). Since the music from the named meeting is included, the field
becomes:

711 22 War Child (Concerts) $d (1998 : $c Modena . . .)

In checking, I searched WorldCat for similar uses, but found none. I then
searched using the examples included in *Bibliographic Formats and Standards*

(p. 7:12–13). I was not able to find the examples "Mostly Mozart Festival. $e Orchestra" nor "Council of Trent" nor "International Symposium on Standardization of Hematological Methods." I wonder in what cases the second indicator "2" is used.

Answer: The second indicator "2" in added entry fields (700, 710, 711) is used only for analytical entries; that is, when the work represented by the added entry is contained within the item being cataloged. Since the second indicator structure was simplified a few years ago as part of Format Integration Phase 1, you can be fairly certain that any 700, 710, or 711 field that does not contain a subfield $t (title) cannot have a second indicator "2".

You would use value "2" when the item in hand contains the work represented by the name-title added entry, for instance, individual musical works found on a sound recording or in a score. You would use "blank in all other cases, including when the added entry is not for an analytic or when no information has been provided as to whether the added entry is for an analytic." Value blank would always be used when the personal, corporate, or meeting name in the 7XX field is *not* accompanied by a title. Use blank also when the work represented by the name-title heading is a related work, not contained within the item in hand.

In the case of your 711 for "War Child (Concerts)," although musical selections from the performance are presented on the disc, the entity represented by the heading "War Child (Concerts)" is not actually contained within the item itself.

Now speaking theoretically, if the entity known as "War Child (Concerts)" had issued (let's say) some sort of declaration of rights for children of war, and Pavarotti had read it at the concert, and that reading were included on the recording, then you could have a heading such as:

711 22 War Child (Concerts). $t Declaration of rights for children of war.

which would legitimately have a second indicator "2" because the work represented by the name-title heading was contained in the recording.

The "Mostly Mozart" example in BF&S on p. 7:12 is doubly incorrect and should be fixed to have a first indicator "2" and a second indicator blank. The "Council of Trent" and "International Symposium on Standardization . . ." examples are OK (though they may have been invented), as they each include a subfield $t. *Newsletter 73 (May 1996)*

3.13 QUESTION: What is the policy for periods after additional authors? I've seen it thousands of ways:

700 1   Fromm, Herbert, $d 1905–1995. $4 cmp, or
700 1   Fromm, Herbert, $d 1905–1995 $4 cmp, or

700 1   Fromm, Herbert. $4 cmp, or
700 1   Fromm, Herbert $4 cmp.

I'm sure you get my drift. Is there any definite acceptable system that has been agreed upon?

Answer: Added entry headings are generally supposed to end in a period unless there is a open date at the end, in which case they end in the hyphen, or if there is some other ending punctuation (period, question mark, exclamation point, closing parenthesis or bracket, double quotation mark, according to LCRI 1.0C). The subfield $4 is an added code and not formally part of the heading proper. So, for example:

700 1   Ozawa, Seiji, $d 1935–$4 cnd   [no period after open date]
700 1   Sitwell, Osbert, $d 1892–1969. $4 lbt   [period after closed date]
700 1   Gedda, Nicolai. $4 prf   [period after forename]
700 1   Sharp, William, $c baritone. $4 prf   [period after addition to name]
700 1   Smith, E. B. $q (E. Brian) $4 cnd   [no period after closing parenthesis]

The form of the personal name heading, of course, would depend on what is found in the authority file or, if there is no authority record, what you come up with by following AACR2 Chapter 22. *Newsletter 72 (May 1999)*

3.14 QUESTION: I have a question about the use of subfield $t for field 700. The instructions for this in the printed version of BF&S reads: "Do not use in AACR2 headings. Enter title information in field 240 or 245, as appropriate." This text is not present in the Web version of the manual. Is this correct (in the printed version)? I checked this against my copy of the USMARC manual and this is not present. There are, certainly, recent records in WorldCat that use the $t. Have we got an error here or am I being particularly dense in this instance?

Answer: This is a clear error in the printed text. The whole passage ("Do not use in AACR2 headings. Enter title information in field 240 or 245, as appropriate.") should be removed. It appears that this was incorrectly carried over from the subfield $t entry in the 100 field, where the passage would be accurate. Thanks for pointing this out. We'll correct it for the next BF&S revision. *Newsletter 68 (November 1997)*

3.15 QUESTION: This question involves a corporate body added entry in which the last word of the name is in quotes. Should I punctuate the 710 like normal English (i.e., 710 20 Corporate body "name.")?

Answer: According to USMARC (it appears on 3/95 revision page X10-p. 11, at the top), "The name portion of a name/subordinate body or name/

title heading ends with a mark of punctuation. The mark of punctuation is placed inside a closing quotation mark." AACR2 seems to offer no guidance. USMARC does say that field 710 ends with a mark of punctuation (X10-p. 10). The LCRI that defines "ending punctuation," LCRI 1.0C, includes "double quotation mark" as one of them. That *might* suggest that when a corporate name ends in a double quotation mark, that serves as the final punctuation, obviating the need for a period on either side of the closing quotation mark. But to be perfectly honest, I'm not sure. I think I'd go with the period within the closing quotation mark, but I don't think there is con-clusive evidence for any of the options. *Newsletter 62 (November 1995)*

3.16 QUESTION: At the OLAC/MOUG meeting, it was generally agreed that the subfield $f could now be discontinued in 700 analytics. I haven't seen any proof of this. Can you tell me what OCLC's position is?

Answer: The justification for omitting subfield $f from most analytical added entries is probably RI 21.30M. It stipulates adding the year of publi-cation for Bible headings (25.18A), for "Works" (LCRI 25.8), and for "Selections" (LCRI 25.9). By implication, the date can be omitted in other cases. *Newsletter 59 (November 1994)*

3.17 QUESTION: I'm cataloging a recording *Origins* by the group Nexus. This recording is (quoting from the notes) "a vivid reproduction of the kind of spontaneous, unrehearsed improvisation that can be experienced at a live Nexus concert." There also is the note under the contents: "all music com-posed by Nexus."

We routinely make 700 author-title added entries, but I have not come across an instance when the "author" is a corporate body. Logically I have no problem with "710 22 Nexus (Musical group). $t Song of the nine iron. $f 1992." However, I have never seen such an entry.

Jazz/rock groups would be a similar case, but most songs (etc.) are com-posed by a person (or a few people) rather than the whole group, and for our catalog we generally find it adequate for popular music to make sepa-rate added entries for the group and for the individual song titles. I have not been able to find an instance of a 710 with a subfield $t attached.

No other Nexus recordings in OCLC use the 710 subfield $t; they use (if anything) 710 followed by 740s for the title added entries. However, for our catalog, a 710 subfield $t would result in more efficient searching. And, in a certain sense, it *seems* logical, as in: "Hey, did you hear the piece [XXX] by Nexus?"

Answer: All sorts of corporate entities have titles associated with them; why can't a musical group? Throughout AACR2 Chapter 25 ("Uniform Titles") are references to works entered under corporate headings (see for instance 25.2E2 and 25.3C2). Actually, I have found at least one musical precedent, albeit an old one, in AACR2 cataloging from the Library of Congress (and you know how I frown on cataloging-by-example). Take a look at LCCN 82-760975 (OCLC #7911443; member-input, not LC MARC Music), a disc by the ROVA Saxophone Quartet. Two of the works on the disc are attributed to the whole quartet and are so traced. One of those works is even in the authority file (n81097265):

110 20 ROVA Saxophone Quartet. $t Trobar clus, $n no. 3.

Newsletter 58 (August 1994)

3.18 QUESTION: Relator codes "itr" (instrumentalist) and "voc" (vocalist) show up on sound recording records but not in the compilation of *OCLC-MARC Code Lists* (1983, with 4/84, 10/84, and 12/85 revisions). If these are legitimate codes, why haven't they been incorporated into OCLC documentation?

Answer: Both of these codes were documented in Technical Bulletin 181 (March 1988). It so happens that the same year, LC began publishing its code lists as relatively inexpensive separate booklets. They had previously been part of the old *MARC Formats for Bibliographic Data*—MFBD—as appendices; their separate incarnations coincided with MFBD's transformation into UFBD, *USMARC Format for Bibliographic Data* in 1988. With these separate publications available, OCLC ceased updating its own code lists, referring users instead to LC's own official works, in this case the *USMARC Code List for Relators, Sources, Description Conventions*, 1990 edition, available from the Cataloging Distribution Service. Although the two codes mentioned have been legitimate since MFBD Update no. 15 in October 1987, you may not encounter them more often because they are among those that LC has chosen not to use. That shouldn't stop you, though. *Newsletter 49 (November 1991)*

3.19 QUESTION: About those pesky little subfields $w, is it OK to change "$w cn" to "$w 1n" after checking the authority file? What exactly does "cn" mean, anyway?

Answer: When you are doing authority work, feel free to change either or both elements of a $w to the appropriate numeric value. Strictly alphabetic subfields $w indicate that the field was matched against the authority file at one of the points when OCLC ran a global conversion, the first time in the early 1980s, the second a few years later. Tapeloaded records are run against the authority file before they are loaded into the OLUC. Of course, the authority file has changed every day since the $w was generated, so "cn" means that the heading was certified correct at only one particular point in time (the same goes for manually input subfields $w, too, of course). The "c" indicates that the name portion of the heading is in authorized AACR2 form; "n" indicates that the title portion (if present) has not been examined. *Newsletter 47 (April 1991)*

[Note: All such subfields $w were removed from WorldCat bibliographic records in 1993.]

CHAPTER 4

Titles

INTRODUCTION

Choice of titles proper, the distinction between titles appearing in field 246 and field 740, parallel titles, caption titles, series titles, and all other manner of titles probably account for a larger proportion of questions than any other single broad category. Every music cataloger's favorite, the uniform title, can be vexatious, from determining whether a title is distinctive or a type of composition, to formulating the correct order of a medium of performance, to figuring out the intricacies of numbering systems.

UNIFORM TITLES

4.1 QUESTION: I am originally cataloging a recording of songs by Russian composers using texts from Western European poets. One of the songs is by Vasily Kalinnikov. The song is entitled "An Liebchens schneeweisse Schulter" and is sung in German. There is no authority record for this in OCLC. Upon consulting *New Grove*, the title of this piece appears in Russian. Normally, you would go with the form in *New Grove*. However, since the piece is originally in German, I am not so sure I should enter it as *Grove* did. My hunch is further backed up by a translation note after the work's listing in *New Grove* ("trans. V.A. Fyodorov"). My instinct tells me to give it the German title as the uniform title. However, I thought I would solicit your views on the issue first.

Answer: The language of the uniform title is determined by the language of the text to which the composer originally set the melody as reflected in the first edition of the musical composition (see AACR2 25.27A1). This may *not* be the original language of text itself. Think, for instance, of Verdi's *Otello*. Although the "original" text is Shakespeare's *Othello* in English, Verdi composed his opera to Boito's Italian translation; hence, the uniform title of Verdi's opera is in Italian. If Kalinnikov composed his song using Fyodorov's Russian translation of Heine's German original, the uniform title of Kalinnikov's song would reflect the Russian text he set. *Newsletter 79* (*November 2001*)

4.2 QUESTION: About halfway through Rule 25.30B1, AACR2 says to use no more than three elements when recording the medium of performance in a uniform title. A little later there are a few exceptions to that, but they aren't relevant here. I've always assumed that meant the *total* number of medium of performance elements, but now notice that all the examples (yes, I know one does not catalog using the examples) shown are for individual instruments. No ensembles. *And* I'm looking at an authority record for a Vivaldi concerto that says, "Concertos, $m woodwinds, horns (2), violin, string orchestra. . . ." Hmm, that's four elements—but one of the elements is an ensemble. There are only three elements for individual instruments. Is the authority record wrong? Or have I managed to misinterpret 25.30B1 all these years?

   Answer: The specific rule for "Solo instrument(s) and accompanying ensemble" (25.30B7) is applied to concertos rather than the "General rule" (25.30B1). Rule 25.30B7 states in part, "For a work for two or more solo instruments and accompanying ensemble, name the medium for the solo instruments as instructed in 25.30B1-25.30B6 followed by the name of the accompanying ensemble." The implication seems to be that the accompanying ensemble is *not* counted in the "do not use more than three elements" statement in 25.30B1. That three-element limit applies only to the solo instruments, which is why the woodwinds are grouped together in accordance with 25.30B5 and its MCD. *Newsletter 79* (*November 2001*)

4.3 QUESTION: In a collective uniform title of the type "Piano music, pianos (2)," should "pianos (2)" go in subfield $t or subfield $m? Initially, I was inclined to keep it in subfield $t since it seems to behave more like a qualifier than a medium of performance. I checked the authority file on OCLC and found that in 11 out of 12 cases, this was the treatment chosen by LC. It was also interesting to note that in the single occurrence of "$m pianos (2)" in an authority record (ARN: 4566639), the bibliographic record cited (86-752268) actually has it as part of subfield $t. OCLC's BF&S does not address this situation but *Music Coding and Tagging* (p. 136) says, "Phrases such as '4 hands' are part of the medium statement *except* when they follow a collective uniform title such as 'Piano music,' in which case they are not subfielded separately. However, consider as a medium statement qualifiers such as 'pianos (2)' that follow a collective uniform title." So, I am happy to comply with this interpretation, but I am curious if you can shed some light on the basis for LC's practice.

Answer: That quote from *Music Coding and Tagging* isn't very clear, is it? Too many mediums or something. In the upcoming second edition, the explanation is somewhat clearer (I hope), both in the description of subfield $a:

> Among the types of parenthetical and other information not separately subfielded are:
>
> . . . Such phrases as "4 hands" and "pianos (2)" that form part of collective uniform titles

100 0	José Antonio de Donostia.
240 10	Piano music, 4 hands. $k Selections
700 12	Sor, Fernando, $d 1778–1839. $t Guitar music, guitars (2). $k Selections.

and in the subsequent descriptions of subfield $m:

> . . . Phrases such as "4 hands" and "pianos (2)" are part of the medium statement except when they follow a collective uniform title such as "Piano music," in which case they are not separately subfielded.

100 1	Poulenc, Francis, $d 1899–1963.
240 10	Piano music, pianos (2)
700 12	Beethoven, Ludwig van, $d 1770–1827. $t Lied mit Veränderungen, $m piano, 4 hands, $n WoO 74, $r D major.
700 12	Hensel, Fanny Mendelssohn, $d 1805–1847. $t Piano music, 4 hands. $k Selections.
100 1	Cooke, Arnold.
240 10	Suites, $m recorders (4), $n no. 2

When the statement of medium is the initial element of the uniform title, as it is in many collective uniform titles, record it in subfield $a in the 240, 630, or 730 field or subfield $t in the 600, 610, 611, 700, 710, or 711 field.

100 1	Schulhoff, Ervín, $d 1894–1942.
240 10	String quartet music
700 12	Blavet, Michel, $d 1700–1768. $t Flute music, flutes (2). $k Selections.
700 12	Boyd, Anne, $d 1946– $t Flute, piano music. $k Selections.

The rationale is that the "pianos (2)" portion is simply an integral part of the initial element, which in these cases happens to be the medium of performance. The one authority record cited that was incorrectly subfielded (no97080415) is a machine-derived record and has been fixed. *Newsletter 76 (September 2000)*

Correction: Thanks to eagle-eyed Wendy Schlegel of the Saint Louis Public Library, who caught the misprint on p. 11 of the *MOUG Newsletter* no. 76 in my answer to the first question. In the Fernando Sor example, the "guitars (2)" designation should *not* be separately subfielded. The example should read:

700 12   Sor, Fernando, $d 1778–1839. $t Guitar music, guitars (2). $k Selections.

The extraneous subfield delimiter was apparently added accidentally in the editing process. *Newsletter 76 (November 2000)*

4.4 QUESTION: I'm working on the Hanssler CDs of Bach's complete works. One CD in particular contains a number of spurious works. There are no headings in the authority file so I will have to come up with some for the 700 fields. I can formulate a basic Bach $t Suites, $m harpsichord, $n BWV 821, $r Bb major, etc. But since this is going to be an original record, I want to make sure that is the correct thing to do with these spurious works that according to *New Grove* have not been attributed to anyone else. Can I enter them under Bach's name and add a 500 note with the BWV numbers in question?

Answer: First, you should check the Schmieder (BWV) catalog to make sure the works have not been attributed. The BWV is the authoritative source, has much more detail than *New Grove*, and is 10 years more current if you've got the 1990 BWV edition. If there is an attribution, make the appropriate composer/uniform title entry. If there is no attribution, you have to go with entry by the title (as examples see authority records nr99022421 and n87113482). Music Cataloging Decision 21.4C1 addresses this question indirectly, but it doesn't really help much:

> When a musical work has been erroneously or fictitiously attributed to a composer, optionally make, instead of the added entry prescribed by 21.4C1, a name-title reference from the heading for the attributed composer and the uniform title which the work would have if it were in fact by the attributed composer to the heading for the actual composer and actual uniform title, or to the title if the actual composer is unknown (see MCD 26.4B). Apply this option when doing so would improve access to the work, e.g., because an added entry under the heading for the attributed composer alone would be lost in that composer's file, or because the work is represented only by a secondary entry in a bibliographic record.

Newsletter 76 (September 2000)

4.5 QUESTION: Serial numbers within an opus number are sometimes considered separate works and sometimes considered excerpts of the opus number. How do you decide when the work is separate and when it's an excerpt? For example, according to the LC/NACO authority file, Beethoven's three string quartets op. 59 are separate works, while Brahms's two clarinet sonatas, op. 120, are considered excerpts. In each case, the set of pieces was published together. I can't figure how one is different from the other, so I can't extrapolate the reasoning when I run into the same situation with a composer who's not in the authority file.

Answer: It all has to do with how the composer (or thematic index compiler, perhaps) numbered things and whether the work or works in question are part of a larger sequence. In the case of the Brahms, he wrote only two sonatas for clarinet and piano, and each was designated as part of opus 120; as a result, their numbering sequence is fully contained within the opus 120 and they are considered excerpts:

Brahms, Johannes, $d 1833–1897. $t Sonatas, $m clarinet, piano, $n op. 120. $n No. 1.
Brahms, Johannes, $d 1833–1897. $t Sonatas, $m clarinet, piano, $n op. 120. $n No. 2.

In the case of the Beethoven string quartets (and the Faure piano nocturnes), the sequential numbering assigned by the composer crosses numerous opus numbers, even though some of those opus numbers happen to have multiple works within them (as Beethoven's op. 18 and op. 59 do). In sequences such as these, AACR2 Rule 25.30C has us add, after the medium of performance, the serial number within the larger sequence and then the opus or thematic index number (plus any numbers within the opus). So the Beethoven sequence goes, in part:

Beethoven, Ludwig van, $d 1770–1827. $t Quartets, $m strings, $n no. 7, op. 59, no. 1, $r F major.
Beethoven, Ludwig van, $d 1770–1827. $t Quartets, $m strings, $n no. 8, op. 59, no. 2, $r E minor.
Beethoven, Ludwig van, $d 1770–1827. $t Quartets, $m strings, $n no. 9, op. 59, no. 3, $r C major.
Beethoven, Ludwig van, $d 1770–1827. $t Quartets, $m strings, $n no. 10, op. 74, $r Eb major.
Beethoven, Ludwig van, $d 1770–1827. $t Quartets, $m strings, $n no. 11, op. 95, $r F minor.

Here, the overall numbering sequence (seventh, eighth, ninth, tenth, eleventh quartet) takes precedence over the opus numbers. The number within the opus number would never be considered an excerpt of, say, "quartet no.

7." All of this can mostly be distilled (in a roundabout fashion) from Rules 25.6, 25.30C, and 25.32, and their respective RIs and MCDs. In short, the difference is whether the complete sequential numbering is contained within a single opus/thematic index number or spread over multiple opus/thematic index numbers. *Newsletter 75 (May 2000)*

4.6 QUESTION: Where do plectral instruments fall in the order of instruments for uniform titles?

Answer: AACR2 Rule 25.30B1 isn't very helpful, outlining the order simply as:

- voices
- keyboard instrument if there is more than one non-keyboard instrument
- the other instruments in score order
- continuo

"Score order" is open to debate in many cases, especially when instruments not usually found in a traditional orchestra are concerned. *New Grove* and *New Harvard Dictionary of Music* agree that harp, celesta, and orchestral piano are usually placed between percussion and first violins (with the solo part of a concerto directly above the first violins, when appropriate). Most examples in the authority file seem to bear this out, although there are some exceptions, which may be incorrect. (Note that many of the records, including two of the three exceptions, are machine-derived headings and have not been verified by humans.)

Bax, Arnold, $d 1883–1953. $t Nonet, $m woodwinds, harp, strings [no97062117]
Bax, Arnold, $d 1883–1953. $t Quintets, $m harp, violins, viola, violoncello [no97062120]
Berg, Josef, $d 1927– $t Sextet, $m piano, harp, strings [no97081194]
Bracali, Giampaolo. $t Quintet, $m guitar, violins, viola, violoncello [no98009992]
Gragniani, Filippo, $d b. 1767. $t Sextet, $m woodwinds, guitars, strings, $r A major [no98000670]
Kœchlin, Charles, $d 1867–1950. $t Quintets, $m flute, harp, violin, viola, violoncello, $n no. 2, op. 223 [nr99006195]
Lloyd, Jonathan. $t Quintets, $m mandolin, lute, guitar, harp, double bass, $n no. 2 [no98039593]
Mozart, Franz Xaver, $d 1791–1844. $t Sextet, $m winds, guitar, strings, $r A minor [no98000671]
Riishøjgård, Knud, $d 1959– $t Quintet, $m piano, flute, clarinet, guitar, violoncello [no98059369]
Süssmayr, Franz Xaver, $d 1766–1803. $t Quintets, $m oboe, guitar, strings, $r C major [n79140426]

Some exceptions:

Flothuis, Marius. $t Quintets, $m flute, violin, viola, violoncello, harp, $n op. 97
   [no98060708]
Hoffmann, E. T. A. $q (Ernst Theodor Amadeus), $d 1776–1822. $t Quintets, $m
   violins, viola, violoncello, harp, $r C minor [n87116196]
Kummer, Kaspar, $d 1795–1870. $t Quintet, $m flutes, viola, violoncello, guitar,
   $n op. 75, $r C major [no98000636]

Newsletter 75 (May 2000)

4.7 QUESTION: For a living composer, how do you decide whether to
pluralize the initial element of a type of composition uniform title, especially
if only one of that type has been written so far?

   Answer: LCRI 25.29A is straightforward on this:

> If the composer is living, use the singular form in the uniform title unless the
> work being cataloged bears a serial number (including 1); in that case, use the
> plural form on the assumption that the composer has written or intends to write
> more works of the type. When cataloging the second occurrence of a work of
> a particular type by a composer, if the singular form has been used in the uni-
> form title for the first work of the type, revise the uniform title to use the plural
> form.

The RI goes on to caution that the medium of performance is not a criterion, that two sonatas are two sonatas and the plural would be used regardless of the instrumentation of each sonata. *Newsletter 75 (May 2000)*

4.8 QUESTION: It seems that in the distant past, there was an effort to
determine the order of subfields $k, $l, $s, and $o in uniform titles. Unfortunately, that's all I remember about it. I have a CD with a boy choir
singing only the soprano line of *Jesu, Joy of Man's Desiring*, with organ accompaniment. Those things make it an arrangement. They are singing an
English translation. In the uniform title, after I get through the composer's
name and the titles, is it $l English; $o arr. or $o arr. $l English? I saw nothing to help in AACR2, LCRIs, or MCDs. Your tagging book, on p. 136 top,
last example under $l, has $o then $l. On p. 139, under $o (the Uhl example), there's $l then $o (with a $k interposed). Is there something I'm
missing here?

   Answer: There was an effort to standardize the order of subfields for
subject heading subdivisions, but I don't recall any similar movement for
uniform titles (which doesn't mean that there wasn't such an effort, of

course, and could be just another sign of aging). When you start adding those subfields $l, $k, $s, and $o, it gets awfully complicated. The only guidance is in rule 25.35A1: "Make additions in the order given. If 'Selections' is added to the uniform title (see 25.32B1 and 25.34C3), add it as the last element or as the next to last element when 'arr.' is used (see 25.35C)." The "order given" is "sketches" (which is not separately subfielded; 25.35B); arrangements (subfield $o; 25.35C); vocal and chorus scores/librettos and song texts (subfield $s; 25.35D-E); and language (subfield $l; 25.35F). Recognizing that the examples in AACR2 are supposed to be "illustrative and not prescriptive" (in the elegant words of Rule 0.14), we can gather from 25.35A1 and the examples throughout 25.35 that the order appears to be: $s, $l, $k. I've got an old LC document called *Descriptive Tabulation: Library of Congress MUMS Format Data for Music Records,* which lists all the combinations of subfields and their frequencies in LC's files as of September 30, 1987. Lots of things have changed since then, but I don't think there has been any substantive reordering of uniform title subfields. The tabulation (looking at fields 240 and 700) bears out the preference for the $s, $l, $k order, although there are stray exceptions. When you throw subfield $o in the mix, it appears as the final subfield nearly every time with only two exceptions. When subfield $l is present, $l is the final subfield in eight out of nine cases. There were two cases where subfield $s followed subfield $o, but no cases in the other order. Considering all of this, the general order of subfields should be $s, $l, $k. When subfield $o is involved, it usually goes at the very end except when the uniform title ends in subfield $s or in subfield $l, in which cases the subfield $o is appended to the subfield preceding the $s or $l. In the case you cite, my guess is:

700 12 Bach, Johann Sebastian, $d 1685–1750. $t Herz und Mund und Tat und Leben, $n BWV 147. $p Jesus bleibet meine Freude; $o arr. $l English.

It's hard to say without access to the uniform titles themselves whether the tabulated exceptions are errors or legitimate variations under certain circumstances. *Newsletter 75 (May 2000)*

4.9 QUESTION: Say you have a sound recording containing two symphonies and one opera overture, all written by the same composer. Would the collective uniform title be "Orchestra music. Selections" (assuming he or she had written more for this medium than these three pieces) or "Selections"? The latter considers the overture part of a vocal work, hence overriding the medium. I seem to remember a rule about this, but I might be wrong. Please refer me to the rule or rule interpretation, if it does exist.

Answer: As far as I have been able to determine, there is no AACR2 Rule, LCRI, or MCD that directly addresses the question (which is what yours

boils down to): Is an orchestral overture to a vocal work considered an orchestral work or an excerpt from a vocal work? AACR2 25.34 deals with
collective uniform titles; I find only one tiny hint, taken shamelessly and
inexcusably out of context, that sheds any light. In the little introductory
paragraph to MCD 25.34B–25.34C, it states in part: "For excerpts from one
work, treat each excerpt the same as a separate work. . . ." But if you think
about it, that sort of makes sense. Given a miscellaneous collection of, say,
marches taken from all manner of compositions by a single composer (independently composed marches, marches from suites, etc.), a collective uniform title that began with the word "Marches" would not be surprising.
That's a roundabout way of suggesting that "Orchestra music. Selections"
sounds correct for the recording of two symphonies and overture you've
invented. After a little searching, I found an LC record of that exact description (91-761850/R/r94; OCLC #25089409) containing two symphonies
(numbers 4 and 5) and an opera overture (*Maskarade*) by Carl Nielsen, with
the collective uniform title "Orchestra music. $k Selections", confirming the
guess. A few other similar collections cataloged by LC are treated likewise.
So, although there doesn't appear to be strict chapter and verse, it looks like
excerpts from larger works may be treated as independent compositions when
collective uniform titles are being formulated. *Newsletter 71 (December 1998)*

4.10 QUESTION: Please bear in mind that this query comes from someone who isn't a USMARC user. As applied to Chopin and Beethoven (to
take a couple of examples at random), presumably we would all agree that
the cataloguer-constructed uniform title "Piano music. Selections" is a "collective title" since AACR 25.34C1 (the specific chapter and verse) is a paragraph within 25.34, Collective titles. The USMARC field for collective
uniform titles is 243. It says so in the format. Why then do USMARC users
seem to use 240 for "Piano music. Selections" and for other similar collective uniform titles (i.e., I'm not talking about "Works", etc.)? Can anyone
point to chapter and verse explaining the logic, justifying the decision, or
even documenting the same? There's nothing in the LCRIs (which seems
fair enough), and the MCDs simply provide examples of use, without explaining how or why the coding was arrived at. UKMARC binds the format much more closely to the cataloging code, and we would expect to input
all types of collective titles in the same field. Splitting different types of collective uniform titles seems, on the face of it, "wrong"; so does mixing two
different concepts in the one field (240). And as for breaking the link between AACR2 and the carrier of the data (the MARC format) in such an
apparently cavalier manner, well. . . . OK, so I exaggerate slightly, but if it
provokes some explanation, perhaps it will have been worth it.

   Answer: Although I am not aware of any rationale for this practice in
USMARC itself, the Library of Congress's *Music File Input-Update Manual*

(compiled by Richard H. Hunter of LC and used internally at LC) excludes
field 243 entirely. Under the description for field 240, there is a note that
reads: "Field 243 (Collective Uniform Title) is not used in records created
by the Library of Congress. Collective uniform titles are contained in field
240. If a 243 field in an imported record contains a correct AACR 2 uniform title, the field should be changed to 240." OCLC has chosen to follow LC's lead in this instance. My suspicion is that the 240/243 split goes
back to the early days of USMARC. Many such distinctions that were expected to be important or useful someday were built in to the MARC formats but turned out to be more unwieldy than helpful. (Remember the 700/
705 and 710/715 splits, with the 7X5 fields limited to performers?) Remember too, that back in the days of catalog cards, collective uniform titles were
supposed to file in front of specific uniform titles, so the 243 may have been
a means to achieve this filing distinction by machine. In the post-card era,
we've lost that difference and so, the need for the separately fielded collective uniform title. *Newsletter 71 (December 1998)*

4.11 QUESTION: We are cataloging several CDs of pieces by Fritz
Kreisler. We have the Lochner biography of Kreisler, which includes a
thematic catalog of works composed and arranged by him. One of the CDs
has two minuets; the first "by Porpora" and the second "by Pugnani." Both
are of course by Kreisler himself; these are two of the many pieces he originally passed off as being composed by earlier composers when in fact they
are new compositions by him. There is an authority record for the "Porpora"
minuet (no97009244). The uniform title is set up as "Minuets, violin, piano,
D major" with cross-references to variations on "Minuet in the style of
Porpora." The problem is that *both* the "Porpora" and the "Pugnani" pieces
are minuets, for violin and piano, in D major. The institution that created
the authority record cited the Lochner book, but apparently failed to notice that the uniform title would match two completely different pieces, both
of which are listed in the Lochner book. My second question is: What's the
best way to handle an authority record that seems wrong? Seems I've heard
lots of alternatives and find I don't know who to contact. My third question is: How do I find out what institution corresponds to a particular NUC
symbol? We no longer have the paper copy of OCLC institutions listed by
NUC symbol, and on the OCLC Web page section where you can search
for participating institutions, there is no way to search by NUC symbol. My
fourth question is: How one would distinguish these two pieces? Locally, we
could choose to make the distinctive titles ("Menuet in the style of Porpora"
and "Menuet in the style of Pugnani") the authorized headings. But that
defeats the luxury of the shared authority file, if you're just going to ignore
it! Besides, we'd make a cross-reference for the "generic" title, and would
still have to distinguish them. I actually had a brainstorm on distinguishing

them—Rule 25.30E1, which allows you to qualify otherwise identical headings by date of composition, publication, or "any other identifying element." I thought of qualifying by who Kreisler ascribed the piece to, namely,

Minuets, violin, piano, D major (Porpora)
Minuets, violin, piano, D major (Pugnani)

I thought that was rather inventive! Maybe put quotes around the names. If I were to go this route, or something similar I might run across in the future, how would that qualifier be subfielded? When one qualifies by date, subfield n is used. But when qualifying by "any other element (e.g., place of publication)" what subfield code would be used? I did check *Music Coding and Tagging* under 240 and didn't find any examples.

Answer: Let's try to take these one at a time. When you've got a conflict such as this or an otherwise incorrect authority record, you should report it directly to the Library of Congress Cataloging Policy and Support Office (cpso@loc.gov) with any appropriate documentation or evidence. In the Participating Institutions search screen (http://www.oclc.org/contacts/libraries/), you can enter an NUC symbol into the "Any Field, Any Text" box and get results. You may get multiple hits, but it's easy enough to distinguish the NUC hit from the others. Although I've got *New Grove* available, I don't really have enough information to say how one would distinguish the two minuets in question. For instance, what are the first edition titles? Judging by AACR2 25.30E1, the dates of composition would be the first choice. I think that qualifying by the composer in whose style it was written, as you've suggested, might be ingenious but according to the same rule, would imply that the parenthetical name is that of the first publisher. Most such parenthetical descriptive words or phrases would not be separately subfielded; this is covered in *Music Coding and Tagging* at the bottom of p. 133 and following. But if the qualifier is a date used as a number to distinguish otherwise identical uniform titles, it would go in subfield $n (see MCAT p. 137). *Newsletter 71 (December 1998)*

4.12 FOLLOW-UP QUESTION: I was thinking I might be able to retire before I had to ask this question. How are we peons supposed to find out the title on the manuscript or first edition? I would solve my Kreisler minuet problems and hundreds of others if I could devise a way to follow 25.27A1 and discover "the composer's original title in the language in which it was presented." Without access to anything that would give the composer's title, we rely on secondary sources. For Kreisler, *New Grove* does not list titles. The Lochner book seems the best there is as far as general availability. It does not even have incipits for everything; some pieces are just listed with who knows where the title came from. Looking through the authority file on his

works in OCLC, most records (largely by LC) choose the generic form as
the authorized one, with the distinctive title (e.g., Précieuse in the style of
Couperin) as a cross-reference. But there are a couple records where the
distinctive title was chosen (e.g., *Rondino über ein Thema von Beethoven*) with
the generic one as the cross-reference. Most authority records quote the
Lochner book as the citation. Looks like LC isn't having much more luck
than I am in deciding which title was Kreisler's and in what language. Or
am I missing something everyone else knows? Besides RISM and occasionally CD liner notes or the foreword to a score, how do you find the
composer's original title, except as filtered through a reference source?

Answer: For titles of first editions, I think we rabble generally rely on thematic catalogs, many (but not all) of which try to give some sort of publication history, often with title page transcriptions. For many (but not all)
composers, *New Grove* does actually try to give original titles, so sometimes
other sorts of secondary sources such as encyclopedias, RISM, and so forth
can be useful. Kreisler is a sort of special case because of his half-joking attempts to pass off what were actually his own compositions as arrangements
he made of existing classic pieces. That would mean that the "first editions"
of most of these Kreisler works are deliberately misleading, presenting Kreisler
as the arranger, with Padre Martini, Francoeur, Couperin, or some other un-
suspecting dead white male as the composer. Here's my guess, based on a check
of some of these Kreisler authority records and without benefit of access to
Lochner. The uniform titles in the generic form of "Type of composition,
medium, key" ("Andantino," "Siciliano," etc.) seem to be among those
Kreisler joke "arrangements" that had a type of composition in their titles.
Those Kreisler jokes that had more distinctive titles ("Chanson Louis XIII and
pavane," "Chasse," "Precieuse," "Preghiera," etc.) were given the more distinctive uniform titles. And those that were first published explicitly "in the
style of" or as "based on a theme by" (that is, those Kreisler did not try to
pass off as composed by someone else and simply arranged by him) received
those distinctive titles ("Rondino uber ein Thema von Beethoven," "Scherzo
in the style of Dittersdorf," "Variationen uber ein Thema von Corelli"), based
on the language of those first editions. Of course, I could be reading too much
into those notes in the authority records. So, do you have your Individual
Retirement Account in order? *Newsletter 71 (December 1998)*

4.13 QUESTION: I'm cataloging some CDs that have the storyteller Jim
Weiss (famous, I guess) retelling various "classics." Often the original classic is a short story or at least a relatively short story (O. Henry's *Gift of the
Magi* or Dickens's *A Christmas Carol*, for example); some are folk tales (e.g.,
Jack and the beanstalk); one CD even has Shakespeare. I have determined
that Weiss has shortened and changed the original substantially to make it
work as a "told story," enough to say the version he's telling is his work rather

than the original writers. The inputting libraries agree with me, giving main entry to Weiss. The CDs nicely give their contents, along with the writer of the original story, play, whatever, when there is one. So I use that as a contents note. *Then* I give name-title added entries for the items on each disc, showing the original writer of the story and the uniform title for the story. Again, the inputting libraries have already done this for the most part. My question (finally): Should the second indicator of the 700 fields be blank or "2"? The work named in the 700 *is* "contained" in the CD—sort of. But in a real sense it's also a "related" work. Which? Not that the second indicator makes an iota of difference in indexing and display of the 700, but don't get me on that soapbox.

Answer: Your final point probably *is* the point: It doesn't make all that much of a difference. That said, what I might suggest is to use your judgment in determining just how much each individual work is Weiss's and how much it is the original (or a translation). Perhaps looking over AACR2R Rules 21.9 and 21.10 (as well as any subsequent rules and RIs that might be relevant) would help. It is suggested generally that adaptations for children are to be entered under the adapter if known, with a name-title added entry for the original, though I find no clear guidance in distinguishing the point at which a contained work becomes a related work. It's discussed in LCRI 21.30M, but not so as to help much. My best advice would be to consider a heading related (indicator blank) when the adaptation is substantial enough to consider it a new work. If it's merely excerpted or condensed, you can probably consider it analytical (indicator "2"). *Newsletter 70 (September 1998)*

4.14 QUESTION: When you have either one or multiple groups of instruments in $m in addition to individual instruments, how do you determine the order of elements in the $m? I'm looking at AACR2 Chapter 25, and I found our favorite rule 25.30B1, but I can't seem to find anything that specifically addresses the ordering of groups and single instruments. An example of a heading is in OCLC #84755796. The uniform title is: "Movements, $m brasses, double bass, percussion." Do you think this was based entirely on score order? I feel like I'm missing something.

Answer: The only guidance in AACR2 appears toward to top of p. 523 in Rule 25.30B1:

Record the medium of performance specifically, but do not use more than three elements except as instructed in 25.30B3. Give the elements in the following order:

voices
keyboard instrument if there is more than one non-keyboard instrument
the other instruments in score order
continuo

There doesn't seem to be anything more enlightening in the RIs or the MCDs about precisely what "score order" might be. It roughly follows the list in 25.30B5 from "woodwinds" through "strings" but that's not really the way most mediums of performance are formulated. Richard Smiraglia in his new *Describing Music Materials* lists what he calls "traditional practice" on p. 178. If Richard is correct, the subfield $m in the uniform title you mention should actually be "$m brasses, percussion, double bass" (as LC has it on OCLC #12912951). I seem to recall somewhere an ordered list that had percussion and other instruments at the end, but I'm probably thinking of subject headings. LC is reportedly working on something that may clarify the concept of "score order." It could end up as an RI or an MCD. *Newsletter 68 (November 1997)*

4.15 QUESTION: If you have a sound recording with works all by the same composer, how many works must there be for you to use a collective uniform title in the 240? I know if you have two works, the first goes in the 240 and the second in a name-uniform title added entry—that's in Rule 25.33. But what about three works? The only guidance I find is indirect, and it's in 25.25A. It doesn't state, but implies, that if you have *more than two* works, you use a collective uniform title. I know—I hate that idea as much as you do, but them's the rules. That means if your CD has two violin sonatas and a capriccio, also for violin and piano, your 240 is Violin, piano music, *not* the uniform title for the first piece. Yet I continually find relatively new cataloging—post-AACR2R anyway—where the first work is recorded in the 240 when there are three works total on the item, rather than a collective title. Am I missing something?

Answer: According to LCRI 25.34B-25.34C, "If a sound recording collection contains three, four, or five musical works entered under a single personal name heading, enter the collection under the collective uniform title appropriate to the whole item. Make name-title analytical entries for each work in the collection." There's also an accompanying MCD that addresses how to treat collections with six or more works entered under the same personal name heading. Catalogers, it seems, are just being stubborn and refusing to create an extra (collective) entry that many consider superfluous. I sympathize. *Newsletter 67 (August 1996)*

4.16 QUESTION: I have a uniform title question that it seems to me I've seen answered elsewhere, but I can't track it down. When one is cataloging a concert aria and/or opera excerpt in which a recitative and aria are both cited together as the title proper, which portion of the text incipit does one use to formulate the uniform title? Using Mozart's *Misera dove son!...Ah! non son'io che parlo*, K. 369 as an example, one might infer that one always uses the aria's incipit, which makes sense (the uniform title in the LC Authority File is "Ah! non son'io che parlo"), given the "weight" of the aria in relation to the often-perfunctory recitative that precedes it. But is this always true? What if one has an extensive, accompanied recitative that almost amounts to a true "cavatina," or even just a case where the incipit for the "introduction" is a common or popularly known title? (Another Mozart aria, *Ombra felice . . . Io ti lascio* comes to mind—I have always known this beautiful work just as *Ombra felice* and couldn't have told you the other part of the title cited in *New Grove* if my life had depended on it.) I guess I want a hard-and-fast rule where probably none should apply. Can you help?

Answer (courtesy of Deta Davis, Library of Congress): The uniform title should be made under the aria. If the piece could be known under the recitative, then a cross-reference should be made from that form (as well as any other form under which it might be known and documented). If the recitative is so extensive as to actually be performed as a stand-alone piece, only then would it receive its own uniform title under the recitative title. *Newsletter 66 (May 1997)*

4.17 QUESTION: Occasionally, I find an authority record that contains "see" references leading from one or more specific titles to a very general title. For example, n81060084 (ARN 605516) for Darius Milhaud contains "Serenade for orchestra" in 400 $t and "Instrumental music. Selections" in the 100 $t. Does this mean I must change a 700 $t or 240 from the very specific "Serenade" to a title that is so general that it is virtually meaningless? I realize that there will be a "see" reference for Serenade, but wouldn't it be better to have a separate authority record for it?

Answer: The authority record you cite is a good example of a particular kind of authority record that has caused no end of trouble over the years for exactly the reason you've pinpointed. These tend to be for some sort of collective uniform title, as here, but that isn't always the case. The AACR2 heading and the reference from the pre-AACR2 form are both pretty easy to understand:

100 10 Milhaud, Darius, $d 1892–1974. $t Instrumental music. $k Selections
400 10 Milhaud, Darius, $d 1892–1974. $t Works, $m instrumental. $k Selections

The remaining "headings" are actually the titles proper (and variations thereof) from items in the Library of Congress's collection (since they are the main creator of this authority file) that have used the AACR2 heading as their collective uniform title. For instance, if you look at the final four references beginning with "2 pianos," you'll find that they were generated when LC cataloged OCLC #31294856 (LCCN 94-704653/R). Look at that bibliographic record and you'll find it has the collective Milhaud uniform title in question. If we searched each of the other "headings" we would be likely to find a corresponding LC record with our collective uniform title and the individual title proper in question (look at #7593011, #10287550, and #15364245, for example). It so happens that the "Serenade for orchestra" doesn't have an obvious LC record online, but it may be for an old NUC record or could have been added by a NACO participant or something. Unless you happen to have the exact item cited, these references are not terribly useful. Worse, as you've discovered, they can be misleading, especially in certain authority file search lists. You should continue to use the most specific uniform title for a particular work. I don't know which of Milhaud's "serenades" you happen to have; if it's op. 71, the authority record is "no 93037928", but op. 62 doesn't have an authority record. I didn't notice any others during a quick glance at *New Grove*. *Newsletter 65 (November 1996)*

4.18 QUESTION: In cataloging a recording of Schubert's *Winterreise*, I found a record with a uniform title that duplicated the title proper. Why is there a uniform title when the title proper is the same thing? I see also that this record has a 505, which I would have guessed to be right, but in another record input by the Library of Congress, there is no 505. So which is right?

   Answer: In a case where the uniform title and the title proper would be the same, no uniform title is necessary (LCRI 25.1). Some libraries input one anyway to accommodate their local systems, which may not display things correctly under certain circumstances. Including a contents note or not is more a matter of taste, local needs, space, and ambition than of right vs. wrong. Libraries that have their 505s indexed or have keyword searching may be more inclined to include them then those who don't. Some catalogers may base the decision to list contents depending on the source of the information: When contents appear on the label, include; when not, don't. But there's no right or wrong. *Newsletter 64 (August 1996)*

4.19 QUESTION: Recently I was trying to catalog "Pavan no. 4" from Melchior Franck's "Newe Pavanen, Galliarden, und Intraden." Making a name-title added entry, everything is fine through Franck's name and subfield $t; there is an LC authority record showing that the authorized form of the collection is indeed "Newe Pavanen, Galliarden, und Intraden." Then I use a subfield $p for "Pavan," and the trouble starts. It would seem that the number of the pavan should be in subfield $n, thus:

$t Newe Pavanen etc. . . . $p Pavan, $n no. 4

But AACR2R doesn't seem to address this situation in Chapter 25 under the discussion about excerpts and parts of pieces. I can't find any examples in BF&S where a subfield $n follows a subfield $p. I'm not sure there should be a comma after subfield $p. There is a pre-AACR2 LC authority record for this very excerpt, and it puts everything in subfield $p: "$p Pavan no. 4", but somehow that seems odd. How should this excerpt be sub-fielded?

Answer: Examples in BF&S are hardly exhaustive. There are a few such examples in *Music Coding and Tagging*, though (p. 137, Visee example at the top, n88660019; p. 139, Leonarda example in mid-page, n83176152; the Caix d'Hervelois example at the bottom of p. 139 has changed). And although the context is different, the Grieg example in rule 25.32B2 shows the same form (n85373695). The subfielding you have suggested

$t Newe Pavanen, Galliarden und Intraden. $p Pavan, $n no. 4

seems to be correct. It is indeed odd, though, that AACR2 does not address the issue directly. The rules dance around it in 25.32, but seem only to imply that this is the way to do it. Unless, that is, we read 25.32A1 to mean that we should identify parts of larger works by "the title or verbal designation and/or the number of the part," with the guidelines that follow to be used in special cases. *Newsletter 64 (August 1996)*

4.20 QUESTION: I am confused about the order of certain additions to music uniform titles. In your *Music Coding and Tagging* are a couple of ex-amples that nicely demonstrate the confusion. (Here I will always omit $f and diacritics.) On p. 136, last example under $l, is:

Moore, Mary Carr, $d 1873–1957. $t Legende provencale. $p Etoile du soir; $o arr. $l English. ($l after $o)

On p. 139, second example under $o, is:

Uhl, Alfred, $d 1909– $t Wer einsam ist, der hat es gut. $l English & German. $k Selections; $o arr. ($l before $o)

Are these different situations (maybe because one has $k Selections)? The second one fits the mnemonic we use to remember the order, except that it doesn't have $s. (The mnemonic is "slicko," for $s $l $k $o.) If the first example is right, we would input it incorrectly. And what if $s were needed? I have read and reread AACR2R 25.35A1, which is fine until the sentence that starts "If Selections is added . . ." but at that point I really lose the thread. Clarification would be very welcome.

Answer: LC's Deta Davis kindly supplied the answer to this vexing question:

> You are on the right track in using 25.35A1 to understand what is happening in these two uniform titles. They are both correct and don't really contradict each other in application. The Moore uniform title was constructed using the principle stated in the second sentence of the rule: "Make additions in the order given." Therefore, the designation for arrangements (25.35C1) comes before the language of a translation (25.35F1). The whole crux of the Uhl uniform title is in the sentence beginning, "If Selections is added. . . ." This supersedes everything else up to this point and you need to think in a new way. "Selections" will always be last. The only time "Selections" has any other subfields after it is when "arr." is added. So, in the Uhl uniform title, there are four elements: (1) the distinctive title, (2) language, (3) Selections, and (4) arr. Element 2 (language) is the only addition that is not designated as last or next-to-last, so it comes second. Regarding the last two elements, let me paraphrase the rule somewhat: add Selections as the last element of the uniform title, or as the next to last element if "arr." is used. Perhaps another way to think about it is without the MARC tagging (and add that later).

Newsletter 63 (May 1996)

4.21 QUESTION: When the music uniform titles "Works" and "Selections" are used with a person's name, must they be accompanied by the date of publication of the item ($s)?

Answer: The music uniform title "Works" would require a date according to LCRI 25.8. That is *not* the case for the music uniform title "Selections," however. Both LCRI 25.9 (paragraph 5 exception) and LCRI 25.34B1 say not to add dates to "Selections" of music. *Newsletter 63 (May 1996)*

4.22 QUESTION: Should "boheme" (as in "La boheme") be capitalized or no? I have seen it both ways in the OLUC.

Answer: In the sense that "boheme" is used in the opera title (as "unconventional" or "artistic" people rather than as an ethnic identifier), I think it should probably not be capitalized. But I have also seen it both ways (including in the authority record n83129419, in the 400 and 670 fields). *Newsletter 63 (May 1996)*

4.23 QUESTION: I have a question about your Q&A on pp. 17–18 of *OCLC Pacific News Update* of July/August 1994 [and *MOUG Newsletter* no. 56 (December 1993) pp. 7–8], on the topic "Generic Titles in Field 245." This was the question about the title proper for the book containing

Glenn Gould's selected letters. Your discussion was thorough, but I'm wondering why you didn't suggest using a "Correspondence"-type uniform title. This provides the access to the idea of "selected letters." Or have I missed something?

Answer: You are, of course, absolutely correct that a uniform title would be appropriate in the Glenn Gould selected letters case. I just didn't get into the uniform title issue at all, partly because such uniform titles are local decisions, but mostly because the question was specifically about the transcription of the title proper. *Newsletter 59 (November 1994)*

4.24 QUESTION: I'm cataloging a recording of Faure piano music where one of the items is Nocturnes 1–5. The uniform titles on the copy I have are:

Nocturnes, $m piano, $n no. 1–3, op. 33
Nocturnes, $m piano, $n no. 4, op. 36, $r Eb major
Nocturnes, $m piano, $n no. 5, op. 37, $r Bb major

I've been mulling this over, and I can't figure out the best way to do this. Faure messed this all up, of course, by giving them separate numbers, then grouping them differently by opus number. There is nothing in the LCNAF and people have made all sorts of different interpretations in OCLC. The way I see it, I have three choices: a) do it the way I've already described; b) group them together as Nocturnes, $m piano, $n no. 1–5 (since Faure did number them separately); c) use only opus numbers and not numbers in the uniform titles (which doesn't really work since Faure gave them the numbers—why did he do that? He must have known it would confuse some poor cataloger.).

Answer: These artists are *so* inconsiderate, aren't they? AACR2 25.32B1, its MCD, and their references to 25.6B all make it clear that your second choice is correct. This is corroborated by the established uniform titles for the various collections of Beethoven's string quartets. Most closely analogous is the uniform title for the "middle" quartets, comprising the three op. 59 quartets, and the single quartets of op. 74 and 95:

Quartets, $m strings, $n no. 7–11   (n82040729)

For both the Faure nocturnes and the Beethoven quartets, individual works are identified first by serial number in the collected sequence, then by opus number, and finally when needed, by serial number within the respective opus. To identify a collection of consecutive parts of the larger "work," the serial numbers in the collective sequence suffice. *Newsletter 57 (May 1994)*

4.25 QUESTION: What is the latest word on initial articles in uniform titles?

Answer: New instructions on uniform titles can be found in *Bibliographic Formats and Standards*. Omit all initial articles and code the filing indicator as "0" in all uniform title fields when inputting current cataloging or transcribing retrospective cataloging. AACR2 25.2C1 specifies that initial articles are to be omitted unless the uniform title is meant to file under that article, as when the uniform title begins with a personal or place name that begins with an article, such as Los Angeles. *Newsletter 56 (December 1993)*

4.26 QUESTION: The name heading and uniform title:

Weber, Carl Maria von, $d 1786–1826. $t Andante e rondo ongarese; $o arr.

is used in OCLC bib records for at least three different works: Weber's arrangement for bassoon and orchestra of his original for viola and orchestra (#24316712, as a 700), an arrangement for viola and piano (#6120983), and an arrangement for bassoon and piano (#12123383, 24814179). Other records show other opinions about what the uniform titles for these three arrangements should be. What is correct?

Answer: A major function of the uniform title is to collect all versions of the same work under an agreed-upon title. Though the uniform title is designed to distinguish among different works, it can gather together, but not necessarily distinguish among, different versions of the *same* work. All of the arrangements of the Weber work you have cited properly have the identical uniform title because they are versions of the *same* work. Other parts of the bibliographic record (title and statement of responsibility area, notes, subject headings, etc.) must be consulted to differentiate the various manifestations of the same work that the uniform title has collected. Assigning the same uniform title to works that are in one sense the same (in that they are arrangements of the *same* work) but are in another sense *not* the same (in that they are *different* settings of the same work), does seem contradictory. Those who formulated the rules on uniform titles opted here for the collocating function to override the differentiating function. That's more or less helpful depending on the situation. *Newsletter 55 (August 1993)*

4.27 QUESTION: Most recordings of musicals omit things like spoken dialogue, musical interludes, and so forth, therefore limiting themselves to the principal songs. However, according to LC, one considers such recordings to be complete if they include phrases like "original Broadway cast." Does this mean we should omit or edit out "$k Selections" in uniform titles and "$x Excerpts" from subject headings, unless the item in some way emphasizes the incompleteness of the contents (e.g., Highlights from . . .). By the same logic, is it OK to make added entries for librettists who are mentioned prominently even though much of their actual work in the collaboration is probably absent from such a recording?

Answer: Music Cataloging Decision 25.32B1 states: "When evidence is lacking as to whether an 'original cast' recording of a musical comedy, etc., or an 'original sound track' recording of a motion picture score contains all the music, do not add 'Selections' to the uniform title." As such, it seems that omitting "Selections" from these uniform titles in AACR2 records would be proper. There doesn't appear to be any corresponding commandment concerning subject headings, but logic would dictate leaving out "Excerpts" as well. Including an added entry for a prominently named librettist seems to be in line with RI 21.23. *Newsletter 54 (May 1993)*

4.28 QUESTION: Is the uniform title "Studies and exercises" followed by the medium of performance applicable to instrumental methods books that do not include the words study or exercise in the chief source? Rule 25.27 states, "If another title in the same language has become better known" it can be used for the uniform title. This seems to make sense for such things as *Rubank's Elementary Methods* for violin, cornet, and so forth.

Answer: As far as I can determine, "Studies and exercises" would never be the uniform title for anything unless the composer named it as such (the new browsable phrase search capability in the authority file reveals no such uniform title). Works such as the various *Rubank's* would probably not need uniform titles at all. The final report of the MLA Bibliographic Control Committee's Working Group on Types of Compositions lists "exercise/exercises" as distinctive and "study/studies" as a type of composition. Perhaps you are thinking of "Studies and exercises" as a free-floating sub-division under subject headings for specific musical instruments or instrumental groups (*Subject Heading Manual* H 1161):

Piano $x Studies and exercises. (sh85101750)
Stringed instruments $x Studies and exercises. (sh85129121)

But those are in the realm of subject headings, not uniform titles. *Newsletter 51 (August 1992)*

4.29 QUESTION: In the uniform title "Quintets, $m violins, violas, violoncello", why are there no Arabic numerals after "violins" and "violas" showing how many of each there are?

Answer: AACR2R 25.30B1 says, "If there is more than one part for a particular instrument or voice, add the appropriate arabic numeral in parentheses after the name of that instrument or voice *unless the number is* *otherwise implicit in the uniform title*" (emphasis mine). In this case, the only possible combination adding up to 5 (quintet) in which both "violin" and "viola" would be pluralized is two of each. Hence, the numerals are implied by the construction of the uniform title and are not to be explicitly included. Of course, where various combinations would be possible, the numerals must be included: "Octet, $m trumpets (2), horns (3), trombones (2), tuba." Where the number of instruments is *not* implied by the title, the numbers must be included where appropriate. *Newsletter 50 (May 1992)*

4.30 QUESTION: If an edition of an opera libretto is in the original language, should that language be added to the uniform title?

Answer: An edition of a libretto in the original language should not have that language in the uniform title (25.35F1, with reference back to 25.5C1), unless two languages are involved, one being the original. In that case, both languages are added, with the original language second, after the ampersand.

Puccini, Giacomo, $1858–1924.
Madama Butterfly. $s Libretto. $l English & Italian.

Newsletter 48 (August 1991)

4.31 QUESTION: Is there, or has there ever been, some sort of designation in uniform titles for a separately published part? "Selections," "Excerpts," "Arranged," and so forth don't seem applicable.

Answer: Checking back through the 1949 ALA rules as well as AACR1 and AACR2R, I don't find anything about parts in uniform titles. Part-ness comes out in the physical description (300), the subject heading subdivision "Parts (solo)," and possibly in a Musical Presentation Statement (256), but not in the uniform title. Take a look at 84-756368/M, for instance. Perhaps you are thinking of the treatment of cadenzas. Separately published cadenzas used to be cataloged under the name of the composer of the larger work with the designation "Cadenzas ([name of cadenza composer])" as the last element of the uniform title. Now, separately published cadenzas are cataloged under their composer's name, with a name-title added entry for the composer of the larger work of which they are a part (see 85-751555/M, for example). *Newsletter 48 (August 1991)*

245 FIELD

4.32 QUESTION: Our local network tells me:

In MARC 21 Update No. 2 (October 2001), the Library of Congress made a subtle change to subfielding practice for field 245, allowing subfield $n

(Number of part/section of a work) and subfield $p (Name of part/section of a work) to follow subfield $b (Remainder of title) as well as precede it. These revisions have been made to the PDF and HTML versions of *Bibliographic Formats and Standards*, 3rd edition. OCLC users may want to annotate their printed copies.

Does this mean that the following example (of mine) could change (using cataloger's judgment, I suppose)?

Was: The fabulous Motown years, reliving the magic. $n Volume 1, $p Roberta Flack $h [sound recording] : $b struttin'.
Could be: The fabulous Motown years $h [sound recording] : $b reliving the magic. $n Volume 1, $p Robert Flack : struttin'.

Answer: Yes, that would be one new way of doing this title. By the way, the change in 245 practice has been folded into the PDF and HTML versions of OCLC's *Bibliographic Formats and Standards*, third edition. The item appears in the "News From OCLC" column in this same issue of the *MOUG Newsletter*, may be found online at the OCLC Web site at http://www.oclc.org/oclc/bit/266/content.shtm#changes, and is in OCLC System News. *Newsletter 81 (September 2002)*

4.33 QUESTION: I have a recording the title of which is: . . . *die Tartaren haben meinen Mann ermordet!* The ellipsis at the beginning has meaning, but, according to AACR2 rules (1.1B1, which, however, does not specifically address this), the ellipsis should not be transcribed. Two questions: (1) Should the ellipsis be included? and (2) If so, should the filing indicator be "4" (omitting "die" and ignoring the ellipsis) or "7"?

Answer: According to LCRI 1.1B1, this title would be transcribed as:

-- die Tartaren haben meinen Mann ermordet!

with a double hyphen replacing the ellipsis and no space between the double hyphen and the first word. This would mean that the filing indicator should be "6".

245 16 -- die Tartaren haben meinen Mann ermordet!

See OCLC #37983869 (LCCN 97-706224) and #26591362 (LCCN 83-751219) as similar examples. *Newsletter 79 (November 2000)*

4.34 QUESTION: I have a question about how to format the 245 for a sound recording record I am working on. There is no collective title on the album itself, nor on its jacket. I'm new at this, so my questions may be pretty basic. If you need the specifics, it is an LP; #3077225 is the best record I can find for it. The person who created this record chose to use the text on the album jacket rather than on the LP itself for the 245. I would like to know (1) Where does the $h [sound recording] go? and (2) What about that "and" shown in two of the examples in Books Format, 245 section (http://www.oclc.org/bibformats/en/2xx/245.shtm), in the part that begins, "If the item lacks a collective title, input the first title in subfield $a"? Here is how I created my 245. Is the $h in the correct place?

245 00   Concerto for piano and wind instruments $h [sound recording] ; Ebony concerto ; Symphonies of wind instruments ; Octet for wind instruments / $c Igor Stravinsky.

Now for part two. These examples are used in Books Format:

245 10   Lord Macaulay's essays ; $b and, Lays of ancient Rome
245 10   Four small dances $h [sound recording] ; $b and, Six Hungarian folksongs

Nowhere that I can find does it give explanation of that "and." Is that something that the cataloger adds between the titles? Or was that word actually part of the text on the material itself? So I could write:

245 00   Concerto for piano and wind instruments $h [sound recording] ; $b and, Ebony concerto ; Symphonies of wind instruments ; Octet for wind instruments / $c Igor Stravinsky.

If this is okay, how many "ands" can/should I use? Just one after the $b?

Answer: Your formulation of the 245 is correct except that you need a subfield $b following the GMD, as follows:

245 00   Concerto for piano and wind instruments $h [sound recording] ; $b Ebony concerto ; Symphonies of wind instruments ; Octet for wind instruments / $c Igor Stravinsky.

Placement of the GMD has changed over the history of AACR2, but according to the 1998 revision, Rule 1.1C2, "In the case of an item having no collective title, give the appropriate designation immediately following the first title (inclusive of part titles [see 1.1B9] and alternative titles, but exclusive of parallel titles [see 1.1D] and other title information [see 1.1E])." For sound recordings specifically, see Rule 6.1G2. Those "ands" in the *Bibliographic Formats and Standards* examples were presumably present on the title page or other source of title, otherwise they would be bracketed. You would need to supply a bracketed "and" only in cases where it might clarify an ambiguous relationship between the titles. In the case you're asking about, you don't need to add anything. *Newsletter 79* (*November 2000*)

4.35 QUESTION: I have what I hope is my last question about subfield $n (or $p) and $b in a 245. We've been copy cataloging each volume in the Hyperion collection of lieder of Robert Schumann. Each disc (so far) has a label thus:

The Hyperion Schumann Edition-1 (or 2, or 3—whatever the number in the set)

Then farther down there is:

Complete Songs–Samtliche Lieder–Melodies Integrales

The Hyperion Schumann Edition *is* the complete songs. No other genres of music are planned to be part of this overall title. The copy we are seeing subfields the 245 thus:

245 14   The Hyperion Schumann edition. $n 1 $h [sound recording] : $b Complete songs = Samtliche Lieder = Melodies integrales.

Reading over your answer to a question I had for you back in 1995, I find these words of wisdom: "Other title information refers to (and should be placed immediately following) the title to which it is attached, whether that title is the title proper or a part title. . . . In fact, looking at the real bibliographic records for the "Dacca University Studies," its "Part C" is exactly what the example [in BF&S under 245] suggests; parts A and B are the semi-annual journals of other university areas (the English Dept. and arts & sciences, respectively)." (Isn't it *scary* that people actually *save* your answers?) My point is that, in the Schumann, "Complete songs" and its parallel titles refer to Hyperion Schumann Edition, *not* just volume 1 of that set. "Complete songs" and so forth, should therefore come right after Hyperion Schumann Edition, *before* the subfield $n. But since you cannot have a subfield $n after a subfield $b, should this title be:

245 14   The Hyperion Schumann edition $h [sound recording] : $b Complete songs = Samtliche Lieder = Melodies integrales. 1

Ick. Not that anyone really cares. Don't think I've met a system that does anything useful with the subfield codes we so carefully put in and worry about.

   Answer: Let's go back to another set of questions and answers in *MOUG Newsletter* no. 62, p. 9, and LC's follow-up answer in no. 63, p. 13. LC's Robert Ewald wrote in part: "LC does not separately subfield a subtitle that comes between the main title and the part title. Instead, the subtitle is treated as part of the main title (e.g., '$a Piano rolls, Gershwin's legacy. $n Volume 2, $p Early years $h . . .' or '$a Piano rolls—Gershwin's legacy. $n Volume 2, $p Early years $h . . . ') or the subtitle is omitted from the title and statement of responsibility area and given in a note." That leads me to suggest this treatment of the title in question:

245 14   The Hyperion Schumann edition, complete songs. $n 1 $h [sound
              recording].

If you consider them important enough, you could mention the partial parallel titles in a note. *Newsletter 79 (November 2000)*

4.36 QUESTION: *Technical Bulletin* 244, p. 2, regarding non-filing indicators doesn't seem to be a change to me. Can you give me an example of how searching practice is changing? The examples in the online BF&S seem to be the same as my old paper copy and neither conflicts with MARC 21. What am I missing?

Answer: Here's how I understand the change in assigning the non-filing indicator. Diacritics and special characters that are associated with the non-filing article *are* counted in assigning the indicator, as always.

245 16 -- The serpent-snapping eye : $b trumpet, percussion, piano, and 4-channel
              computer-synthesized sound / $c Roger Reynolds.

Diacritics and special characters that are associated with the first filing character *are not* counted in assigning the indicator, which is a change from previous practice.

245 02   L'Été australien à Montpellier : $b 100 chefs-d'œuvre de la peinture
              australienne : Musée Fabre Galerie Saint Ravy, Montpellier, France.
245 14   Die ägyptische Helena $h [sound recording] : $b Oper in zwei Aufzügen
              / $c Richard Strauss ; [Text] von Hugo von Hofmannsthal.

In OCLC, there is no change in searching, as WorldCat has always compensated for such cases as these. *Newsletter 79 (November 2000)*

4.37 QUESTION: I have been finding some "strange" sound recording records on OCLC. The one that I am working with now is very odd. I'd like your input on it since I really can't justify how the cataloging agency cataloged this particular title (OCLC #43981816). My disc has "Mozart Strauss" as the prominent feature on the disc itself. The disc then lists the three pieces at the bottom. It then lists the performers and conductor. These people are not "prominent" on the disc. I can't see how 6.1B1 is applied here since the performers are not prominently mentioned even on the container or the insert over the composers' and their works.

Answer: My guess is that the cataloger based the decision on LCRI 21.23C, determining from AACR2 21.23C and D proper that "Mozart Strauss" was presented in such as way as to constitute a collective title. LCRI 6.1B1 (which deals with transcribing the title proper, not choosing the main entry) doesn't state it explicitly, but the implication of the whole RI (looking in particular at its second paragraph) is that, although a single composer name would not ordinarily be a candidate for title proper, the names of more than one composer could be so considered. Looking at the fourth example in LCRI 21.23C (*Music of Chabrier and Massenet*) and seeing that the main entry was under the orchestra, the cataloger followed suit. If you check the AACR2 definition of "prominently" (AACR2 Rule 0.8), it says merely that it must be found in one of the prescribed sources of information for that area and class of material. So, if the orchestra and conductor were both on the chief source (the disc/label), that's "prominent" enough. AACR2 21.23C1 says that if there are two or more principal performers, enter under the first named. Anyway, that's my guess. *Newsletter 77* (*November 2000*)

4.38 QUESTION: I have a "split CD" to catalog, with two different rock bands on it, little information, and no title other than their band names, "Wat Tyler" and "Xpensive Dogs." Could you give me a couple of examples in OCLC to look at, and maybe a suggestion of how the title might look?

Answer: We need to look at a few rules and RIs on both titles proper and items without a collective title. Rule Interpretation 6.1B1 allows us to use the name of a performer as a collective title proper. The RI's head is still in the vinyl era (if an RI can be said to possess a head; it was issued in 1989) and says in part: "If the chief source being followed is the label of a sound recording and the decision is to treat the name as a title proper but one name appears on the label of one side and another name on the second side, transcribe the two names as individual titles (separated by period-space)." (Makes one wonder who writes these RIs. William Faulkner?) Your instance seems to be the CD-era equivalent of this, and that's how I'd suggest handling it. There is additional corroboration in the rule about items with no collective title, 6.1G2 and its reference back to the general rule 1.1G3 and its RI, which suggest pretty much the same. So I think your title field would be:

245 10   Wat Tyler $h [sound recording]. $b Xpensive Dogs.

After some searching I couldn't easily find any examples, though. *Newsletter 77* (*November 2000*)

4.39 QUESTION: I'm cataloging a bunch (100–150?) of original cast recordings. Now that I'm about a fourth of the way through, a question occurs to me. If there is a statement on the disc itself, to the effect that this is a cast recording, it typically reads "Original Broadway Cast Recording" or "Original Cast Recording." In some instances, though, the statement "Original Broadway Cast" appears, without the word "Recording." I've been blithely transcribing all of the above as other title information, but it seems to me that "Original Broadway Cast" is really a statement of responsibility. Should we regard the phrase "Original Broadway Cast" as a statement of responsibility rather than other title information?

Answer: If we look at AACR2 rules 6.1B1, 6.1E1, and especially 6.1F1, and their respective LCRIs, it's clear that performers in the so-called "popular" idiom *may* be included in the statement of responsibility. Without getting into the debate over "popular" versus "serious" and the performer's intellectual responsibility, my gut feeling is that musicals would be grouped with operas in this respect, in that the performer's responsibility generally does not go beyond "performance, execution, or interpretation." LCRI 6.1F1 would have us shy away from including performers of musicals in the statement of responsibility. I don't really have a problem with including the statement "Original Broadway Cast" as other title information, since the missing word "recording" seems to be a logical implication. (If that makes you uncomfortable, you could add the missing word in brackets.) Alternatively, you might relegate it to either a quoted note by itself or as a quoted introduction to a 511 note that details the performers. *Newsletter 76 (September 2000)*

4.40 QUESTION: I am originally cataloging a piece of music entitled "Gran trio concertante" by Valentino Molino. I noticed other records of this same work in OCLC read "Grand trio concertante." One might apply AACR2 1.0F and write "Gran[d]" in the 245. However, on the title page, the cover, and the title page verso, the spelling is "Gran," which leads me to believe that perhaps this is a variant spelling of this title, rather than an omission of the letter "d." This is further given credence by the fact that the preface gives the title on the original manuscript as "Grand trio . . ." so maybe this is a variant form of the title. However, I am not totally sure about this, and so if you could please share your thoughts on the matter, I would be most grateful.

Answer: Since the variant spelling appears virtually everywhere on your item and does not seem to be a title-page typo, I think it's safe to assume that this is a true variant spelling for this particular edition. Because the original edition had the spelling "Grand," however, it also sounds like this spelling would be the proper uniform title. You could also supply a 246 title with the "Grand" spelling. *Newsletter 76 (September 2000)*

4.41 QUESTION: I have a question regarding the correct order to list uniform titles for two works by the same composer on a compact disc. On the disc label, the works are listed separately. So, to give an example, the 245 for two works by Sibelius (this is not what is on my CD) would be:

245 10   Finlandia $h [sound recording] ; $b Tapiola / $c Sibelius.

This is the order that they are listed on the disc label, so that is how you would transcribe it in the 245. However, they actually appear in the opposite order in the recording (this would be noted in a 505). So my question is, would you list the uniform titles to reflect the order that they are listed on the disc label (first the 240 for *Finlandia*, then the composer/title 700 for *Tapiola*), or would you list them in the order that they actually appear on the recording (first the 240 for *Tapiola*, then the composer/title 700 for *Finlandia*)? I realize that this would be made easier if there were three or more pieces on the recording, because then you could just give a collective uniform title, and do the 700s in the recorded order at the end, but no such luck this time. I checked AACR2 and the appropriate MCDs with no luck.

   Answer: AACR2, the LCRIs, and the MCDs don't seem to address this issue directly, as you discovered. But I think we can take LCRI 21.29 on the "Order of Added Entries" and extrapolate commonsensically from the statement, "For arrangement within any one grouping, generally follow the order in which the justifying data appear in the bibliographic description. If such a criterion is not applicable, use judgment." Since you are using the label as chief source and transcribing its order of the works as the non-collective titles, I think it's reasonable to keep the 240 uniform title and the 700 composer/title added entry in the same order as the transcribed titles, that is, *Finlandia* first (240; of course, in this case, the 240 would be omitted according to LCRI 25.1, as it exactly duplicates the title proper, but the principle stands) and *Tapiola* second (700). That also has the fortuitous effect of keeping the uniform title in the 240 and the first title in the 245 in harmony, referring to the same work. By the way, since the contents are already outlined in the 245, I don't think you really need a formal 505 note. Instead, a 500 note should be sufficient, to the effect that the works are actually in the reverse order from that indicated on the label. *Newsletter 75 (May 2000)*

4.42 QUESTION: We have several fragments of scores that are not identifiable, except that John Philip Sousa is the composer and they seem not to be from the same work. We wondered if (a) all of these could be included in one record (yes, according to AACR2?), and (b) could we use the phrase "sketch score" to describe these fragments, since they appear to be incomplete motifs, not fleshed out. I have never heard or seen that phrase used before but that doesn't mean much. Many of these fragments are parts of vocal scores of Sousa's operettas, I think. Some have never been published.

Answer: You may compile such miscellaneous sketches into a single record, though you'll have to supply (I am supposing) some comprehensive (bracketed) title. If they can be identified as some particular genre of works, as you suggest, you would use the collective uniform title for that genre with the qualifier "(Sketches)" as per AACR2 25.35B. If they cannot be narrowed down, you'll need to be more general (such as "Selections [Sketches]"). The "(Sketches)" qualifier is not separately subfielded.

100 1   Sousa, John Philip, $d 1854–1932.
240 10   Operas. $k Selections (Sketches)
245 10   [Sketches for miscellaneous operettas].

If you do a search on "beet, sket" you'll find lots of examples to get ideas from. The specific phrase "sketch score" is not familiar to me, but there's no reason why you couldn't use it in a supplied 245 title. *Newsletter 74* (*November 1999*)

4.43 QUESTION: What do we do when a CD is reissued under a different title than the original release, with the new title taken from a different song title on the CD, but the new title is misspelled everywhere on the new release? In hand I have a CD with the publisher number "Classic 7724," published by Classic Sound, Inc. (Norcross, Georgia), performed by Art Blakey and the Jazz Messengers. The title on all parts of the CD reads *Rucerdo*; the song list reads: "Buttercorn lady," "Rucerdo," "The theme," "Between races," "My romance," "Secret love." There are no dates whatsoever on the CD, but it is obviously a reissue, although I've been unable to determine the date of the original issue. On the Web, I found an Art Blakey discography that lists and pictures a 1966 album titled: *Buttercorn lady* (Limelight 82034) with the exact same song list, except the one song is titled "Recuerdo" and not "Rucerdo." "Recuerdo" is a legitimate word in Spanish. As far as I know "rucerdo" isn't a word in any language. I feel sure the item I have in hand is a (possibly unauthorized) retitled reissue of the 1966 album. I really don't like having to exactly transcribe a title that is so obviously wrong and without meaning in any language. Here's how I'm thinking of describing the item:

100 1   Blakey, Art.
240 10   Buttercorn lady
245 10   Recuerdo $h [sound recording] / $c Art Blakey and the Jazz Messengers.

246 1 $i Title on disc label and container misspelled as: $a Rucerdo
500   Originally issued in 1966 under the title: Buttercorn lady.

Is this description acceptable?

Answer: Since you have determined through your research that the item is some sort of reissue, incompetent though it may be, you should include that information in the record as you have in your proposed 500 field. Although I don't believe that the use of the original release's title as a uniform title would be called for, a related title 740 for *Buttercorn Lady* would be fine. The use of that uniform title under Blakey's name implies first of all that he is the composer of the entire collection and secondly that these pieces were composed, presented, and intended as a collection by that composer. Since Blakey is the main entry by reason of his being the chief performer rather than as composer (or so is my guess), a uniform title is not appropriate here. Regarding the misspelled title, AACR2 1.0F would have you transcribe the title as it appears, followed either with "[*sic*]" or "i.e." and a correction. The latter would seem to be the way to go in this case. LCRI 21.30J gives guidance about access to both the incorrect and corrected form of the title.

245 10   Rucerdo [i.e. Recuerdo] $h [sound recording] / $c Art Blakey and the Jazz
          Messengers.
246 3   Recuerdo

You could use the same "i.e." technique in the 505 field where the title is incorrect. *Newsletter 74 (November 1999)*

4.44 QUESTION: Determining the title proper of compact discs has become increasingly problematic. We've had several examples of a disc containing several pieces by one composer with a nice collective title, then one piece at the end by a different composer. I've found one example by LC where they cataloged it as if the second composer did not exist, then added a note, something to the effect of "Also includes [name of piece] by [name of composer]" and made an added entry for it. That seems eminently reasonable to me, but I only saw that one example. Have you run into this? The one I'm facing now has the collective title *Classic Oboe Etudes* [by] Barret, Brod, Ferling, and then right after that on the face of the CD: Britten: *Six Metamorphoses after Ovid*. The Britten takes up 12 minutes of the total 60 minutes of music on the CD. The copy I'm working from solved it thus:

100 10   Zupnik, Marilyn $4 prf (she's the oboist)
245 10   Classic oboe etudes $h [sound recording] / $c Barret, Brod, Ferling. Six
          metamorphoses after Ovid / Britten.

One should only use principal performer main entry when you have a collective title. This title is only "kind of" collective; the first half of it is. Any clues or suggestions?

Answer: You're right about not being able to use principal performer as the main entry for sound recordings in the so-called "serious" idiom when there is no collective title (21.23D1b) and I agree that in the instance you cite, there is no truly collective title. I've seen other similar examples where LC has fudged this when there's a little piece (often by the same composer) added to fill out the disc in addition to a major work (#31488546, #32550767, #30948194), or when there are miscellaneous pieces added to something(s) larger (#40053240, #39079360, #35564446, #34477490). Though I see the commonsense advantage of this practice, it strikes me as a sort of lazy shortcut. Since LC resorts to it on occasion, I can't really argue against it. But whether you choose the no collective title option or the "also includes" note option here, the question of the main entry remains. As I read 21.23D1b, the only choice you have for the main entry is the heading for the first work, in this case the Barret etude. *Newsletter 73 (August 1999)*

4.45 QUESTION: In most (maybe all) of the chapters in Part I of AACR2R, Rule X0.B1 lists the chief sources of information, followed by a sentence that states, "If information is not available from the chief source, take it from the following sources (in this order of preference): . . ." and then lists things like container, accompanying material, and the ubiquitous "other sources." My question is at what point do you bracket a title that does not come from the approved chief sources? If I have no title at all on the face of my CD nor on the insert, which shows through the jewel case, but do have a perfectly acceptable title on the spine or back of the jewel case, do I bracket the title? Or if I have a set of slides where the only place I find a title is on the accompanying material, do I bracket it? I think I never have bracketed such titles, just put them in the 245 and added a note saying where I found the title. I now realize that I have adjusted that rule in my head to: if the title is not on the chief source but is somewhere else on the item or on things that come with the item (e.g., accompanying material, containers), give it without brackets and with a note. If the title comes from outside the item (e.g., publisher's catalogs, my own head) then bracket and add a note. But that's not exactly what AACR2R says. It lumps accompanying material, containers, and "other sources"—which to me means things outside the item, including cataloger-supplied titles—all together, as if titles from all these places should be recorded in the same way. Can you clarify?

Answer: AACR2 Rule 1.0A1 says, "Enclose in square brackets information taken from outside the prescribed source(s)." In most of the Part I chapters, the prescribed source for the title and statement of responsibility area is the chief source of information. Definition of the "chief source" differs from chapter to chapter but it tends to cover a wide choice of sources, its name notwithstanding. In Chapter 5 for music, for instance, it eventually says, "Use the title page or title page substitute (see 2.0B1) as the chief source of information." The phrase "title page substitute" covers a lot of ground, judging from 2.0B1 and the specific information in each chapter. In the sound recordings chapter, 6.0B1 in part says, "Treat accompanying textual material or a container as the chief source of information if it furnishes a collective title and the parts themselves and their labels do not." In the graphic materials chapter, you find similarly broad interpretations of "chief source" in 8.0B1, concluding with, "In describing a collection of graphic materials as a unit, treat the whole collection as the chief source."

This is all pretty confounding, as you've noticed. I think it generally boils down to using square brackets when the cataloger is supplying information, when information comes from a source external to the piece in hand (a publisher's catalog, for instance), or when the title and statement of responsibility have a mixed heritage (when a subtitle appears only on a container, for example, but is included as other title information with a title from a sound recording label).

245 10   Steel wheels $h [sound recording] / $c [principally] written by Jagger/
         Richards.
245 00   From dusk till dawn $h [sound recording] : $b [music from the motion
         picture].
500   Subtitle from container.
245 10   [Euro-Landerkarte 1:800.000. $p Deutschland : $b mit Ortsnamenverzeichnis
         und Entfernungstabelle].
500   Title derived from publisher's catalog.

You will want to indicate in a note the source of information when appropriate. *Newsletter 73 (August 1999)*

4.46 QUESTION: Those of you who have been cataloging as long as I have will recall the fairly frequent occasions when an LP would have on its two labels the names of two different performers, say, Rosa Ponselle on side one and Lily Pons on side two. No other collective title was available. In such a case, RI 6.1B1 comes into play, and the two names would be transcribed as individual titles separated by a period-space: "Rosa Ponselle. Lily Pons." Fast-forward to the CD era, and now we sometimes encounter examples where the appropriate collective title to employ consists of the names of the performers found on the label. Do we extrapolate from the LP-centric RI and separate the two names with a period-space, or should we use some other form of punctuation? In my example, the possibilities include:

Jack Teagarden's Big Eight. Pee Wee Russell's Rhythmakers

Jack Teagarden's Big Eight, Pee Wee Russell's Rhythmakers
Jack Teagarden's Big Eight ; Pee Wee Russell's Rhythmakers

(And where does subfield $h go?) The RI appears to need updating, but in the meantime I would appreciate any thoughts my fellow catalogers might have on the matter.

Answer: Extrapolation is the way to go, I think, when there is no usable collective title anywhere (including the container and its spine). This means we are dealing with the two names as individual, non-collective titles, so they need to be separated by period space, with the GMD intervening:

245 00   Jack Teagarden's Big Eight $h [sound recording]. $b Pee Wee Russell's
               Rhythmakers.

Of course, you would also have a 740 for the second non-collective title. *Newsletter 72 (May 1999)*

4.47 QUESTION: I'm cataloging a CD with a fake URL for a title and am wondering exactly how to deal with it. An exact transcription would be:

etsu://wind
ensemble@
cbdna.in.concert
3.1.1996.edu

The typeface is perfectly uniform throughout. So, do the line breaks separate words? Should the backslashes be retained, even though they would be used to distinguish the statement of responsibility? I know that according to AACR2, I do not have to transcribe punctuation exactly—but are these symbols "punctuation" or computer coding or perhaps there is no difference (since punctuation is coding for human language)? I also know that if I put a colon after "etsu" our indexing system thinks that everything after the colon is other title info (even without the subfield $b—GRRRR!). And regardless of how I transcribe it, I know I'll put in plenty of added titles. My impulse is pretty straightforward: "ETSU Wind Ensemble @ CBDNA in concert, 3-1-1996.edu $h [sound recording]."

Answer: We're probably going to be seeing a lot more of these "clever" imitation URLs as the Web further infiltrates our culture. This particular one seems to be combining and/or confusing the URL convention of "access method-colon-slash-slash" with the e-mail address convention that includes the "at" sign and "dot-edu". LCRI 1.1B1 offers a little guidance on how to treat punctuation that, in other contexts, would be ISBD. If it is possible (and does not violate sense) to keep the spaces surrounding the punctuation in question closed up, there is no problem. Remember that most ISBD punctuation (certainly the colon and the slash) would have blank spaces on each side. That being said, I would transcribe the title almost exactly as it appears:

245 00   etsu://wind ensemble@cbdna.in.concert 3.1.1996.edu $h [sound recording].

Although I find nothing in AACR2 or the rule interpretations to tell us how to treat line breaks, I have chosen to retain as spaces those breaks that serve to separate words (between "wind" and "ensemble" and between "concert" and the numeric date), but to close up the space between the "at" sign and "cbdna" to follow the electronic address convention. If you transcribed it this way (and there is no one "correct" transcription, of course), providing a 246 with all the spaces closed up might be wise. As you've indicated, any number of additional 246s could be appropriate (including your own transcription impulse), but try to use discretion (as well as LCRI 21.30J). *Newsletter 71 (December 1998)*

4.48 FOLLOW-UP QUESTION: Upon reflection and careful perusal of AACR2, I had changed my mind and tentatively transcribed the title as you suggested, except without the line breaks (plus an added title *with* breaks—the reverse of what you suggested, actually). My reasoning behind this was that URL and e-mail addresses wouldn't have breaks, so a "faux URL" address wouldn't either. Does this make sense to you or would you still include the line breaks?

Answer: Your solution makes just as much sense as mine. Maybe even a bit more, since you are being more faithful to the conventions for electronic addresses, whereas I am still a slave to the English language. Either alternative seems perfectly acceptable to me. One thing I had neglected to mention, especially if you choose to go with no breaks, was that you might optionally want to include some sort of 500 note explaining the character of the title. This would be in the spirit of LCRI 1.0E, perhaps something like, "Title is presented as a pseudo-Uniform Resource Locator." *Newsletter 71 (December 1998)*

4.49 QUESTION: Source of information, AACR2 6.0B1 reads: "When information is not available on the defined chief source, take it from (in order of preference): Accompanying textual material, Container, Other sources." MCD 6.0B1 reads: "Consider information which can be read through the closed container including information on the front cover of a booklet inserted in the container to be on the container." I often find a third source, the container, more informative than the second, the accompanying material. Is the phrase in parentheses (in order of preference) really restrictive? That is, if there is no collective title on the chief source, and there seems to be a collective title in the accompanying material, but the container contains the most complete collective title, may I transcribe that title? Would "In order of preference" here mean whichever of these has the most useful information? If there isn't a comprehensive title in the chief source, you look at next, accompanying material, and if there is nothing there, you go on to the container?

Answer: When you have no collective title on the disc or label, you may use the most complete, comprehensive, and/or useful collective title you find elsewhere, whether it is on the accompanying material, container, or other source. Explain the source of that title in a 500 note, of course. Remember that even if you choose one of these titles as the collective title proper, you may still transcribe and give access (in field 246) to any other useful titles you find in other places.

245 04 Les Araucans du Chili $h [sound recording].
246 1 $i Parallel title on container: $a Araucanians of Chile
246 1 $i Additional title on container: $a Musique des Araucans du sud Chili

Newsletter 70 (September 1998)

4.50 QUESTION: Is the spine considered to be part of the container? How should we indicate in a note that a title is from the container spine?

Answer: The spine of a sound recording is considered part of the container, so you really have a number of choices about how you designate a title found on the spine. Using the 246 field, you can simply choose second indicator "8", which will generate the "Spine title:" designation. But you may also supply your own introductory phrase (using second indicator blank and subfield $i for the text) such as "Title on spine of container:" or "Title on container spine:" or whatever you are comfortable with. If the title chosen for the 245 is from the spine, you may likewise phrase the 500 note as you please, for instance:

500 Title from container spine.
500 Title from spine of container.
500 Title from spine.

Any variation is acceptable. *Newsletter 70 (September 1998)*

4.51 QUESTION: Although these are invented examples, the situations are very real. For each, the question is how the 245 should read (including ISBD punctuation), particularly, what is the title proper and what is other title information? The mix of "type" words and non-"type" information in the examples is deliberate and parallels the real situations. The examples are both scores.

Trio   [big print, bold]
A Night in Bavaria   [smaller print, not bold]
For   [continuing the smaller print]
Violin, Violoncello, and Piano
By
John Doe   [slightly larger print, but smaller than Trio]
Op. 23   [the smaller print]
Waltz   [big print, bold]
From A Big Piece Op. 74   [smaller print, not bold]
By
John Doe

My fellow scores cataloger and I can think of more than one way to do each of these examples, depending on which particular rules you follow, especially general rules or music-specific rules. How would you do these?

Answer: The first thing to remember is that there is no single "correct" way to create a catalog record. Although there are certainly wrong ways to transcribe such things as titles and statements of responsibility, there may be several equally acceptable correct ways. As long as the information is accurate and reasonably complete, it's probably not worth agonizing over whether a comma might be more helpful than a colon in a particular instance. Besides, the rules, RIs, and MCDs are not a lot of help in making such a decision. Cataloging is an art more than a science. That being said, my two alternatives (there could be others) for the first example are:

245 00   Trio, a night in Bavaria : $b for violin, violoncello, and piano, op. 23 / $c by John Doe.

or

245 00   Trio : $b a night in Bavaria : for violin, violoncello, and piano, op. 23 / $c by John Doe.

There is no concrete guidance in the rules, but you can find an example (albeit in the Sound Recording chapter; and yes, I know that the examples are illustrative, not prescriptive) much like the first possibility as the third example in Rule 6.1G2 (both the original text and the "Amendments 1993" version):

Prelude, the afternoon of a faun

In the second alternative, the relationship is more of title and subtitle, though you could optionally give access to the other possibility in a 246 field:

246 3   Trio, a night in Bavaria

In both cases, you'd want to give access to the more substantive part of the title:

246 30   Night in Bavaria

Keeping the opus number as part of the title instead of trailing off after the composer's name is justified in Rule 5.1B1, regardless of which alternative you choose: ". . . if one or more statements of medium of performance, key, date of composition, and/or number are found in the source of information, treat those elements as other title information."

There's not much more guidance about your second example, either. My guess is that when you have a nondistinctive title (such as "waltz" in your example), the further identification as being "from" some larger work is retained as part of the title proper to give it some distinction. This is in the spirit of making other nondistinctive titles distinctive through additional information in the title proper.

245 00   Waltz from A big piece, op. 74 / $c by John Doe.

Again, there are examples to back this up (Rule 5.1F1, second example) but nothing really explicit in the rules. If the opus or other number belongs to the "big piece," I'd keep it with the title of the big piece, as in the subfielding above. If the opus or other number is associated with the smaller part of the big piece, I'd probably set it off with a space-colon-space and a subfield $b to suggest its association with the entire subfield $a rather than just the "big piece." This doesn't entirely fulfill your need for AACR2 chapter and verse, but it's the best that I can come up with given that imperfect tool called AACR2. *Newsletter 70 (September 1998)*

4.52 FOLLOW-UP QUESTION: As a follow-up, another possibility we came up with is:

245 00   Trio for violin, violoncello, and piano, op. 23 : $b a night in Bavaria / $c
         by John Doe.

That puts all the correct information up with the "type" word (AACR2 5.1B1) but really goes against the rule of transcribing things in the order they are found on the chief source (AACR2 1.1B1, 1.1D1, 1.1E2, etc.). What's your take on this possibility? (We would, of course, provide the 246 30 Night in Bavaria.)

Answer: The option of putting the distinctive title information at the end is tempting but, as you point out, it does go against the rule about keeping the order found in the item, so I wouldn't advocate it. It could easily lead a subsequent cataloger into inputting a duplicate based on perceived title differences. In both of your questions, a good argument can be made for making the single words "Trio" and "Waltz" the respective titles proper, though I think there is nothing in the rules to explicitly sanction this decision or my own preference. To explain my own preference, I am thinking back to when we first started using ISBD punctuation. At that time, we ended up with lots of titles proper that consisted of single, nondistinctive words that went nowhere in expressing to anyone the identity of the work in question. In those early days, all the distinctive stuff (medium, key, numbers) was relegated to other title information. It was ugly, it wasn't helpful, and it wasn't user-friendly. We quickly (well, quickly in cataloging rule bureaucracy terms) came to our senses and declared (in AACR2r 5.1B1) that medium, key, date of composition, and number were part of the title proper when present with a name of a type of composition. My preferred answers to both of your questions are in that same spirit of including distinctive information in a title proper when the title is the name of a type of composition and when the presentation on the chief source allows it. But I reiterate that I find no definitive answer in the rules, either way. *Newsletter 70 (September 1998)*

4.53 QUESTION: What is the proper capitalization for titles in the 245 field of AV materials? I quoted AACR2 saying only the first word is capitalized even if it's an article, unless it is a personal name, etc. There seem to be a lot of AV records in WorldCat that have the second word capitalized, and I wanted to know what OCLC policy is.

Answer: Only the first word of a title (in English) is capitalized, even if it is an article. You will see many records in WorldCat with the second word capitalized, and will hear lots of confusion on the matter, because the original text of AACR2, 1988 revision, said (Rule A.4D1): "If an article is the first word of the title proper and the main entry is under the title proper . . . , also capitalize the next word" (p. 568). Of course, the title is most often the main entry in Visual Materials records. With the "Amendments 1993," however, Rules A.4A through A.4H were deleted and had new versions of them substituted, eliminating the capitalization of the second word when the title is the main entry. The Amendments are also full of changed capitalizations throughout the text, which are repercussions from that revision. *Newsletter 69 (April 1998)*

4.54 QUESTION: A while back you gave some good advice about cataloging 45 rpm records. Looking at p. 22 of CSB no. 75, the examples seem to indicate a new approach to "without collective title" items: the examples have 246 subfield $a with both titles (245 subfields $a and $b, etc.), *and* there is the example with the 700 author/title. But, there is a Note between 2) and 3) saying to use 246s only for titles occurring in 245 subfield $a. I have been doing these 45s (usually title main entry) with 740s for the flip side and doing just fine; do I need 246s now, and author/title access for bands *and* writers?

Answer: The LCRI in question (21.30J) deals with title added entries. The section you refer to ("Items Without Collective Title") concentrates mostly on the changes wrought by the revised placement of the GMD in the "Amendments 1993" to AACR2, the resulting revised placement of subfield $b, and the expanded use of field 246 after Format Integration. Using the 246 for the complete string of titles without intervening GMD or subfielding was an attempt by LC to accommodate the machine environment (see the RI's "Introduction" for more details on that). They reasoned that such previously unsubfielded title strings should remain accessible in the 246 even though they were now formulated differently in the 245 under the new practices. You would use this 246 string only for non-collective titles found in 245 subfields $a and $b. If there were any subsequent titles (usually with different statements of responsibility) in 245 subfield $c or after any "Other" title information, these would not be included in the 246 string. If your two sides of the 45 have different statements of responsibility, so that the flip side ends up farther along in 245 subfield $c, do not add the 246 for a string of both titles. If both titles have the same statement of responsibility and are not separated by other title information, the 246 string would be appropriate. In both cases, the second title by itself would still properly have a 740.

245 00   Title A $h [GMD] / $c statement of responsibility. Title B / statement of
             responsibility.
740 02   Title B.
245 00   Title A $h [GMD] ; $b Title B / $c statement of responsibility.
246 3   Title A ; Title B.
740 02   Title B.

The "Note" is stating that, in addition to this title string use of 246, you would use 246 for varying forms of the title in 245 subfield $a. (This is an exception to the rule that 246 is used only for comprehensive titles that could cover an entire item.) Any variations on other titles found in 245 would be handled in 740s. Author/title added entries all around ("author" generally being the first named composer here) would be appropriate. The performer(s) would be traced separately, without title, generally. *Newsletter 67 (August 1997)*

4.55 QUESTION: I am cataloging a bunch of 45 rpm records. I have seen on OCLC, older examples of 245 fields with "Tune / $c Artist", and newer examples of both "A" side and "B" side titles in the 245 separated by subfield $b, with a 505, and/or a 246 or 740. Could you give me some "title" and tracing guidance with these records? There doesn't seem to be much about 45s around.

Answer: You've seen different practices in cataloging 45 rpm discs both because things have changed over the years and because you have different options available. AACR2R 6.1G gives details on cataloging sound recordings without a collective title (usually the case with 45s), allowing the item to be cataloged as a unit or each side (title) to be cataloged separately. The latter isn't done much any more and is frowned upon by LCRI 6.1G1 and LCRI 6.1G4; but it's still an option, linking the two records with 501 "With" notes. If you check AACR2R 1.0H1a and its reference to 6.0B1, you'll see that you can treat the two labels on a disc as a single source. In the unlikely event that the 45 happens to have a collective title, it would go in the 245 and the individual titles (and respective statements of responsibility, if appropriate) in a 505. Lacking a collective title, both titles would go in the 245 and you would not need a 505; how the statement(s) of responsibility would be formulated depends on whether they are both the same or different. Rule 6.1G2 (make sure you're looking at the updated "Amendments 1993" version with the GMDs resituated following the first title), has examples for both common statements of responsibility (example two; though it has three titles, the idea is the same) and different statements of responsibility (example four). If you had a collective title in the 245, you could trace the individual titles from the 505 in separate 740s. For an item without a collective title, you could trace the second title from the 245 in a 740. *Newsletter 64 (August 1996)*

4.56 QUESTION: The insert to a recording I'm working on (OCLC #32533876) says "Summersongs is the first of 'John McCutcheon's Four Seasons,' a series of family albums celebrating each season of the year." The 245 is "John McCutcheon's four seasons: summersongs." An LC record for the CD has the same 245 and no series (OCLC #32535949). Is there no series because the 440 would be identical to the 245?

Answer: Judging simply from the information in the records that you have provided, I would have been inclined to include a 4XX/8XX. The LC record for the CD is copy cataloging, which LC generally doesn't change much, so I'm not sure that we can take the absence of a 4XX as anything definitive; we also do not know how the potential series information might have been presented on the CD, if at all. But if a title proper and a series title were the same, you would indeed include both. *Newsletter 64 (August 1996)*

4.57 QUESTION: Down in the 245 $b of OCLC #20914187, the Soch. number for "Evgenii Onegin" is given as 20, although it should really be Soch. 24. What do you do when information on an item is known to be incorrect?

Answer: Information in the 245 is supposed to be transcribed from the chief source, whether it is right or wrong. If it's wrong, as is the case here, it should be so noted (with "[*sic*]") or corrected (with "[i.e. . . .]"), both under AACR2 (Rule 1.0F) and (as this is pre-AACR2 cataloging) under AACR1 (Rule 132A2). If you've got the item (or a surrogate) in hand and the item really does not read "Soch. 20" as the Cyrillic LC copy says, we'd want to ask the inputting library before changing it, as there may well be different versions. *Newsletter 64 (August 1996)*

4.58 QUESTION: In a 245, when subfield $b follows a subfield $n or $p, does the subfield $b refer to the immediately preceding subfield ($n or $p) or to subfield $a? There are two examples on BF&S p. 2:24–25. In the subfield $n discussion, last example (Dacca University studies), does it mean that subfield $b, "semi-annual journal of the Faculty of Commerce" is other title information for subfield $n, "Part C", or is it other title information to subfield $a, "Dacca University studies"? BF&S, p. 2:25, subfield $p discussion (actually starts on previous page), last example (Solar photovoltaics) uses subfield $b, "a bibliography with abstracts." Is this other title info to subfield $p, "Quarterly update" or to subfield $a, "Solar photovoltaics"? We are cataloging a bunch of the Goals 2000 videos (the educational initiative of the U.S. government). Life would have been simpler if we had set up a series for "Goals 2000, a satellite town meeting" since each video starts with this title. The first couple we did, however, it seemed there would be no more, so we used the above as the title, with a subfield $p for the specific subject for a given video. These portion titles tend to be quite long and split quite nicely into main and other title parts. So we are left with:

245 00   Goals 2000, satellite town meeting. $p Math and science $h [video-
             recording] : $b education for the 21st century.

This assumes that $b is other title information to $p (Math and science). But I'm not sure that this is what BF&S is trying to say. In short, I guess the question is: if the title in subfield $n or $p has other title information connected with it, does it go in subfield $b? (assuming there is no previous subfield $b, since it's not repeatable). And if there was a previous subfield $b—for other title information, for the title proper—it would not be repeated here (after $p), just punctuated with a space-colon-space?

Answer: Other title information refers to (and should be placed imme- diately following) the title to which it is attached, whether that title is the title proper or a part title. That other title information goes in subfield $b unless there is a previous $b. In fact, looking at the real bibliographic records for the "Dacca University studies," its "Part C" is exactly what the example suggests; parts A and B are the semi-annual journals of other university areas (the English Department and arts and sciences, respectively). *Newsletter 63 (May 1996)*

Comment: Robert B. Ewald, Cataloging Policy Specialist in LC's Cataloging Policy and Support Office offers this clarification:

> You are correct that LC follows AACR2 and places the GMD following the part title (AACR2 Rule 1.1C2). But LC does not separately subfield a subtitle that comes between the main title and the part title. Instead, the subtitle is treated as part of the main title (e.g., "$a Piano rolls, Gershwin's legacy. $n Volume 2, $p Early years $h . . . " or "$a Piano rolls—Gershwin's legacy. $n Volume 2, $p Early years $h . . . ") or the subtitle is omitted from the title and statement of responsibility area and given in a note.

This appears to be an LC policy that, as far as I can tell, appears neither in AACR2 nor in any LCRI (or MCD). It helps explain why, as the original question noted, we don't see any examples with subfields $a and $b along with $n and/or $p. *Newsletter 63 (May 1996)*

4.59 QUESTION: What is the order of subfields in the 245, when you have $a, $b, $n, and $p? Let's say you published a book (to make things simple) and the title page reads as follows:

MADMEN, MISFITS, AND MORONS
A chronology of music catalogers I have known
by O. C. Elsie*
PART I—Your Favorite Cataloger Here*
[*Names have been changed to protect the satiric]

It seems to me the 245 would read as follows:

245 10 Madmen, misfits, and morons : $b a chronology of music catalogers I have known. $n Part I, $p Your Favorite Cataloger Here / $c O.C. Elsie.

(This is assuming this book is a complete bibliographic item, that other music catalogers will be the subject of separate books.) Everything I can find in AACR2R and BF&S talks about the relationship between subfield $n and/ or $p in relation to the *title proper*—in other words, the rules and examples always seem to talk in terms of subfield $n and/or $p following subfield $a. I am given direction on what to do if the other title info applies to the *part*

($n and/or $p) but not what to do if the other title info applies to the title proper when you also have subfields $n and/or $p present. I can't think of any other way to catalog the book I made up for you; it seems reasonable; it just seems odd there is no example with subfields $a and $b along with $n and/or $p.

Answer: Subfields $n and $p can only be used following $a or other sub-fields $n or $p. Of course, you can punctuate so as to indicate the relationship of the part/section title/number to the other title information.

245 10   Cranks, curmudgeons, and compulsives : $b a chronology of music cata-
          logers I have known. Part II, Your Favorite Cataloger Here / $c O.C. Elsie.

That's why it says under $n and $p in BF&S that they qualify the title proper (subfield $a) and why $b says, "If the *other* title information has a part or section number or name, enter the number or name in subfield $b, not in subfield $n or $p." *Newsletter 62* (*November 1995*)

4.60 QUESTION: My question is about *22146597. At the top of the disk it says in large print:

Marlborough Music Festival
40th Anniversary

Below that in smaller print: Johann Sebastian Bach
    Then in even smaller print, the various works are listed:

14 canons (not "Fourteen") . . .
Orchestral suite no. 2 . . .
Orchestral suite no. 3 . . .

Performers, in small print, are also listed on the disc. What goes in 245: the various titles, or "Marlborough Music Festival 40th Anniversary" as a collective title? Or would "Marlborough . . ." be put in a 500 "At head of title:" note?

Answer: The record online (#22146597) suggests that the "Marl-borough . . ." might be a series, though it's not coded as such. From your description, "Marlborough . . ." sounds as though it could be a reasonable collective title, with the individual works listed in the contents. If there is some other obvious collective title on the container, you could alternatively use that, but "Marlborough . . ." seems to fit that bill. *Newsletter 62* (*November 1995*)

4.61 QUESTION: We get a lot of stuff with the performer's name on the disc plus "Greatest hits." Would the 245 be, for example, "John Denver $h [sound recording] : $b greatest hits." *or* "Greatest hits $h [sound recording] / $c John Denver," assuming that the size of the lettering is the same and equal prominence appears to be given to both? "Greatest hits" seems to me to be awfully generic and not much use as a title proper. What about a 246 here?

Answer: This one is hard to generalize about; it depends on typography and prominence. All else being equal, I'd lean toward "Greatest hits" as the title proper, generic as it may be. But no matter which option you choose ("Name $h [GMD] : $b greatest hits" or "Greatest hits $h [GMD] / $c Name", it's probably a good idea to enter the other alternative in a 246. *Newsletter 62 (November 1995)*

4.62 QUESTION: This question has to do with whether you need a period at the end of a 245 when you have a GMD but no statement of responsibility. I have found plenty of examples both ways. The USMARC documentation clearly shows periods at the end. Sample MARC records I've looked at in the Nancy Olson books, Carolyn Frost book, and so forth don't show periods, but they also don't show brackets around the GMD. BF&S does not show periods. I have always been under the impression that if you have brackets at the end of most all MARC fields, you don't need a period. Is this clarified anywhere?

Answer: According to LCRI 1.0C (under the section "Punctuation—ISBD, etc."), here's the lowdown: "Within the paragraph that precedes the physical description area, separate each area from a succeeding one with a period-space-dash-space, and give this separator in addition to all other ending punctuation except a period." A footnote says that "'ending punctuation' refers to one of the following when it is the very last mark: period, question mark, exclamation point, closing parenthesis or bracket, and double quotation mark." In short, when a GMD, enclosed in brackets, concludes the 245 field, follow it with a period. By the way, even when the brackets have been omitted (OCLC now recommends explicitly entering those brackets), a period should follow the GMD. The OCLC print program is supposed to provide the brackets (for cards, that is) correctly, with the period following the closing bracket. *Newsletter 61 (August 1995)*

4.63 QUESTION: The 1993 Amendments to AACR2 made for some big changes in the placement of General Material Designations (GMDs) in the 245 field. Can you clarify the changes for me?

Answer: The changes mostly affect items that have no collective title, and you'll notice revisions of such examples scattered throughout the 1993 Amendments. The GMD (in subfield $h) now follows the first title in items lacking a collective title. This standardizes the position of the GMD directly following the complete title proper or the first title (where there is no collective title) in almost all cases and should simplify the cataloger's decision making. The presence of the subfield $h now dictates that second and subsequent titles will be contained in subfield $b rather than in subfield $a where there is no intervening statement of responsibility in a subfield $c. Let's look at some schematic examples of the new practice.

245 10   First title $h [GMD] ; $b Second title ; Third title / $c Statement of responsibility.

Under the old practice, the GMD would have followed the last title and preceded the statement of responsibility. Note that a semicolon separates the first title and GMD from the subsequent titles. Yes, I know it looks funny, but let's keep in mind that we made up all of this ISBD stuff in the first place. Remember how funny it *all* looked back in the days of the revised chapters to AACR1? Relax. You'll get used to it.

245 10   Title proper $h [GMD] = $b Parallel title / $c Statement of responsibility.

This example is unchanged from the old practice.

245 10   First title $h [GMD] / $c First statement of responsibility. Second title / Second statement of responsibility.

Under the old practice, the GMD would have been at the very end of the field.

245 10   Title proper $h [GMD] : $b remainder of title / $c Statement of responsibility.

This example is unchanged from the old practice. Note that a colon still separates the title proper and GMD from the other title information.

245 10   Title proper. $n Number of part, $p Title of part $h [GMD] / $c Statement of responsibility.

Again, unchanged from the former practice. The GMD follows all elements of the title proper, including the number and/or title of a dependent part.

245 10   Title proper : $b remainder of title. $p Dependent title $h [GMD] / $c
Statement of responsibility.

The GMD still follows the entirety of the title proper, including any dependent title or part numbering.

245 10   Title proper, or, Alternative title $h [GMD] / $c Statement of responsibility.

Alternative titles are still considered part of the title proper, and are not separately subfielded.

245 10   First title ; $b and, Second title / $c Statement of responsibility.

Use subfield $b for titles subsequent to the first when there is no collective title, even if no GMD is present. This is to provide consistency in content designation and is a change from previous practice. *Newsletter 58 (August 1994)*

4.64 QUESTION: How am I to treat the title of this book of Glenn Gould's letters? Existing OCLC records have something similar to the following 245 field:

245 10   Glenn Gould : $b selected letters / $c edited and compiled by John P.L.
Roberts and Ghyslaine Guertin.

They relegate *Selected letters* to the subfield $b with no 740 access to that title. If I were cataloging from scratch, I would probably choose *Selected letters* as the title proper. I have always found AACR2 1.1B inadequate as a guide for determining title. Rule 1.1B2 directs us to include author statements in titles when they are integral parts of the title. By inference, I conclude that they should *not* be included otherwise, hence my view that the title proper of the book should be *Selected letters*. What do you think?

Answer: About the Glenn Gould *Selected letters*, AACR2R is not terribly helpful, as you point out. With generic titles of this type, many catalogers try to add distinction by including what would otherwise be a statement of responsibility as part of the title information. I think you are right that the implication of 1.1B2 is *not* to include a statement of responsibility as part of the title proper when it is not an integral part of that title. Coupled with 1.1B3 and 1.1F3, this would suggest your solution of *Selected letters* as the title proper and Glenn Gould as a statement of responsibility. Records from the British Library (UKM, #28583474), the National Library of Canada

(NLC, #26257382), and Princeton University (PUL, #28714143) remind us that this is open to interpretation. All three are consistent in not giving access through a 740 to the generic title *Selected letters*, and I think this is correct. Even if you were to have this as the title proper, I would be inclined not to trace it, though most LC AACR2 examples I found actually trace the phrase. This may not be a valid reflection of LC practice, though. Since many of my searches started with the phrase "selected letters," my findings are hardly random. Tracing such a generic title would certainly be an acceptable local practice.

Looking at LC AACR2 records really doesn't help much anyway, since there are examples of just about any choice you'd want to justify. Many use "Selected letters" as the title proper and the name as statement of responsibility, but virtually all that I looked at also traced that generic title, as I mentioned (examples: #24121923, #26127979). Some put the name and the generic phrase together in 245 $a and trace the generic phrase (#15549499). Others put the name and the generic phrase together in 245 $a and do not trace the generic phrase (#23942071). Some put the name in 245 $a, the phrase in $b, and trace the phrase (#16683734, though here the name includes a title of address). Others put the name in 245 $a, the phrase in $b, and do not trace the phrase (#21525113).

My suggestion would be to use one of the existing records (they are all roughly equivalent in quality) and simply edit it as you see fit for your own use. *Selected letters* as the traced title proper and "Glenn Gould" as part of the statement of responsibility are perfectly respectable choices. But clearly, there is no single right answer. *Newsletter 56 (December 1993)*

4.65 QUESTION: What's the current policy on General Material Designations (GMDs), what fields they belong in, and how they should be input?

Answer: The new *Bibliographic Formats and Standards* document includes revised instructions about GMDs. When inputting current cataloging or transcribing retrospective cataloging, include any applicable GMDs only in field 245. GMDs in all other fields should now be omitted, in accord with LC practice. In OCLC, GMDs are now required, when applicable, for both Level I and Level K input. Following USMARC guidelines, you should now enclose GMDs in brackets. Use only those GMDs that appear on p. 11 of BF&S (based on LCRI 1.1C) for current cataloging. These changes in GMD practice were made in consultation with OCLC's Cataloging and Database Services Advisory Committee to bring OCLC practice into conformity with LC practice and USMARC guidelines. OCLC staff is looking into the possibility of scanning the OLUC to remove GMDs from fields other than 245. *Newsletter 56 (December 1993)*

4.66 QUESTION: Has there been any change to AACR2 rule 6.1F1 that I might have missed? Suddenly, the names of performers, conductors, etc.

seem to be appearing in the 245 subfield $c for "serious" or "classical" music when said performer, etc. is the main entry. Rule 6.1F1 says this is a no-no. Might people be doing this to circumvent local system peculiarities such as one where main entries don't display when subfield $4 is present?

Answer: There is an RI 6.1F1 (dated January 5, 1989, in LCRI 2nd ed.) that "allows performers who do more than perform to be named in the statement of responsibility. Accept only the most obvious cases as qualifying for the statement of responsibility." This would preclude most "classical" performers, and I'm unaware of any other change to that rule. Perhaps some catalogers are mistakenly thinking that a 1XX field must be justified by a corresponding mention in field 245. Of course, justification can be anywhere in the record. *Newsletter 53 (November 1992)*

4.67 QUESTION: I have a John Cage score title page (the score is a reproduction of a holograph) with a small transcription problem. The "original" t.p. reads: 27'7.614" for a percussionist. However, the 7.614" has a single line marked through it, and above it is written: 10.554". In the 245, I transcribed the title as 27'10.554" as that seems to have been Cage's intention. Neither AACR2R nor the RIs seem to address this type of problem. What do I do?

Answer: RI 1.0E goes on at some length, but offers only the barest hint of help: "As judged appropriate, use notes to explain and added entries to provide additional access." I would probably transcribe the 245 as you have and formulate a 500 note saying basically what you have just said, something like:

500   Characters 7.614" of original title, 27'7.614" stricken with single line; 10.554" written above it.

Then trace the "original" title. Without further information, I won't venture a guess on the correct uniform title, if one is needed. *Newsletter 46 (November 1990)*

4.68 QUESTION: When a 245 field *ends* in a subfield $h (i.e., no further title info, statement of responsibility, etc.), should one add a *period* at the end of the subfield? For example, should the field look like:

245 00   Most-played hits of mediocre rockers $h sound recording
or
245 00   Country heartbreak hits $h sound recording.
or
245 00   Disco doomsday $h sound recording .

I know that the system supplies brackets in subfield $h, but I'm not clear as to how the end-of-field period relates to the brackets.

Answer: Save your keystrokes. The OCLC system will supply not only the brackets but also the final period after a field-ending subfield $h. The first example will print correctly as:

245 00   Most-played hits of mediocre rockers $h [sound recording].

Glenn Patton and I figure that the second example would print with a period both within and outside of the brackets, but we won't even venture a guess as to how the third one might turn out. For further information on the complexities of the subfield $h, please refer to Appendix B of the Scores and Sound Recordings format documents. *Newsletter 42 (November 1989)*

246 AND 740 FIELDS

Mini-Lesson

4.69 Over the years, what started out as the "mini-lesson" portion of my column evolved into the Q&A section. But occasionally another mini-lesson seems appropriate. The advent of Format Integration Phase 1 in January 1995 brought the 246 field out of the world of serials and into the larger bibliographic universe. Since then, many questions about the use of 246 and 740 have arisen. This little "cheat sheet" on 246/740 should help you apply the fields correctly.

[Note: My earlier understanding of the 246 field was mistaken regarding its use for comprehensive titles *only*. So as to avoid further confusion, I have corrected some of the following text, questions, and examples to reflect the additional use of the 246 for any variants of the first title when there is no collective title.]

246   Varying Form of Title (Repeatable)

Use for uncontrolled variants of the title for the *entire* item and for any variants of the first title when there is no collective title.
First Indicator

- 0   Note, no title added entry
- 1   Note, title added entry
- 2   No note, no title added entry
- 3   No note, title added entry

Second Indicator

   blank No information provided

Use when no information is provided as to the type of title; includes corrected forms of title, "at head of title" data, binder's titles, colophon titles, container titles, and titles from sources other than 245; use also for additional title added entries formulated because of the presence of abbreviations, ampersands, numbers, symbols, and so forth. Information on the type of title may be provided in subfield $i (Display text). *No* print constant is generated.

245	12	A hundred folktunes [*sic*] from Hardanger = $b Hundert Volksmelodien aus Hardanger : op. 51 . . .
246	30	Folkstunes from Hardanger
246	30	Volksmelodien aus Hardanger
246	31	Hundert Volksmelodien aus Hardanger
246	3	Hundred folk tunes from Hardanger
246	3	100 folkstunes from Hardanger
246	3	100 folk tunes from Hardanger
246	3	Folk tunes from Hardanger
246	3	100 Volksmelodien aus Hardanger

245	00	Regionmusiken $h [sound recording].
246	1	$i At head of title: $a Verbunk

245	10	Live at Moers Festival $h [sound recording] . . .
246	1	$i Additional title on container: $a Live at International New Jazz Festival

245	10	Father & son $h [sound recording] . . .
246	3	Father and son

0   Portion of title

Use for part or section titles (245 subfield $p), alternative titles, portions of the title proper, and other title information for which access is desired, and initialisms or full forms of title (245 subfield $b) not already the title proper. *No* print constant is generated.

245	14	Der Ring des Nibelungen. $p Götterdämmerung . . .
246	30	Götterdämmerung

245	13	Il principio, or, A regular introduction to playing the harpsichord . . .
246	30	Regular introduction to playing the harpsichord

245	00	Greg and Steve present We all live together : $b plus song & activity book, leader's guide . . .
246	30	We all live together

245	00	ANSCR : $b the alpha-numeric system for classification of recordings . . .
246	30	Alpha-numeric system for classification of recordings

1   Parallel title

> Use for titles in another language than that of the title proper. NO print constant is generated.

> 245 10   Alternative instrumental music $h [sound recording] = $b Alternative Instrumentalmusik.
> 246 31   Alternative Instrumentalmusik

2   Distinctive title

> Use for special titles that appear in addition to the regular title on an individual issue of an item. Print constant: "Distinctive title:". *Not* generally used outside of serials.

3   Other title

> Use for other titles that appear on the piece but are not specified by other second indicator values; subfield $i is not being used to provide text. Print constant: "Other title:". *Not* generally used outside of serials.

4   Cover title

> Use for titles from the cover. Print constant: "Cover title:".

> 245 00   Sonata 1 : $b Six sonatas, c. 1700 . . .
> 246 04   Sonata 1 in D major

5   Added title page title

> Use for titles, usually in another language, found on a title page preceding or following the title page used as chief source, or on an inverted title page at the end of the publication. Print constant: "Added title page title:".

> 245 10   Makbet : $b balet v dvukh deistviiakh . . .
> 246 15   Macbeth

6   Caption title

> Use for titles found at the head of the first page of music or text. Print constant: "Caption title:".

> 245 00   Impromptus für Klavier, op. 5 . . .
> 246 16   Impromptus über ein Thema von Clara Wieck

7   Running title

> Use for titles printed at the top or bottom margin of each page of a publication, and for eye-readable headers in microfiche. Print constant: "Running title:".

245 10   Quadrilles . . .
246 17   Herz's quadrilles

8   Spine title

> Use for publisher-supplied titles found on the spine. Print constant:
> "Spine title:".

245 10   Back at the chicken shack $h [sound recording] . . .
246 18   Back to the chicken shack

Subfield $i   Display text

> Use for text to be displayed when none of the other second indicator
> display constants are adequate. When subfield $i is used, second indi-
> cator must be blank. Subfield $i precedes subfield $a at the beginning
> of the field.

245 04   The Bluegrass album $h [sound recording].
246 1 $i Vol. 3 has title: $a California connection

245 00   Stück für 2 Klarinetten in B . . .
246 0 $i Parallel title on caption: $a Piece for 2 clarinets

Field 246 does not end with a mark of punctuation unless the last word
in the field is an abbreviation or other data that ends with a mark of punctuation. Initial articles are generally not recorded in field 246 unless the in-
tent is to file on the article.

740   Added Entry—Uncontrolled Related/Analytical Title (Repeatable)

Use for uncontrolled analytical titles of independent works contained
within the item except for any variants of the first title when there is no collective title, and for uncontrolled titles of related works external to the item.
First Indicator

0-9   Nonfiling indicator

Second Indicator

blank   No information provided

> Use when added entry is not for an analytic or when no information is
> provided as to the entry's character.

245 14   Das Land des Lächelns $h [sound recording] : $b romantische
          Operette in drei Akten . . .
500   Rev. version of the composer's Die gelbe Jacke, the text for which
          is by Viktor Léon.
740 0   Gelbe Jacke.

2   Analytical entry

Use when the item in hand contains the work represented by the added entry.

245 00   Album lyrique ; $b and, Derniéres pensées . . .
246 3   Album lyrique ; and, Derniéres pensées
246 30   Album lyrique
740 02   Derniéres pensées.

245 00   Sinfonie Nr. 1 $h [sound recording] : $b Fogli ; Sinfonie Nr. 2 : Ricordanze ; Sinfonie Nr. 3 : Menschen-Los . . .
246 30   Fogli
740 02   Ricordanze.
740 02   Menschen-Los.

245 00   2 ballate for 3 voices or instruments . . .
505 0   Gram piantágli occhi -- Caro singnor.
740 02   Gram piantágli occhi.
740 02   Caro singnor.

Newsletter 60 (April 1995)

246/740 Questions and Answers

4.70 QUESTION: My question concerns items without a collective title. If Title 1 and Title 2 each had a parallel title, would they be in 246s or 740s? I recall someone at the MARC Format Subcommittee saying titles in the 246 refer to the whole and the 740 holds titles that are a part of a whole. This makes sense to me and my inclination is to put the parallel titles in 740s, but I can be easily convinced that a parallel title is a parallel title first and an analytical title second and should go in a 246.

Answer: That someone at the MARC Formats meeting was probably me. As I understand things right now (and we're *all* getting used to this new stuff), any analytic (part of the whole) title goes in a 740. That would include parallel titles of your Title 1 and Title 2. In other words, a title is a whole title (246) or an analytical title (740) first, then a parallel, caption, cover, and so forth title. *Newsletter 60 (April 1995)*
[Note: As we came to know later, this answer is partially incorrect in that varying forms of the first title, when there is no collective title, are also coded 246, even when they are not comprehensive.]

4.71 QUESTION: I've just encountered my first FI bib record in OCLC and of course have a question about it. It's a CD with four works by Xenakis; works two through four are listed in the $b of the 245 and also in separate 246 fields with second indicator "5". I would have been more inclined to use 740s, viewing the titles as analytic. I was curious about the use of second indicator "5", added title page title. If the $b titles in the 245 are distinctive but vary from the form of title in the 700 $t, would a 246 be appropriate? And if so, what should be the second indicator? The choices don't seem to fit the situation very well.

Answer: The Xenakis record that you encountered was incorrect in its use of the 246 field, and I have since corrected it. You have it right in your note, and the distinction is fairly simple: Use 246 for uncontrolled variants of the title for the entire item and for the first title when there is no collective title; use 740 for uncontrolled analytical titles of subsequent independent works contained within the item and for uncontrolled titles of related works external to the item. When you have no collective title, as in this instance, each of the individual distinctive titles in the string after the first could be traced in 740s. Also note that the second indicator structure of the 740 field has changed with Format Integration. *Newsletter 60 (April 1995)*

4.72 QUESTION: I'm cataloging Nelhybel's *Trois danses liturgiques*, which would formerly have had title added entries:

```
740 01   3 danses liturgiques.
740 01   Danses liturgiques.
```

I am doing these both as 246 10. First indicator "1" is supposed to generate a note, which I don't want to do, but the instructions for 246 say that a note is *not* provided if the second indicator is "0" or "1". (I am assuming that second indicator "0" is applicable for titles such as this. Also, if I were cataloging a piece with the title, say, *Chorale prelude on Lobe den Herren*, I suppose that if I wanted a title added entry for *Lobe den Herren*, it too would be 246 10.)

Answer: For the Nelhybel title added entries, I would use:

```
245 10   Trois danses liturgiques . . .
246 3    3 danses liturgiques
246 30   Danses liturgiques
```

That first 246 has first indicator "3" (no note, title added entry), second indicator blank. The first 246 has a blank second indicator as it is formulated because of the presence of a number given in an alternate form. The second 246 has second indicator "0" because it is a portion of the title proper (number dropped).

Same goes for your *Lobe den Herren* example, portion of title proper.

```
245 10   Chorale prelude on Lobe den Herren . . .
246 30   Lobe den Herren
```

Newsletter 60 (April 1995)

4.73 QUESTION: I have the following situation:

100 1   Schubert, Franz, $d 1797–1828.
240 10   Piano music. $k Selections
245 10   34 valses sentimentales $h [sound recording] : $b D. 779 ; 12 valses nobles
         : D. 969 ; 2 scherzi : D. 593 / $c Franz Schubert.

I am trying to follow the latest rule interpretations about title tracings on this, which is easy enough except for the matter of MARC tagging under Format Integration. What I think I should do is trace the variant forms of the 245 $a using a 246 (since LC has decided to trace the $a anyway because of the new GMD placement, etc.), but this flies in the face of advice from LC given at MLA, which said if a title refers to a portion of the item being cataloged, trace it using 740 with indicators "02". What I have done in my first pass at the above record is to trace the 245 $a as follows:

246 1   Vierunddreissig valses sentimentales (The language of the chief source is
         principally German; the French titles are actually those supplied by Schubert
         to the works in question)
246 1   Valses sentimentales

and then handled the tracings for the "12 valses nobles" using 740s, including the concatenated Title A ; Title B. (I am assuming that Title C would not be included since it is a nondistinctive, generic title that LC would not trace either singly or in concert with the preceding titles.) This seems inconsistent, and I would feel much better about it if you were to tell me, "No, use 740s for all of them."

Answer: Variants of the first title "Vierunddreisig valses," "Valses sentimentales," "12 valses," and so forth would be 246s. Any tracings for the individual titles and their variants after that ("Valses sentimentales," "12 valses," etc.) would all be 740s. In this case, I also think you would not do the "concatenated" title thing either because the title proper of this item was not changed by the new subfielding practice; it would have ended before the other title information regardless. If we're looking at RI 21.30J, it is represented by schematic example 17 or 18 (the last two under "Items without a collective title") rather than example 1. Titles A and B have to be immediately adjacent in order to justify the title added entry for all of them strung together. *Newsletter 60 (April 1995)*

4.74 QUESTION: Now that format integration is a fait accompli, who is going to go through the 30-odd million bibliographic records in the OLUC and make the changes from MARC field 740 to 246? Will it be our good and tireless friend, Algo Rithm?

Answer: We're keeping track of everyone who asks this question and its variations and are going to send each of them their assignment of a share of the database to go through and correct. Seriously though, there is no way an algorithm could be devised that would be able to distinguish the 246 uses from the 740 uses, so that option is not possible. The change in tagging became effective starting on February 1, 1995, after which the new definitions have been required. Users are welcome to change existing records from before that date via Enhance, minimal level upgrades, and so on, but there can be no systematic attempt to fix records retrospectively. We will have to learn to live with the pre- and post-practice, as we have done with ISBD, AACR2, and so forth. Later this year, though, we will be running some conversions to do away with certain fields, and so on for which a one-to-one switch is possible. Those will be announced periodically in PRISM News. *Newsletter 60 (April 1995)*

4.75 QUESTION: In your mini-lesson on 246/740 in the *MOUG Newsletter* no. 60, the example under 246 second indicator "8" was for a title on the spine of a sound recording. I had assumed that second indicators "2" and "3" weren't really used, and "4"—"8" were only for nonbook print materials (scores, maybe maps). The definitions really seemed to have print materials in mind (which makes sense, since they were intended for print serials when developed). Sound recordings, however, do tend to have a spine-like part: the narrow left edge of an LP album cover, the left edge of a cassette case, and the left and right edges of a CD case. So if OCLC wants us to define spine title as including those parts, we'll do that. I had been using subfield $i with "Title on container spine:". What about videos? The container has a spine, often with a title and other stuff on it. Unfortunately, the cassette itself also has a spine, which may also have a title and other stuff on it, though not as often. I would be inclined not to use second indicator "8" here; I can be more specific here with subfield $i "Title on container spine:", or "Title on cassette label:" (if there is no label in the usual place on the front of the cassette), or "Additional title on cassette:" (if there is a label on the cassette spine in addition to the label on the front of the cassette). This does happen, and the two labels tend to have different titles. Would you ever use second indicator "4" (cover) for a nonprint AV item? It's already been decided that the cover of the booklet that shows through the top of a CD jewel case is actually the "container."

Answer: What should dictate your use of a particular 246 second indicator is the propriety of the particular display constant associated with it. If it fits (my mind keeps screaming, "you must acquit"), use it. If you need to change it in any way, for more detail or clarity, go for the blank second indicator and formulate your own introductory phrase for the subfield $i. In

other words, if you want to use "Title on container spine:", that's fine; use
the blank indicator and $i. The same goes for any video variations, container
spine, cassette spine, cassette label, what have you. There may be instances
where you would find the second indicator "4" useful for nonprint AV, but
I would imagine that in most cases, you will want to be more specific, again
using blank and $i. *Newsletter 63 (May 1996)*

4.76 QUESTION: What should the second indicator be in a 246 field
when the title variant in that 246 refers not to the 245, but to *another* 246?
Here's an example from a video. There's no title at all on title frames; the
cassette label reads: *Joe Allard's saxophone and clarinet principles;* the container reads: *Joe Allard's saxophone & clarinet principles.* Thus:

245 00   Joe Allard's saxophone and clarinet principles . . .
246 30   Saxophone and clarinet principles
246 1 $i Title on container: $a Joe Allard's saxophone & clarinet principles
246 3?   Saxophone & clarinet principles

The last 246 is a portion of a title found in the 246 just preceding it. At first
I decided that the indicator should be "0", for "portion of title." But portion of *what* title—the one that appears anywhere on the item, or the one in
the 245? So then I decided blank, "for titles not accommodated by other second indicator values." That seemed safe. Does OCLC have an opinion?

   Answer: You've made the right choice in going for blank. Referring back
to my 246 cheat sheet in *MOUG Newsletter* no. 60, one of the uses of second indicator blank is "titles from sources other than 245." Had I known
then what I know now about 246 (we were so innocent back in those days),
I'd have been clearer in saying that variants of most titles from other 246s
should have blank second indicators. The "Portion of title" referred to in
second indicator "0" is strictly "portion of title that appears in 245." *Newsletter 63 (May 1996)*

4.77 QUESTION: When a sound recording has no collective title, and the
245 is just a string of individual titles, is one supposed to make a 246 of the
long, strung-together version of the title? The various sources I've consulted
don't seem to agree on this. Which reminds me . . . I thought that the 1993
Amendments to AACR2 standardized and simplified the placement of the
GMD. Yet, in many of the guides, cheat sheets, and other documents relating to format integration that I've seen, the GMD continues to jump about
merrily, as if the 1993 Amendments never happened. Did I miss something?

   Answer: LC recommends a 246 for the uninterrupted string of titles
(minus the GMD and subfielding) so as not to lose the access to that string

we had before the 1993 Amendments to AACR2 (which placed the GMD in such cases at the end of the string). Why anyone would purposely want to search an arbitrary string of titles like that is a mystery to me, and I think LC is being compulsive or silly in this instance. Their guidelines for the 246 do stipulate that use, however.

Any document issued since the GMD placement change announced in the 1993 Amendments that does not have the GMD directly following the title proper, the last part of the title proper, or (where there is no collective title) the first title is simply incorrect. *Newsletter 62 (November 1995)*

4.78 QUESTION: I have a question about one of the records we submitted as part of an Enhance application. The title proper is *Three Cummings sky choruses* and the uniform title is "Cummings sky choruses." You wondered whether I needed to add a 246 for "Cummings sky choruses." The reason I didn't is that it's identical to the 240, which is searchable in both OCLC and our local catalog (searchable as a stand-alone title, not as a 100/ 240 combo). Why would one want to add such a 246?

Answer: Call me a stickler (I've been called worse), but I consider decisions about 246 titles to be entirely independent from the presence of any uniform title. The bibliographic functions of controlled uniform titles (unique identification, differentiation, collocation) and uncontrolled title added entries (pure access) are different. Fields 240 and 246 may be treated differently by different systems, in terms of both indexing and display. LCRI 21.30J (a 27-page dissertation interpreting a 13-line rule) acknowledges these differences in section 8 of its "Guidelines for Making Title Added Entries for Permutations Related to Titles Proper." It is labeled "LC practice" and reads: "Do not make title added entries for uniform titles. There may, however, be instances in which a title added entry is the same as the uniform title (e.g., cf. subsection 7d) immediately above." The subsection referred to regards titles proper that begin with separable statements of responsibility. It mandates the creation of a 246 for the title minus the statement of responsibility, then goes on to say: "Note that this applies regardless of whether a uniform title has been assigned the work or not, since the function of providing access through a varying form of title is separate and distinct from the function of collocation provided through a uniform title." I guess someone at LC is a stickler, too. *Newsletter 80 (May 2002)*

4.79 QUESTION: If an item has a uniform title, would you add a 246 if it were identical? I have in mind OCLC #34500346:

```
100 0    Teresa, $c Mother, $d 1910–
240 10   Simple path. $k Selections
245 10   Meditations from A simple path / $c Mother Teresa.
```

Answer: That would depend on a number of things. In this case, the 246 and the uniform title would *not* be quite identical (the uniform title includes "Selections", remember) and might subsequently file far removed from a 246 entry. You have to consider whether you need to generate a note and/or an added entry regardless of the 246's resemblance to any other heading. Also remember that the 246 is an uncontrolled title and the uniform title is, by definition, a controlled title, no matter how much they may look alike. They perform different functions, are formulated according to different standards, and their status really should be considered independently of each other. *Newsletter 64 (August 1996)*

4.80 QUESTION: I keep reading MARC 21 and BF&S and keep having questions on the 246. Here's one more: Both of these sources strictly limit what kinds of other title information can be put in the 246. The only time you can use 246 has something to do with full form vs. initialisms. Does this stricture mean that, if the title proper has other title information that, by itself, is a useful title, it cannot go in a 246? Such as:

245 10 Opera festival $h [sound recording] : $b arias from famous Italian operas.

Assuming that I think the other title information functions as a useful title, would "Arias from famous Italian operas" go in a 246 or a 740? Looking at the MARC 21 definition and scope of 740, it seems that other title information is not something you can put in the 740, either.

Answer: Other title information or portions of other title information fall under 246 second indicator "0" ("Portion of title"). So in your example, you would have:

246 30 Arias from famous Italian operas

This is justified in the first paragraph of the code "0" definition in MARC 21: "Value '0' indicates that the title given in field 246 is a portion of a title for which access or an added entry is desired, but which does not require that a note be generated from this field." The information that follows in MARC 21 (about titles in subfield $p, alternative titles, initialisms/full forms in subfield $b, etc.) are stated to be examples, but do not exhaust all the possibilities. *Newsletter 76 (September 2000)*

4.81 QUESTION: The definition of field 246, third paragraph, says, "For items including several works but lacking a collective title, field 246 is used only for titles related to the title selected as the title proper, usually the first work named in the chief source of information. Titles related to other works are recorded in field 740 or other 7XX." It's the "usually the first work" part that bothers me. If you couldn't find a collective title on your sound recording and the chief source had two titles, each with a parallel title, I thought both parallel titles went in 740s, since neither pertained to the entire sound recording. This rule seems to say that the parallel title of the first work goes in the 246, and the parallel title of the second work goes in a 740, to wit:

What I think:

245 14   The firebird $h [sound recording] = $b L'oiseau de feu ; The rite of spring
         = Le sacre du printemps / $c Stravinsky.
740 02   Oiseau de feu.
740 02   Sacre du printemps.

What BF&S seems to say:

245 14   The firebird $h [sound recording] = $b L'oiseau de feu ; The rite of spring
         = Le sacre du printemps / $c Stravinsky.
246 31   Oiseau de feu
740 02   Sacre du printemps.

Who's right?

Answer: On the 246, MARC 21 explicitly states that 246 is to be used for titles related to the title chosen as the title proper (the first title) when there is no collective title. That is the exception to the comprehensive title rule. So your second example is correct (if you add a 740 for "Rite of spring"). *Newsletter 76 (September 2000)*

4.82 QUESTION: I sometimes find the expression of "p. 4 of cover." For example, see LC bibliographic record no. 96-126668, tag 246 ($i Each piece has on p. 4 of cover : $a30 variatsii iz baletov russkikh khoreografov); and check out LCRI 1.6 "If an unnumbered phrase indicating a broad subject or category appears only on page 4 of cover. . . ." Does "p. 4 of cover" mean the back cover? Do you usually use this expression in everyday life, or is it a professional term?

Answer: After checking a bunch of places, I was unable to find any explicit explanation of the "pages of cover" issue. There is LCRI Appendix D, which (in part) defines "Preliminaries": "'Cover' in the list of sources means pages 1, 2, 3, and 4 of cover. . . ." I've always read page 1 of cover to be the front cover; page 2 of cover to be the verso (inside) of the front cover; page 3 of cover to be the inside of the back cover; and page 4 of cover to be the outside of the back cover. That does seem to be the implication of the Rule Interpretation. Like many other cataloger's terms (for instance, the limited meaning of "score" to exclude music for a solo instrument), these "page of cover" references would probably not be used in real life, where we'd likely say "back cover" or "inside of back cover." *Newsletter 72* (*May 1999*)

4.83 QUESTION: I have a question about the 740 tag, subfield $h [GMD]. I seem to recall reading on AUTOCAT that in *Bibliographic Formats and Standards* there is a misprint and that subfield $h can be used in OCLC, although *Bibliographic Formats and Standards* says "do not use." I could not find this message searching the AUTOCAT archives, so could you please clarify this for me. Is that a misprint?

    Answer: No, it's not a misprint. Subfield $h for GMDs $h should be used only in the 245 field. LCRI 25.5D says not to use GMDs in uniform titles. Not using GMDs in the 740 and other added entries is covered in LCRI 21.29: "Although a general material designation (GMD) is given in the title and statement of responsibility area (LCRI 1.1C), do not use a GMD in added entries, including added entries for titles, series, and related works." *Newsletter 68* (*November 1997*)

4.84 QUESTION: Can you direct me to whatever authority exists for the practice of adding a date in subfield $f to analytic entries for musical compositions? I see this in records for sound recordings all the time, but I can't find any reference to it in AACR2, in LCRIs, or in Richard Smiraglia's book (at least the edition I have).

    Answer: Subfields $f used to be added routinely to analytic entries for sound recordings, although the practice has been abandoned by most institutions in recent years. LC Rule Interpretation 21.30M stipulates adding the year of publication to analytical added entries for the Bible (25.18A) and the collective uniform titles "Works" (LCRI 25.8) and "Selections" (LCRI 25.9) only. If you follow this last reference, you will discover the instruction not to add the date (among other things) to the collective uniform title "Selections" when applying Rule 25.34B, regarding collections of various types of compositions by a single composer. Finally, LCRI 25.34B1 states, "Do not add a date of publication, etc., to the uniform title 'Selections' when this is used for collections of musical works by one composer." In other words, current practice for sound recordings analytical added entries is to add the date only to Bible headings and to the collective uniform title "Works". *Newsletter 69* (*April 1998*)

4.85 QUESTION: We've been cataloging several videodiscs with one program on side one and another program on side two, for example, side one entitled The brain, and side two entitled The heart. The 245 is simple:

245 04   The brain $h [videorecording] ; $b The heart . . .

But then on the disc label for side one it says The human brain. We can't make this a 246 because it applies to only half the item. So it seems to me we have to use:

500   Title on disc label, side 1: The human brain.
740 02   Human brain.

So, are there still times when we use a 500 note with a 740 for a varying title?

Answer: Yes, you will still need to use 500 notes for variant titles that are not comprehensive and are related to, or justify, 740s. *Newsletter 63 (May 1996)*

Correction: In the *MOUG Newsletter* no. 63, the answer to one question did not agree with LC practice. For items without a collective title, added entries for titles relating to the first title in the 245 field (subfield $a, the title proper) go in field 246, not 740. *Newsletter 64 (August 1996)*

4.86 QUESTION: Now that we all have the basics of 246 fields down, I'm wondering whether there is an order to multiple 246 fields. BF&S says first to list those with second indicator "0", then those with second indicator "1", which makes a certain amount of sense. Then it says to put the others in "the note printing order." What might "the note printing order" be? I figured AACR2R order, which is Source of the Title Proper first, then Variations in Title, then Parallel Titles and Other Title Information. This "order" is actually contrary to what BF&S says. I would just as soon invoke Weitz's First Law and put 246s in whatever order seems most reasonable. I also know that LC has given some guidelines, but they are for books, and I can't make much sense out of their statement anyway.

Answer: It's hard to give concrete rules about the order of 246s because sometimes they generate notes and sometimes they don't, sometimes they have to intermingle with explicit 500 notes and sometimes they don't. I guess those with second indicators "0" and "1" go first because they generally don't need to generate notes; that is, they usually restate part of what has already appeared in the 245 and do not have an introductory display constant in any case. Remember that you probably wouldn't use second indicator "1" for a parallel title not already in the 245. Any other parallel title would likely need further clarification and therefore require second indicator blank, anyway.

246 1# $i Parallel title on container: $a Chants de la Synagogue de Florence

The stipulated order of 246s doesn't contradict AACR2; in fact, the "note printing order" of BF&S is supposed to encourage following AACR2. But let's be honest: AACR2 doesn't say much about the order of those notes, either. "Source of title proper" notes (5.7B3, 6.7B3) would usually be 500s rather than 246s because they don't often contain a title, only refer to the one in field 245. "Variations in title" (5.7B4, 6.7B4) and "Parallel titles and other title information" (5.7B5, 6.7B5) cover the rest, leaving a good deal up to cataloger's judgment. In short, you get to put the notes in what you consider to be their "most reasonable" order, after all. *Newsletter 62 (November 1995)*

4.87 QUESTION: I have the following situation:

100 1   Wellman, Samuel.
240 10   American pieces
245 10   Four American pieces : $b opus 69 : for piano solo / $c Samuel Wellman.

My question is in regard to the second indicator in the 246 for "4 American pieces," which I did as:

246 33   4 American pieces

since the instruction in *Bibliographic Formats and Standards*, Rev. 9503 says "Use [second indicator "3"] for titles not specified by other second indicator values and not identified using subfield $i," despite the caveat, "Used primarily for serials." It was the best guess I could hazard, since it is merely an alternative tracing for the complete title and that doesn't seem to be covered by any of the other indicator values. What do you think? (Of course I will do a second 246 with indicators "30" for "American pieces," too.)

Answer: Take a look at the bottom of p. 2:28 (Rev. 9503) in BF&S. This would qualify as an "alternate form of title" (substituting &/and, numerals/text, etc.), second indicator blank. You don't need a subfield $i in this case.

246 3   4 American sketches

would be the way to go. *Newsletter 61 (August 1995)*

4.88 QUESTION: We are having a problem with the definition of "cover title" as it applies to compact discs, for use in the 246. Is it "insert" or "container"? Would the "insert" be acceptable since the container, strictly speaking, is nothing but a clear plastic case? Should the 246 use second indicator "4" for Cover title or blank with $i Title on container?

Answer: According to Music Cataloging Decision 6.0B1, "For compact discs and cassettes, consider information which can be read through the closed container (including information on the front cover of a booklet inserted in the container) to be on the container." That suggests to me that we can consider the title on the booklet's cover to be a "container title." In the past, we haven't usually called this a "cover title" for a sound recording, in accordance with AACR2R 6.0B. As such, I'd suggest using 246 second indicator blank with an appropriate subfield $i such as "Title on container:". *Newsletter 61 (August 1995)*

4.89 QUESTION: I'm cataloging a Hindemith score entitled *Sonatas for piano*. The title page is a quasi-list title page, because below that title, one finds the titles for each sonata, thus:

First Sonata
(Edition Schott 2518)

Second Sonata
(Edition Schott 2519)

Third Sonata
(Edition Schott 2521)

(I am dying to know what happened to Edition Schott 2520!) This particular score is the *First Sonata*. It is obviously a complete bibliographic entity, in addition to the fact that it has its own publisher's number. So the 245 appears thus:

245 00   Sonatas for piano. $p First sonata / $c Paul Hindemith.

So far, so good. Now, this sonata is also known as *Der Main* after the poem that inspired it, as it says in a little note on the t.p. verso. I'd like to make a title added entry for *Main*. The question is, do I make it a 740 or a 246? My gut says 246, since the item in hand, as described in the 245 is just the *First Sonata*. But my gut has been wrong before.

Answer: Your gut is right this time, but how you want to present the information is up for grabs. If you use a quoted 500 note from the t.p. verso,

246 3   Main

would be appropriate. If you're not going to use a quoted note, but want to indicate the source of the title, something like this would be the way to go:

246 1 $i Additional title on t.p. verso: $a Main

By the way, Edition Schott 2520 was the *Sonata 2 1/2*, of course. *Newsletter 61 (August 1995)*

4.90 QUESTION: The item I need to catalog is a multivolume set with a collective title. Each volume is described by listing in a contents note. There are no individual authors. We approached this by making analytical added title entries using 740/02. One title in a contents note has distinctive other title information. Could we include this other title information in 740/02 as well?

Title A -- Title B : other title information -- Title C.
740 02 Title A.
740 02 Title B: other title information.
740 02 Title C.

Or is it possible to use 246? While you're at it, could you clarify your definition of 740: "Use for uncontrolled analytical titles and for titles of related items. Use field 246 for uncontrolled varying forms of title for the entire item." What do you mean by "varying forms of title" and "entire item"?

Answer: Regarding your first question, whether you would include the other title information in the 740 depends on the title itself and how meaningful or distinctive Title B is alone. I don't think we can generalize on this one. Again depending on the specific titles, you could trace Title B both without and with its other title information, if that seems appropriate. You might find some guidance in AACR2 RI 21.30J. Usually, I'd say that a distinctive Title B is enough to trace in most cases. Since your Title B is the title of only one volume in a multipart set, using 246 for Title B would be incorrect.

The difference between 246 and 740 is fairly simple. Field 246 is used for forms of the title for the whole item; that is, any title that is, or could be, the equivalent of the title for the entire item, most commonly found in the 245 (if there is a collective title). Field 740 is used only for analytical titles of independent works contained within the whole item and for titles of related works external to the item. An "uncontrolled title" is one that has not been manipulated; that is, it's not a uniform title. *Newsletter 61 (August 1995)*

4.91 QUESTION: We have an item with a part title and a parallel title for the part: 245 10 Title in Polish. $p Part title in Polish = $b Parallel title in German. Parallel part title in German / $c Statement of Responsibility. My question is, when coding 246 for parallel part title, should we code for part title or for parallel title? Is there a hierarchy for this kind of thing?

Answer: These 246s sure are subject to all sorts of permutations, aren't they? Though I don't feel strongly about this, I'd lean toward coding a parallel part title as second indicator "0", "Portion of Title" (and one of the non-note-generating first indicators, since it already appears in the 245). That appears to imply a default hierarchy in second indicator order, but I wouldn't want to insist on that. *Newsletter 61 (August 1995)*

4.92 QUESTION: How does one construct name/title added entries in sound recording records for a composition done by two composers? Does one do a separate 700 12 for each composer with the same subfield $t?

Answer: As far as I can determine, AACR2 does not specifically address this issue. But judging by two cataloging examples from LC, it appears that their practice is to give a name/title added entry for the first composer only, and to ignore the second composer. This is the case for two recordings of *Double music*, co-composed by John Cage and Lou Harrison (look at 85-743193/R, OCLC #14520226 and 92-750520/R, OCLC #25370662). As much as I frown upon cataloging by example, sometimes it comes in handy. If you feel compelled to include a name/title added entry for the second composer, however, it could certainly be justified by reference to such rules as 21.29D, 21.30A1, and 21.30M1. *Newsletter 53 (November 1992)*

Correction: In the Q&A portion of my *MOUG Newsletter* column for issue no. 53, the first question dealt with name/title added entries on a sound recording record for a composition by two composers. Judging by LC cataloging examples and in the absence of any seemingly relevant rule, I deduced that only the first composer should have a name/title added entry and that the second should be ignored. This part of the answer was accurate, but then I went on to suggest that an added entry for the second composer could be justified by such rules as 21.29D, 21.30A1, and 21.30M1. Charles Herrold of the Carnegie Library of Pittsburgh (CPL) kindly brought to my attention the LC Rule Interpretation to 21.30M, part of which I had overlooked.

> The relationship that is expressed between works by means of an added entry, either analytical or simple, is limited to a single access point, namely, that of the main entry. An added entry in the form of the main entry heading for a work provides the sole access to the work it represents in the tracing on the catalog record for another work; do not trace in addition any added entries for that work's title (when main entry is under a name heading), joint author, editor, compiler, translator, etc.

Newsletter 54 (May 1993)

SERIES

4.93 QUESTION: One of the general catalogers here tells me that that LC is no longer using 490/0 for untraced series, but is either authorizing them for tracing or using 500 notes. She argues that there is really no such thing as an untraced series field any longer. I'm trying to confirm this. Are you aware of any recent decisions by LC that discourage or prohibit using the 490/0? What do you recommend to libraries that want to allow access to their 490/0 headings? Do you recommend changing them to 400–440 and creating an in-house authority heading, setting up the system to access 490s, or moving them to notes?

Answer: LC decided in August 1989 (that's stretching the definition of "recent" just a bit too much) to trace all series being newly established, but did not change the trace/non-trace status of series already established. The decision is documented in LCRI 21.30L. OCLC users should follow the trace/no-trace decisions found in series authority records when they input original records. Users are *not* obligated to follow this guideline locally; that is, they don't have to trace every series in their own local copy of a record. Changing all of your existing series 490s to traced series would be quite a chore and I don't recommend moving the headings to note fields. I would think that getting your local system to index all 4XX/8XX fields would be the best solution, if your system does not already do so. The OCLC keyword "series" search includes 490s, for instance. *Newsletter 76 (September 2000)*

4.94 QUESTION: In a 440, does subfield $v always refer to subfield $a or can it refer to a preceding subfield $n and/or $p? For instance, on BF&S page 4:11, last example under subfield $p discussion, does "no. 39" refer to *Journal of polymer science* or to Part C, *Polymer symposia*?

Answer: Generally, subfield $v would refer to whatever it happens to follow, be it $a, $n, or $p. It would depend on the formulation of the series titles and numbering systems, which can be quirky and convoluted. *Newsletter 63 (May 1996)*

4.95 QUESTION: In *MOUG Newsletter* no. 56 (December 1993, p. 8), you answered a question about initial articles in uniform titles. Exactly which fields are considered uniform title fields? X30s, of course, and 240. The new BF&S document clearly states that one is to code the second indicator as zero and not to use initial articles. What about the 440? When used, it should contain the authorized form of the series (i.e., the "uniform" series title). BF&S, however, does not carry the injunction about not using a filing indicator; so it sounds like the 440 is not included in the set of fields considered to be uniform titles; and therefore we should continue to input initial articles and use a filing indicator. The plot thickens with the 740 field, which clearly is *not* a uniform title field. BF&S there says to "follow LC practice," which is to delete the initial article and use a first (filing) indicator of zero. If we're doing it for the X30s, the 240, and the 740, why not the 440? Can you clarify this?

Answer: Some of the pronouncements about uniform titles result from the capabilities (read: limitations, at least in the past) of LC's system. But some also result from the differences between the "pure" uniform title areas and those areas that are derived from descriptive information or that have a mixed function.

By "pure" uniform title areas, I mean X30s and 240, which have filing indicators; and subfields $t in various places, which do not have filing indicators. The texts in these areas are constructed, often *very* artificially, to fulfill a few specific purposes (you know, collocation and all that). Because they are constructed (even though they sometimes look just like transcribed information, in the case of many distinctive titles), doing so without superfluous initial articles seems a good idea (and, it's the law). With subfields $t, of course, it's especially important since most systems have no way of ignoring initial articles there.

Field 440 serves a dual function, as it is both a transcribed, descriptive field *and*, coincidentally, a uniform title field. The initial article should be retained here because of the field's transcription function, with the filing indicator compensating for it. This is similar to the function that the 245 serves for many distinctive titles that do not require constructed uniform titles (at least until we have 1XX $t in bibliographic records). We also transcribe the initial articles here, and compensate for them with filing indicators.

In a different sense, field 740 also serves two functions. Though it's not a uniform title, it is somehow "constructed" from information elsewhere (245, 500, etc.), but it also (usually) directly reflects transcribed information. I'm not sure why LC has chosen not to transcribe initial articles in 740s, but I guess it's partly because of the field's "constructed" nature (and the desire to save a few keystrokes). *Newsletter 57 (May 1994)*

4.96 QUESTION: Is the following series treatment acceptable?

```
490 1   Traced series title ; $v 1–3
830 0   Traced series title ; $v 1.
830 0   Traced series title ; $v 2.
830 0   Traced series title ; $v 3.
```

Answer: For series tracings in a master OLUC record, users should follow RI 21.30L. In this case, because the numbers are consecutive, the 490 should have been input as a 440, without the need for the 830s. If the numbers were not consecutive, the proper form would be:

```
490 1    Traced series title ; $v 3, 5, 7, 9
830 0    Traced series title ; $v 3, etc.
```

Some local systems require a separate tracing for each number, but such local practices should not be retained in a master record. *Newsletter 48* (*August 1992*)

4.97 QUESTION: While upgrading a DLC minimal level record (Encoding Level 7), I found that the series wasn't traced but needed to be. It happens to have an initial article. Now, I know that initial articles are excluded from series uniform title authority records and that they are included in the bibliographic 4XX field as part of the description. Should I tag it a "490 1" with the article, then trace it without the article in an 830, or use the nonfiling indicator in a 440 field?

Answer: Feel free to use the nonfiling indicator in a 440 field. The former practice was due to limitations of LC's online system in handling non-filing indicators; LC's limitations needn't concern us when we edit LC minimal-level records in OCLC's online system. *Newsletter 46* (*November 1990*)

4.98 QUESTION: What should be done with numbers associated with untraced series such as "Schirmer's library of musical classics"?

Answer: Practices have varied so much over the years that people are justifiably confused about these things. Many phrases that once were considered series and placed in the series area of bibliographic records (such as "Edition Peters") are now considered Music Publisher Numbers. Now these are placed in notes and in 028 fields. Some such phrases are still considered as series, albeit untraced. I have encouraged people to input these numbers in 028 fields as well (coded so as not to generate additional notes), giving extra access to notoriously hard-to-search music records. Although they are not entirely consistent in the practice, the Library of Congress seems to be doing the same thing more often than not. *Newsletter 40* (*August 1989*)

CHAPTER 5

Description and Related Fields

INTRODUCTION

Coded information about the time and place of an event, about historical period, about language, and about instrumental and vocal forces strike some catalogers as redundant of natural language information in other parts of the record. Although that is true as far as it goes, coded information is also more easily manipulated by systems, more and more of which are using the data found in coded fields. The core areas of edition, publication and distribution, and physical description are central to the identification of bibliographic items. Publishers, places, pagination, specific material designations, and all sorts of dates generate their share of questions.

DATE/TIME/PLACE OF EVENT

5.1 QUESTION: During a recent training session it was mentioned that LC was no longer using 045, 047, and 048 fields. What happened to the LC guidelines that used to come with the MARC format? I seem to recall some statement about them going away, but are LC usage guidelines available somewhere? Do you know if they are still using the 033?

Answer: Although LC no longer inputs 045, 047, and 048 (and hasn't done so since October 1991), the specifications remain in MARC 21 documentation, as they are still valid fields. When LC uses copy cataloging from other sources, they do not remove these fields, so you will still find them in LC records (and in records created before October 1991, of course). As far as I am aware, LC continues to use field 033 when appropriate. The current edition (1999, with updates) of LC's internal *Music and Sound Recordings*

Online Manual no longer has LC usage specifications for 045, 047, and 048 (that is, it simply says that LC no longer uses them), but 033 remains. I've heard of no plans to remove any of these fields from MARC 21. Lots of libraries continue to use these fields and the choice about their inclusion is entirely up to you. *Newsletter 78 (May 2001)*

LANGUAGE CODE

5.2 QUESTION: After 15 years at this, it has just now occurred to me that there may be two ways to read the instructions coding the first indicator of 041 as a "1" = "Item is or includes a translation." To use first indicator "1", does the whole item have to be or include a translation? Or just some of it? (It's the word "includes" that is tripping me up.) I'm cataloging a recording of a bunch of arias and songs by a soprano. Most are in Italian, but the three songs are in English. Two of those songs were originally in Russian. So two tracks out of 16 are sung in translation. Do I use first indicator "1" or not?

   Answer: The variations are endless, aren't they? Yes, this would be considered to "include" a translation. The wording reads "is or includes," I think, to cover items that *are* translations (and so may not contain a single word of the original language) as well as items that contain, in whole or in some part, both the original language and at least one language of translation from the original. You will, of course, want to indicate (in some sort of appropriate note) the fact that the two songs in question are English translations from the Russian. *Newsletter 79 (November 2001)*

5.3 QUESTION: In #17156763 field 041 has a first indicator of "0" (no translation in sight). To be correct this would have to apply only to the sound emanating from the disc. It is not a translation. It is German. But, the program notes are in three languages and the libretto is translated from the German into three languages. The answer must be that only subfield $d has no translation in sight. Therefore, indicator "0" is correct. If we take into account the other written translations the indicator should be "1". Is "0" the correct indicator?

   Answer: The value of the first indicator of field 041 in both Scores and Sound Recordings is determined by consideration of the main content of the item itself, not of any accompanying material. (There is one exception. When a score includes a translation of the vocal text printed as text, it is considered to include a translation.) For the recording in question to be considered to include a translation, it would have had to be sung in a language other than German, the original. So for a sound recording, when subfield

$d contains only the original language(s), the first indicator is "0". *Newsletter 76 (September 2000)*

5.4 QUESTION: Field 041, subfield $b, says, "Do not enter language codes that already appear in subfield $a." Since sound recordings don't use subfield $a, can we ignore that sentence, meaning that you *can* enter language codes that already appear in subfield $d? For instance, if you have an opera sung in French, and there's a synopsis in French and English and German, you'd have:

041 0b $d fre $b engfreger

Your *Music Coding and Tagging* book, middle of p. 90, has this situation, so I'm guessing that the sentence does apply only to subfield $a, not subfield $d. (Though I can't fathom what the difference would be, as subfield $d just substitutes for subfield $a in sound recordings.)

  Answer: Regarding the 041 subfield $b question, I have taken MARC 21 at its word, though I'm not sure my interpretation is correct. For music (specifically Sound Recordings), it reads "subfield $b contains the language code(s) of material accompanying sound recordings if the accompanying material contains summaries of the contents of a nonmusic sound recording or summaries of songs or other vocal works (not translations of the text(s)) contained on a music sound recording." Both the general definition and the audiovisual materials definition emphasize the use of the subfield $b when the language of the summary differs from that of the text or the sound track. The music explanation does not mention this restriction and I can only guess that it's because subfield $a is not used for sound recordings. *Newsletter 76 (September 2000)*

5.5 QUESTION: What is the Language Code if you have a sound recording that is a collection of music, almost all of it instrumental but with voices on a few of the selections. Is it "N/A" or do you pick the language(s)?

  Answer: The Language Code(s) would reflect the language(s) of the sung texts, in the fixed field and in the 041, if appropriate. If it isn't clear from the contents note or somewhere else in the record, you could include the details in a 546 note:

546   Third and sixth works sung in Latin.

as an example. *Newsletter 75 (May 2000)*

5.6 QUESTION: *Bibliographic Formats and Standards* says that the first language code in field 041 must agree with the Language code in the fixed field, and that, in the absence of a field 041, the system uses the code in the Language fixed field to determine filing in certain title and heading fields. What happens when the 245 title is in one language, but the 041 subfields $a or $d and/or the fixed field code is for the content of the item in hand and it differs from the 245 title? Does this confuse the system as far as indexing? This scenario happens to me a few times a month. For example, a sound recording of Rossini opera excerpts called *Rossini in Vienna*. The 245 is in English, but the 041 subfield $d and the Language fixed field coded "ita." Basically, it is an American label production with program notes in English, but the sung content of the album is Italian.

Answer: As long as the relevant filing indicators are correctly coded (in fields 130, 222, 240, 243, 245, 440, 730, 740, and 830), the system will generally be able to keep its indexing ducks in a row. There may be cases where an initial article incorrectly included in a corporate heading would cause the heading to be indexed wrong. For instance, if the Language code for an item was "N/A" and there was a 710 that read "I Musici", the system would not know that the "I" is an Italian article meant to be ignored. (The correct heading would have been "Musici" [n83129444], anyway.) Something similar can happen when an initial article is incorrectly included in one of the indexed title fields that lack a filing indicator (fields 212, 246, 247, 780, and 785). For instance, if the Language is coded "fre" and there is a 246 that includes an initial article "The", it will be included as part of the indexed title since it is not recognized as an English article meant to be ignored. In most cases, if you make sure the filing indicators are correct and that initial articles are neither included in corporate headings nor transcribed in fields without filing indicators, there should be no indexing problems. *Newsletter 74 (November 1999)*

5.7 QUESTION: In BF&S, field 041, p. 0:98 subfield input standards at the top, subfield $a is shown as mandatory (for VIS, COM, SCO, REC only). Subfield $d is only required if applicable. Ah, since REC does not use subfield $a, using subfield $d in its place, should subfield $d be mandatory for REC? I'm a little hazy on the meaning of "Required if applicable." The text for 041 seems to be saying that if I have a libretto or other accompanying material, say, in a CD booklet, I have to code 041. Catalogers aren't doing that; everyone is acting as if everything but subfields $a (or $d for REC) is optional, including me. Are all of us all wet?

Answer: "Only mandatory for VIS, COM, SCO, REC" really is misleading, a legacy of OCLC's split of the single USMARC "Music" format into the two formats, Scores and Sound Recordings. If we look at USMARC

(Appendix A, p. 9) we read of 041 subfield $a, "Only Mandatory if applicable for Computer files, Music, and Visual materials." My guess is that we translated USMARC's "Music" format into OCLC's SCO and REC without thinking it through entirely. Both USMARC and BF&S make clear elsewhere that you don't use 041 subfield $a in sound recording records. Subfield $d is "Required if applicable" rather than mandatory for sound recordings because so many recordings don't have a sung or spoken text associated with them, all instrumental recordings, for example. Now "Required if applicable or readily available" is a multifaceted standard. As BF&S (p. xii or http://www.oclc.org/bibformats/en/about/ in the online version) puts it: "Data is readily available from: (1) The item in hand; (2) Other bibliographic records in the Online Union Catalog; (3) OCLC Authority File records. Data is applicable if: (1) AACR2 1988 rev. instructs you to enter the data when it applies; (2) It is necessary to justify the existence of an added entry (AACR2 1988 rev. rule 21.29); (3) It is essential for efficient access to, or effective processing of, records." If you are cataloging a sound recording that has only one language associated with it (that is, spoken/sung text, printed text/libretto, notes, etc., all in a single language without any translations being involved anywhere), the language coded in the fixed field is enough and you can dispense with the 041 all together. If there were no meaningful language code in the fixed field because the recording is instrumental (Lang: N/A), for instance, and there were some other language associated with the item such as the language of program notes that are mentioned in notes, field 041 would be required in an I-Level record. Regardless of the contents of the Language fixed field, if there were more than one language or a translation associated with any language aspect of the item (that is, spoken/sung text, printed text/libretto, notes, etc.), an I-Level record would need field 041 if those language aspects were mentioned in notes or elsewhere. Many catalogers do neglect to input field 041 when it would be required in an I-Level record (for Core-Level sound recordings records, only subfields $d and $h would be required if applicable), but this is substandard. If it's worth mentioning in a note or elsewhere, it's worth coding correctly. Although you may not be all wet, you might want to start pricing dehumidifiers. *Newsletter 71* (*December 1998*)

5.8 QUESTION: What is the accepted practice for coding the Language fixed field for scores of vocal works that contain interlinear or supralinear text in several languages, including the original language? The only guidance I can seem to find is a statement such as that in *Music Coding and Tagging*, p. 29: "If no predominant language can be determined, the codes are recorded in alphabetical order in the 041 field and the first is recorded in the Language fixed field." That raises other questions: 1) What are the marks of predominance—the language of the title page, the language of the text printed above others in the score? Does dissonance between these two sources produce a lack of predominance? 2) Is there some pronouncement that documents this concept, or is it one of those "common sense" things that everyone knows about but me? Putting this question in concrete terms: What is the coding for a G. Schirmer vocal score of *The Magic Flute*? The title page is in English; the text is printed interlinearally in German and English, the German on top.

Answer: Determination of prominence isn't an exact science. (So, what in cataloging is?) I think it tends to be common-sensical, but I doubt that there's universal agreement on it. USMARC doesn't give much guidance, but I'd consider the language(s) of the title page, the original language of the work, and the language(s) of the translation. Not having your Schirmer *Magic Flute* in hand, I can't say for sure, but it sounds like it may have been intended as an English translation. In that case, the predominant language may well be English (title page, interlinear text translation). Although you are supposed to ignore accompanying material in this determination, you might also keep in the back of your mind the language(s) of any preliminaries (preface, table of contents, etc.), indexes, and so on, but only as a minor corroborating factor. Ultimately, when all other things are equal, you may want to base your final decision on the language of the title page (first title), if only to keep the 245, the 041, and the Language fixed field in synch. That's the direction I would go when there is dissonance. Remember: Don't agonize. *Newsletter 67 (August 1997)*

5.9 QUESTION: The recording I'm cataloging features totally instrumental versions of folk songs. The texts of the songs are included in the program notes, but those words are not sung on the recording. How should the Language fixed field and field 041 be coded?

Answer: Because the texts are not sung, we cannot, strictly speaking, call them printed versions of the sung or spoken texts. Record the language(s) of the program notes and the unsung song texts in subfield $g of the 041, *not* in subfield $e. Of course, because the recording is instrumental, the Language fixed field would be coded N/A. *Newsletter 62 (November 1996)*

5.10 QUESTION: We are told to use the 041 field when, among other things "the language of the summaries abstracts, or accompanying material differs from the language of the main item." In the case in hand, I'm cataloging a CD accompanied by program notes. Fixed field "Lang" is coded N/A. The program notes are 21 pages long, with 18 of the 21 pages in English. Pages 19 and 20 contain the words to *Ode to joy* in German, with an English translation. Would you recommend adding a 041, subfield $g and $h in this case? If so, how would I code these two subfields?

Answer: This is exactly the sort of situation in which you would want to add field 041. First, though, if this is a recording of Beethoven's Symphony no. 9, then the Language Fixed Field should be "ger" for the choral finale, rather than "N/A", which would be for a purely instrumental recording. If this is the case, you would need "$d ger" in the 041 for the language of the sung text. From what you've described, here is your 041:

041 1 $d ger $e gereng $h ger $g eng

The subfield $e covers the printed German and English texts; subfield $h, the original language of the printed text; and subfield $g, the language of the program notes. *Newsletter 61 (August 1995)*

5.11 QUESTION: I'm in a quandary here concerning the instructions for the 041 languages field in the new Bib formats document. We have a recording with works being sung both in the original language and in translation. The original languages vary. In the old sound recordings format under instructions for 041 subfield "h" there was a paragraph that read: "If the recording contains separate pieces, some of which are translations and some of which are originals in various languages, do not use field 041. In fixed field 'Lang,' enter the code for the language of the major portion of the text. In case of doubt, use code 'mul.'" I cannot seem to find any guidance on what to do in this situation in the new Bib formats document. Am I missing something that appears somewhere else in the new formats document, or has something changed that I'm not aware of?

Answer: Some things certainly got smushed around in creating the single BF&S volume, but I think the essence of what you're asking still appears on p. 0:89, from the top all the way down to the "History" heading. As far as I am aware, policy has not changed, and you may continue to code as you have previously. *Newsletter 60 (April 1995)*

5.12 QUESTION: In 041, can subfield $h be used after a subfield $g?

Answer: Subfield $h may appear after a subfield $a, $d, $e, or $g; however, it is meaningful only in relation to its preceding subfield, so it can never appear alone. Perhaps confusion arises because only when the $h relates to $a in scores or $d in sound recordings will the first indicator be "1" (for translation). Both format documents happen to mention the use of $h after $g in the 041 $g sections. *Newsletter 49 (November 1991)*

5.13 QUESTION: I'm cataloging a Russian edition of a Tchaikovsky opera; it has a preface in Russian, which I've mentioned in a 500 note. Since both the libretto and the preface are in a single language, do I need to include a field 041 in addition to coding the Language Fixed Field "rus"?

Answer: When everything is in the same language and no translation is involved, 041 is not needed; the Language Fixed Field is sufficient to cover both the libretto and the accompanying material. However, note that if you have an instrumental work, with "N/A" in the Language Fixed Field, any accompanying material mentioned in a note would need a corresponding 041 field. *Newsletter 46 (November 1990)*

TIME PERIOD

5.14 QUESTION: Working with a bunch of photocopies of music manuscripts, I've found that some composers include the time of completion of the work along with the date. Some even include the date and time the work was begun. Should this information be included in the catalog record? If so, how precise can it be according to the correct coding?

Answer: The complete information can certainly be included in a 500 note. Field 045 subfield $b has provisions for the coded inclusion of the year, month, day, and hour (yyyymmddhh). The hour information, figured on a 24-hour clock, is optional. If you have a range of dates/times such as a starting point and an ending point, you can enter them in separate subfields $b with the appropriate indicator.

045 0 $b 1953062917
500   At end: June 29, 1953, 5 P.M.

Newsletter 46 (November 1990)

NUMBER OF INSTRUMENTS/VOICES CODE

Mini-Lesson

5.15 The treatment of soloists in the 048 field has caused considerable confusion over the years. However, the Music Section at the Library of Congress has been kind enough to share its own guidelines on the matter with us. Special thanks to Deta Davis, Harry Price, and the rest of the Music Section for all their trouble. The LC guidelines are reprinted here pretty much as I received them, save for some editorial changes and conversion of the field examples into OCLC format. The bracketed comments and examples are my own.

For solo voice(s) and one instrument, or piano 4 hands, or 2 pianos, assign subfield $a for voice(s):

```
500   For soprano and piano.
048   va01 $a ka01
500   For vocal quartet (SATB) and 2 pianos.
048   va01 $a vc01 $a vd01 $a vf01 $a ka01 $a ka01
```

[This is the case *regardless* of whether the accompanying medium has been reduced from larger forces. This is a change from existing OCLC guidelines and contradicts examples in the format documents.

```
500   For medium voice and piano; acc. originally for orchestra.
048   vi01 $a ka01]
```

For solo voice(s) and 2 or more instruments (except 2 pianos), assign subfield $b for voice(s):

```
500   For tenor, flute, and piano.
048   $b vd01 $a wa01 $a ka01
```

For chamber music, always assign subfields $a:

```
500   For violin and piano.
048   sa01 $a ka01
500   For flute and continuo.
048   wa01 $a ke
```

For solo instrument(s) with ensembles, assign subfield $b to solo instrument(s).

```
[650 0 Concertos (Trumpets (3) with string orchestra)
048 $b bb03 $a oc ]
```

For solo instrument(s) with acc. arr. for piano, assign subfield $b to solo instruments.

```
[500 For trombone and orchestra; acc. arr. for piano.
048 $b bd01 $a ka01 ]
```

Obviously, each case must be judged on its own merits. Whatever you do, don't agonize over it. *Newsletter 42 (November 1989)*

EDITION

5.16 QUESTION: What is OCLC policy for shape-note editions of hymnals? I would assume that if two versions of a denomination's hymnal were published, one in standard and another in shape-note notation, one would enter a new record in the database for one that does not appear. That would

seem to me to be in the interests of both ILL and local library users, but I
would like to have it confirmed. If the notation is announced with a title
page or verso statement of "Shape-note edition" or "Standard edition," I
am also extrapolating to choose to enter the data in a 250, rather than a 254,
field. Unfortunately, this problem did not come up in either your or Richard
Smiraglia's manuals, and I don't see a statement about it in AACR2 Revised
or the LCRI that I have. I'm looking forward to your guidance.

Answer: A hymnal issued both in standard notation and shape-note versions would certainly justify separate records. If there were a statement such
as "Shape-note edition" or "Standard edition," it would be a legitimate edition statement, suitable for field 250. It might need to be bracketed, depending on its source (see AACR2 5.0B2). If there is nothing that could be
construed as an edition statement, I think you can use AACR2 Rules 1.2B4
and 5.2B3 (and their respective RIs) as justification for supplying one along
those lines. As far as the possibility of using 254 instead of 250, remember
that 254 is used for statements of the physical format of the item (score,
miniature score, part, etc.). Actually, I think there is a somewhat relevant
example in the first edition of *Music Coding and Tagging* on p. 161, the
twelfth one down.

250   Neue Ausg. in modernen Schl¨usseln.

It's not as pure as your example because it's got the clear "new edition"
in there, but I think the rest means something like "in modern notation."
Hymnals are published in all sorts of versions: with and without accompaniment, in different voice ranges, and so on. Generally, they could all be
cataloged separately. *Newsletter 68 (November 1997)*

PUBLICATION/DISTRIBUTION

5.17 QUESTION: I have the following score:

Title page: Sonata for viola : in d minor = Sonate fur Viola, d moll / Michail Glinka
    ; completed and edited by V. Borisovsky.
Cover: Sonata : in d minor for viola / Michail Glinka.
Plate number: M.R. 1034.
Publisher on title page: Breitkopf & Hartel ; Musica Rara.
This copyright statement is on page 1: "c1961 by Musica Rara, London
assigned 2000 to Breitkopf & Hartel, Wiesbaden."

This is a reprint of the Musica Rara edition (see OCLC #368085 or OCLC
#49599492) with a new title page and cover. My question goes to which
date(s) to use and if/how to mention the copyright statement. Should I only

use 1961 and list both Musica Rara and B&H as publishers, or does the 2000 date need to be incorporated as well? This copyright statement is throwing me and I am not quite sure how to deal with it. I hope you can give me some advice.

Answer: These apparent republications are always confusing, and I'm never sure myself how to treat them. It's complicated by at least two other factors: changes in copyright laws over the years, and publishers who may or may not be presenting the publication information accurately. So here is my best guess based on the information you've presented. Since we've got a new title page with a new first publisher and place, let's consider it a new publication. Since I have no idea what the copyright "assigned to" really means, but it does clearly refer somehow to the new publisher, let's treat that as an inferred date of publication. So here's my suggested 260:

260   Wiesbaden : $b Breitkopf & Hartel ; $a London : $b Musica Rara, $c [2000?], c1961.

DtSt would be "t" and the Dates would be "2000, 1961." I have no idea if that's correct, but it seems like a fairly reasonable guess. *Newsletter 81 (September 2002)*

5.18 QUESTION: On bracketed dates, is there ever a "p" or "c" situation such as [p1967] or [c1982]? I never see it, and I guess it's because we don't know if it should be "p" or "c"?

Answer: Brackets are used for transcribed areas in only a limited number of situations, mainly to correct inaccuracies (Rule 1.0F1) and to indicate that information is taken from outside the prescribed source(s) (Rule 1.0A1 and elsewhere). Since the prescribed sources for the publication, distribution, etc. area of Sound Recordings (6.0B2) include "Chief source of information [disc and label, and as outlined in 6.0B1 for other recording formats], accompanying textual material, container," it would be rare for an explicit phonogram copyright date (a "p" date) to be bracketed. Remember that, if publishers are doing things correctly (always a questionable assumption), a run-of-the-mill copyright date (a "c" date) should not refer to a recording itself but to something else associated with the recording, be it package design, program notes, accompanying material, or whatever. As such, these "c" dates can be used only as inferred dates of publication and so must be bracketed, but without the "c" designation. I highly recommend Richard Smiraglia's new *Describing Music Materials* (Soldier Creek Press, 1997), which has a clear and concise section about dates on pp. 48–49. *Newsletter 69 (April 1998)*

5.19 QUESTION: The sound cassette in question has the RCA and the Bluebird logos on the label; the RCA, Bluebird, and BMG logos on the container spine; and RCA with the dog and record player, General Electric U.S.A., BMG logo, Bluebird logo, "Manufactured and distributed by BMG Music, New York, N.Y. Printed in U.S.A." on the container. Should the 260 be:

260   New York : $b Bluebird, $c p1992.

or

260   New York : $b Bluebird : $b Manufactured and distributed by BMG, $c p1992.

and what about RCA?

Answer: Either treatment of the 260 is OK, though LCRI 6.4D1 suggests following the option of including the distributor, making the second choice better for a full-level record. RCA is correctly excluded in accordance with AACR2 rule 6.4D2. *Newsletter 53 (November 1992)*

5.20 QUESTION: I see lots of inconsistency in the abbreviations used in place names in field 260. Should we be using the forms found in Appendix B of AACR2R or the standard two-character Postal Service abbreviations?

Answer: According to Rule Interpretation B.14, the Postal Service abbreviations are used only if they appear on the piece (and in exactly the form on the piece, regarding capitalization and punctuation). In all other cases (when supplying the name of the state or when abbreviating it from the full form that appears on the piece), use the form in Appendix B.14. *Newsletter 50 (May 1992)*

PHYSICAL DESCRIPTION

5.21 QUESTION: At a recent workshop, one of the participants said she had heard that it was OK now to say "1 compact disc" in the 300 field for a sound recording. Is this true or apocryphal?

Answer: No doubt this is apocryphal (as well as inevitable and unfortunate) fallout from the revision of AACR2 Chapter 9, specifically 9.5B1, which allows the use of so-called "conventional terminology to record the specific format of the physical carrier." As things stand right now, this applies to Chapter 9 Electronic Resources *only* and cannot be carried over to other chapters and their treatment of other types of materials. The wisdom of this change was a matter of heated discussion at MLA in Las Vegas. I personally share the strong consensus of distaste for this idea, even while recognizing that the floodgates have been opened. It's only a matter of time before Rules 5.5B and 6.5B (as well as the corresponding rules in many of the remaining chapters) are contaminated by the same sludge—I mean, updated in the same spirit. In Las Vegas, the various subcommittees of the Bibliographic Control Committee were talking about the possibility of drawing up guidelines for such "conventional terminology" so as to preserve some uniformity in description. This is in anticipation of rules changes that have not yet taken place, of course. In the meantime, the current wording of Rule 6.5B still holds, and the wording "1 compact disc" *cannot* be used in field 300. *Newsletter 80 (May 2002)*

5.22 QUESTION: I have parts to a brass ensemble accompaniment. Half of the parts are 26 cm. and half of them are 28 cm. How do you notate that in the 300 field? By the way, it works like this: one of the first trumpet parts is 26 cm., the second first trumpet part is 28 cm.; the same is true with each of the other parts. We are often given permission to make photocopies of parts and this is why I have this problem.

   Answer: Referring to AACR2 2.5D3, you could give the range of sizes as 26–28 cm. Because the size difference is relatively small, however, you could ignore it and record the size simply as 28 cm. without doing serious damage to the integrity of the record. *Newsletter 78 (May 2001)*

5.23 QUESTION: In cataloging scores, tag 300, I'm noticing a real divergence in actual practice as opposed to BF&S. A lot of institutions are putting parts for a score in subfield $e routinely rather than keeping them in subfield $a, or, if there is a size differential or intervening illustrative matter, putting them in a second subfield $a.

   Answer: Using subfield $e for parts is incorrect. It's an honest mistake, though, because the "+" convention (as in "+ X parts") looks just like the construction for the accompanying material that would properly go in subfield $e. Please report these incorrect records, or feel free to change them yourself on minimal-level records. *Newsletter 77 (November 2000)*

5.24 QUESTION: I have a page-numbering question concerning an item that is two scores. Usually, the two scores have equal page numbering, so the solution in this case would be, for example, "2 scores (55 p. each)." However, since one of these scores has a short appendix, one of the scores has one more page than the other. The only place that seems to have any kind of information relating to this situation is MCD 5.5B1. It gives the example of "46, 39 p. of music." However, that refers to a single score with two different page-numbering schemes. The only thing I can think of to do is "2 scores," just like you would do for "2 parts."

Answer: As I see it, there are two options, depending on how strictly we want to read the rules. Rule 5.5B2 reads in part, "If the item consists of different types of score . . . give the details of each in the order of the list in 5.5B1, separated from each other by a space, plus sign, space. Add the pagination or number of volumes as instructed in 2.5B." So if these are actually two different types of score (say, a full score and a condensed score), there's no problem. But if we stretch the letter of the rule to include differently paginated scores of the same type (say, both full scores), you could describe them as such:

1 score (55 p.) + 1 score (56 p.)

The other option, and the one I think I'd prefer since it is simpler (and requires no stretch, lazybones that I am), resorts to Rule 2.5B21 (which LC locally chooses not to apply, but we needn't feel restrained by that). It reads, "If the volumes in a multivolume set are individually paged, give the pagination of each volume in parentheses after the number of volumes." The example shows the paginations separated by a semicolon, space. This would result in:

2 scores (55; 56 p.)

In either case, you might want to mention the presence of the short appendix in a note, if appropriate. *Newsletter 76 (September 2000)*

5.25 QUESTION: Recently, I found a Web site with guitar tablatures for Nanci Griffith's songs. This particular site has only the tabs, no scores. For a Web site, there is no 300 field, but for a paper version, would the 300 field be something like:

300   30 p. of music : $b ill. ; $c 28 cm.

Also, would the subdivision "$v Scores" apply to the subject heading? I searched OCLC but couldn't find an example of anything with just the tabs, although I did find things with scores and tabs.

Answer: For reasons that have never been entirely clear to me, LC has generally excluded chord diagram books from their music file. So if the site you cite consists of chord diagrams, it would be considered Type "a". I answered a related question in *MOUG Newsletter* no. 69 (April 1998, p. 16). Such an item would be described simply as "p." rather than as "p. of music" since chord diagrams are not considered to be music, bibliographically. That would also suggest that the form subdivision "$v Scores" would not be appropriate. Check out #33407843, #38174460, and #9394154, for example. *Newsletter 76 (September 2000)*

5.26 QUESTION: In what kind of situation was script-L used in the pagination of pre-AACR2 records? I suppose it implies that the book has a blank or unnumbered leaf or leaves preceding the text. Is this definition correct? And how were they counted? According to the present rules, one leaf counted as "1 [script-L]" not as "2 [script-L]." Is this true in the older catalogs?

Answer: In pre-AACR2 records, script-L was used to indicate leaves (defined in AACR2 as "One of the units into which the original sheet or half sheet of paper, parchment, etc., is folded to form part of a book, pamphlet, journal, etc.; each leaf consists of two pages, one on each side, either or both of which may be blank"). The old rules required a much more detailed pagination than does AACR2 currently, so blank and unnumbered sequences (which might now be ignored) especially at the beginning or end of the main pagination were often described as so many leaves. A single leaf (or sheet of paper) would have been counted as "1 leaf" if numbered or "[1] leaf" if unnumbered. There are still instances under AACR2 when such leaves would be included in the pagination, but the words "leaf" and "leaves" are now spelled out (see such rules as 1.5B2, many in the 2.5B and 4.5B sequences, for instance). *Newsletter 75 (May 2000)*

5.27 QUESTION: In hand is a two-page fragment of a vocal score. Would this be described in the 300 field as "1 vocal score," despite the fact that it is obviously incomplete? Also, how best to describe it in a 500, as "fragment" or "score fragment" or some other phrase?

Answer: The way you've described this in the 300 ("1 vocal score ([2] p.) ; $c 35 cm.") seems fine, but I'm not sure if the copy you have is actually missing pages or if this item is simply something that was broken off in the middle and is as complete as the item ever was. If the former, look at AACR2 2.5B16 and at LCRI 1.7B20. If the latter, you might expand the "Score fragment" note to explain that it's a sketch that breaks off after so many measures, or whatever is appropriate. *Newsletter 74 (November 1999)*

5.28 QUESTION: How do you describe a score in the 300 field when the score is in a cover that is 28 cm. high, but the music is to be played horizontally, so it is 21 × 28 cm.? Which dimension would go in the 300 field?

Answer: The implication of AACR2 2.5D1 (in reference back from 5.5D) is that the height is the measurement of the binding (that is, the spine), so that would be the determining factor. If the item is bound along the 28 cm. side, the dimension in 300 subfield $c would be 28 cm. If the item is bound along the 21 cm. side, the dimension would be 21 × 28 cm., according to Rule 2.5D2. Guess it doesn't really matter which way the title reads. *Newsletter 70* (*September 1998*)

5.29 QUESTION: I'm cataloging a "conductor's score" and can't seem to find the proper information for where and how the term should be entered in the record. Should the physical description be just "1 score" with a musical presentation statement indicating what kind of score it is? Or perhaps "conductor's score" should only be in a note? Could the uses of "miniature score" be used as models for "conductor's score"?

Answer: First you might want to check the AACR2 definition of "piano [violin, etc.] conductor part" (p. 621) to see if what you have fits; publishers are notoriously unreliable about applying such descriptions, at least for the purposes of cataloging. If it fits, you may use the appropriate designation (for instance, "1 piano conductor part") as the SMD in the 300 field. If it does not fit, look at rule 5.5B1 and its MCD to see if any other designation fits; again if not, describe the item as "1 score" in the 300. If the designation "conductor's score" appears on the item itself, it would be appropriate as a 254 if it refers merely to a particular physical manifestation of the score. If creating the "conductor's score" involved some sort of intellectual work (arrangement of the music, for instance; with or without an indication of just who is responsible), it should instead be part of the statement of responsibility. If the publisher's use of the term is somehow quirky and what you are trying to describe is not otherwise made clear in the record, you may optionally further explain the format of the score in a 500 note. *Newsletter 67* (*August 1997*)

5.30 QUESTION: One of our catalog librarians was asking for a definitive definition of what constitutes a "score" vs. "p. of music." We were looking at AACR2R plus Richard Smiraglia's book and I couldn't find an answer. The piece in hand is a collection of songs with piano accompaniment for a single voice. We own only one of the four volumes.

Answer: The distinction is really fairly simple, though the everyday language use of the term "score" for any piece of printed music is what causes the confusion. If we look at the AACR2 definition of "score" we find: "A series of staves on which all the different instrumental and/or vocal parts of a musical work are written, one under the other in vertical arrangement, so that the parts may be read simultaneously." In other words, to describe an item as a "score" in the physical description, the music must be for more than one voice or instrument. As a result, most music for a solo unaccompanied voice or for a solo instrument must be described as "p. of music" (or "v. of music" or "leaves of music" according to 5.5B1). One exception is a "part," defined by AACR2 as "the music for one of the participating voices or instruments in a musical work." Any music for two or more voices and/or instruments would be described as a "score" or one of the appropriate terms also listed in 5.5B1 and defined in the AACR2 glossary. Thus, a collection of songs for solo voice with piano accompaniment would be described as a "score." *Newsletter 67 (August 1997)*

5.31 QUESTION: Would you consider these two records to be duplicates? One has in the 300, "1 score (46 p.)" whereas the other has "2 scores (46 p. each)." I ask this because it involves a general principle involving the publication of scores for 2 pianos. I suspect that the publisher issued one score, and that it was necessary to buy two copies; the approach in the second record implies that two scores were issued together, which of course sometimes does happen.

Answer: They sound like duplicates. When two identical copies are required for performance, it has always seemed to me a holdings question, not a question of bibliographic description in the 300. (A 500 note to that effect might be appropriate, though: Two copies needed for performance.) Please *do* report such cases as duplicates. *Newsletter 60 (April 1995)*

5.32 FOLLOW-UP QUESTION: In a related matter, I always report records that have, say, "1 score (2 v.)" vs. "1 score (2 v. in 1)" as duplicates, assuming that in the latter case the volumes were bound together after publication, and should not have been cataloged this way. The conservative approach, which seems to be an OCLC principle concerning the merging of duplicates, would allow both records to stand. Should I stop reporting these cases?

Answer: On this question of "2 v." versus "2 v. in 1" it's more difficult to generalize. If the latter is a local binding decision, these are duplicates. But I've seen cases where things have been issued both ways, and those have to be considered legitimately separate records. When you report such possible duplicates, any evidence to help determine who did the binding (publisher or library) is useful. I'll usually send the query on to the inputting library. *Newsletter 60 (April 1995)*

5.33 QUESTION: Can you clarify the description of scores in the collation? According to AACR2 a score is "a series of staves on which all the

different instrumental and/or vocal parts of a musical work are written. . . ."
Using this definition then, it would seem that "1 score (xx p.)" should be
used for all musical works that have more than one instrument even if the
publication is a collection of works. The collation "xx p. of music" would
be used for all works with only one instrument, that is, piano or guitar, regardless of whether it is a collection of works.

Answer: The way you have described things is exactly the way I understand them. *Newsletter 54 (May 1993)*

5.34 QUESTION: For a recording I'm cataloging, I've found LC cataloging copy in the Music NUC. It's got three physical description fields, each
for a different recording format, and each prefaced with the publisher's number for that format. What do I do about these? Can I code it as LC copy?

Answer: Back in the early and mid-1970s before they were creating
MARC records for recordings, LC experimented with these multi-carrier
collation records; they are briefly explained in the 1976 text of AACR Chapter 14, revised. (A brief history of the practice can be gleaned through reference to the following *Music Cataloging Bulletins*: 2:7 [July 1971] p. 4;
2:11 [November 1971] p. 3; 3:11 [November 1972] p. 3; 7:2 [February
1976] p. 3; and 9:4 [April 1978] p. 2. Cessation of the practice was announced in the Spring 1978 *Cataloging Service*, bulletin 125, p. 9. If you
leaf through the 1973–1977 Music NUC cumulation, you're bound to find
a few examples.) If you intend to use this LC cataloging as the basis for your
own, transcribe only the physical description for the item you have in hand
and ignore the others. Transcribe the appropriate publisher's number(s) in
the correct place for the cataloging rules that are being used; of course, create
a 028 field. If your physical format is the first one in the LC record, consider the cataloging LC and code it as such (Source code: blank; LCCN in
010 subfield $a; DLC in 040 subfield $a). Otherwise, consider it original
cataloging, and put the LCCN in a subfield $z of the 040 field. Further
guidelines for the transcription of retrospective copy can be found in *Bibliographic Input Standards*, 3rd ed. *Newsletter 39 (May 1989)*

CHAPTER 6

Notes

INTRODUCTION

No area of the bibliographic record is as varied as the notes, so it's no surprise that the questions concerning them are just as wide-ranging. Queries about how to formulate notes about language, source of title, performers and other credits, accompanying material, and the like pale in comparison to the number about contents notes. The rules give little guidance about contents notes relative to their complexity and the limited supply of punctuation marks at our disposal.

LANGUAGE

6.1 QUESTION: A question has come up concerning the appropriate tag for inputting a note regarding program notes that are written in various languages (these program notes are ones that are inserted in a container). Would it be more appropriate to use a 546 tag or a 500 tag to input such a note in a sound recording record? We have seen either tag used in various records found in the OCLC database.

Answer: Notes about program notes, including any language information about those program notes, belong in field 500. Only notes limited to discussions of the language of the main content of the item (for a sound recording, the language(s) of sung text and of any printed text(s) and translation(s) of the sung text) would be coded as field 546. If the note goes much beyond this sort of information, it's best to code it as 500.

546   Sung in French.
546   Words of the songs in Xhosa language; English translations included.

500   The 1st song, based on a Lebanese traditional song, with Arabic words in pho-
       netic romanization; the 2nd song with English words selected by the composer.
500   Program notes by Kurt Hoffmann in English, French, and German on con-
       tainer.

Newsletter 79 (November 2001)

6.2 QUESTION: Should I be using the 546 tag for the language of song
texts in scores? I have always seen just 500 used, except for sound recordings. Is this something new since I was a student? I'm kind of embarrassed
that I've been putting language in a general 500.

   Answer: That depends on how long ago you were a student. Until Format Integration about five years ago, the language note field 546 was valid
only in Serials and the Archival Control formats. Now, 546 should be used
for language notes in all formats, including Scores and Sound Recordings.
Use 546 only when the note is devoted pretty much exclusively to the lan-
guages/scripts of the item's main content; notes including information about
the languages of program notes, for instance, would be coded 500. *Newsletter 76 (September 2000)*

6.3 QUESTION: Regarding field 546 for sound recordings, is 546 repeatable? For example, if there were a note for language of sung text and a note
about libretti in xyz languages, are they both coded 546? I'm also unclear
on the use of $b.

   Answer: Field 546 is repeatable. A note such as "Sung in French" would
be a 546, but if the other note in question includes information beyond the
language(s) of the libretto (such as mention of program notes, the number
of pages, the author of the notes, etc.), it should be a 500 instead. Subfield
$b has to do with the alphabet, typeface, and the like, if that happens to be
important; I don't imagine it will be used much for recordings. *Newsletter
61 (August 1995)*

SOURCE OF TITLE PROPER

6.4 QUESTION: If the list title page is used as chief source for a score,
do you need a 500 to that effect? I know we make a note for "Caption title"
or "Cover title." Same thing here?

   Answer: Since a list title page is, by definition, a title page, I don't believe you need to mention it as the source of the title. AACR2 5.0B1 doesn't

seem to make any special provision in this regard for list title pages. *Newsletter 63 (May 1996)*

DURATIONS

6.5 QUESTION: Sometimes a score will include a duration note that is a range ("Duration: ca. 17:00–18:00", for instance) rather than a single time. How should we code this in field 306?

Answer: Code the 306 for the longer duration. *Newsletter 49 (November 1991)*

PERFORMER/CONDUCTOR

6.6 QUESTION: This is something I don't know and have been afraid to ask. I keep seeing in OCLC records for sound recordings (including some fairly recent records), space-semicolon-space in field 511. As far as I can determine from the current AACR2 rules (i.e., 6.7B6), they do not now prescribe any such exotic punctuation conventions (although I vaguely remember that they did years ago). The examples have semicolons following words in the normal manner. Am I missing something? What is the basis for this extrapolation of ISBD conventions into a note field? Has it become correct again?

Answer: First, we must keep in mind the statement found in AACR2R's General Introduction 0.14: "The examples used throughout these rules are illustrative and not prescriptive. That is, they illuminate the provisions of the rule to which they are attached, rather than extend those provisions. Do not take the examples or the form in which they are presented as instructions unless specifically told to do so by the accompanying text." Since 6.7B6 does not address punctuation and the rules on punctuation of notes (6.7A1 and 1.7A) do not directly address such internal punctuation, the examples in 6.7B6 should not be taken as establishing any punctuation rules. In fact, 1.7A3 states in part, "If data in a note correspond to data found in the title and statement of responsibility . . . give the elements of the data in the order in which they appear in those areas. In such a case, use prescribed punctuation. . . ." Because the 511 note is a logical extension of the statement of responsibility, and 1.1A1 states, "Precede each subsequent statement of responsibility by a semicolon," and 1.0C1, paragraph 3 states, "Precede each mark of prescribed punctuation by a space and follow it by a space . . . ," it seems that the space-semicolon-space practice is at least acceptable. As far as I can determine, the last official word on this topic appeared as MCD 6.7B6 in the December 1992 issue of *Music Cataloging Bulletin*, based on a memo from Bob Ewald in LC's Cataloging Policy and Support Office. It cites several examples in various AACR2 rules (including also 7.7B6 and 9.7B6) that variously followed and did not follow prescribed punctuation. It should be noted that, although the MCD was citing the 1978 and 1988 texts of AACR2, these discrepancies still appear in the 1998 text, as well. The issue was discussed at LC and Mr. Ewald reports in part:

> The consensus of the discussion was that prescribed punctuation in the note was not required by rule 1.7A3 since the note does not necessarily reflect exact transcription from the source from which the data are taken. On the other hand, the presence of prescribed punctuation in the 1988 rule 9.7B6 indicates that prescribed punctuation is not forbidden, and in fact may be useful when the note contains a long listing of entities performing a number of different functions. Conclusion: Standard punctuation (semicolon-space) or prescribed punctuation (space-semicolon-space) may be used when making the notes called for [in] AACR 2 rules 6.7B6, 7.7B6, 9.7B6.

In other words, one is not required to use prescribed punctuation in field 511, but it is often helpful in making the note more readable. *Newsletter 79* (*November 2001*)

6.7 QUESTION: If a record album jacket has two photos of the composer conducting the orchestra, but it doesn't *say* anywhere that the composer is conducting, may one add that information in the 511 field, and if so, would one be obliged to explain that the information came not from the text, but from a picture?

Answer: Since no conductor (the composer or otherwise) is credited anywhere and the visual evidence strongly suggests that the composer and conductor are one and the same, that seems to be a fairly safe assumption. Since we don't ordinarily state the source of information for the 511 field, I don't think you would need to justify this little curiosity explicitly. If you feel compelled, you might want to add a question mark after the "conducted by the composer" statement, but that's up to you. It does make one wonder if the publisher is trying to pull a fast one, doesn't it? *Newsletter 55* (*August 1993*)

DISSERTATIONS

6.8 QUESTION: We just noticed that a bunch of our records have been modified by OCLC ("OCL" added to 040 field). The only change we were able to identify is that the degree indication in 502 fields has been changed from "D.Mus." to "D. Mus." (adding a space before "Mus."). Can this be for real? I had consciously used "D.Mus." based on the usage shown in our university's register of academic appointees. Is someone at OCLC or some program at OCLC actually searching out "D.Mus." and changing it to "D. Mus."?

Answer: My colleague Robert Bremer occasionally runs a macro to correct such spacings. Here is Robert's explanation. (I had asked him if he based the correction on the example in LCRI 1.7B13, which has the space between Ph. and D.):

> "D. Mus." is one of a whole group of academic degrees where spacing is routinely adjusted via a macro. However, the spacing is determined by RI 1.0C, which would have you treat an abbreviation consisting of more than a single letter as if it were a distinct word, separating it with a space from preceding and succeeding words or initials. Actual usage doesn't figure into it—"Ph. D." for example, is probably more commonly found as "Ph.D." in real life and is actually illustrated that way in rule 2.7B13. The spacing in all these kinds [of] academic degrees have an impact on keyword searching, which has made it worthwhile to periodically run the macro to adjust them.

Newsletter 78 (May 2001)

CONTENTS NOTES

Mini-Lesson

6.9 Nowhere in AACR2 or its Rule Interpretations is there much discussion about the correct construction of formal contents notes, particularly concerning punctuation. The newly published *Notes in the Catalog Record: Based on AACR2 and LC Rule Interpretations*, by Jerry D. Saye and Sherry L. Vellucci (Chicago: American Library Association, 1989), deals with contents notes in admirable depth and with numerous examples. Although there is a wide range of possible combinations, including the incorporation of statements of responsibility, indications of sequence, and certain elements of physical description, a few general types can be distilled.

Individual titles either with or without statements of responsibility arc separated by a space-hyphen-hyphen-space:

505 0   King Porter stomp -- New Orleans joys -- Grandpa's spells -- Kansas City stomp -- Wolverine blues -- The pearls -- Thirty-fifth Street blues / Charles Levy -- Mamanita -- Frog-i-more rag -- London blues -- Tia Juana / Gene Rodernich -- Shreveport stomp -- Mamanita -- Jelly Roll blues -- Big foot ham -- Bucktown blues / Boyd Senter -- Tom cat blues -- Stratford hunch -- Perfect rag.

505 0   G-Dur op. 6 Nr. 1 / Georg Friedrich Handel -- G-Dur Nr. XXI : Propitia sydera / Georg Muffat -- d-Moll op. 3/11 / Antonio Vivaldi -- g-Moll : fatto per la Notte di Natale / Arcangelo Corelli.

505 0   Sonata for cello and piano / Benjamin Lees (28:00) -- Elegy / Gabriel Faure
         (6:12) -- Fantasiestucke, op. 73 / Robert Schumann (10:18).

Titles sharing the same statement of responsibility are separated by a space-
semicolon-space:

505 0   Variazioni su un'aria nazionale di Moore : in re maggiore / F. Chopin --
         Danze spagnole : op. 12 ; Danze polacche : op. 55 / M. Moszkowski.
505 0   Suite no. 1 in E-flat, op. 28, no. 1 / Gustav Holst -- English folk song suite
         ; Toccata marziale : for military band / Ralph Vaughan Williams -- Suite no. 2
         in F, op. 28, no. 2 ; Hammersmith : Prelude and scherzo, op. 52 / Gustav
         Holst.

For multipart works, separate the larger designation (collective title, title
of an opera, volume, etc.) from the individual titles with a period-space:

505 0   6 concerti per l'organo, opus 7. No. 1 in B flat major, HWV 306 (18:50) ;
         No. 2 in A major, HWV 307 (13:09) ; No. 3 in B flat major, HWV 308
         (14:47) ; No. 4 in D minor, HWV 309 (15:55) ; No. 5 in G minor, HWV
         310 (12:06) ; No. 6 in B flat major, HWV 311 (7:55) -- In F major, with-
         out op. no., HWV 295 (13:06) -- In D minor, without op. no., HWV 304
         (11:51).
505 0   Nabucco. Sinfonia -- Luisa Miller. Sinfonia -- La traviata. Preludio Atto I ;
         Preludio Atto III -- I vespri siciliani. Sinfonia -- Un ballo in maschera.
         Preludio Atto I ; Preludio Atto II -- La forza del destino. Sinfonia.

For multivolume items, set apart volumes with space-hyphen-hyphen-
space:

505 0   [1] Nos. 1, 3, 5, and 7 -- [2] Nos. 2, 4, 6, and 8.
505 0   [v. 1] Sonata in G minor, for oboe & continuo, op. 1, no. 6 ; Trio sonata
         no. 2 in D minor, for 2 oboes & continuo ; Sonata in C minor, for oboe
         & continuo, op. 1, no. 8 ; Trio sonata no. 3 in E-flat, for 2 oboes &
         continuo -- v. 2. Trio sonata no. 1 in B flat ; Trio sonata no. 4 in F major
         ; Trio sonata no. 5 in G major ; Trio sonata no. 6 in D major.

Obviously, only a few examples are noted here, though many more complex situations can be dealt with by combinations of these practices. *Newsletter 40 (August 1989)*

Contents Notes Questions and Answers

6.10 QUESTION: We just hit another weird one. In a multivolume set
that is being cataloged on one record (not analyzed), the last volume is titled
Duos. The pieces in this volume are by several different composers. This is

the only volume in the set that has a collective title for the volume. For all the rest, there are just titles of pieces, maybe a half dozen or fewer pieces per volume. Except in the *Duos* volume, there is only one composer per volume. The pattern for all but the last volume is clear:

1. <Title1> ; <Title2> ; . . . / <Composer1> -- 2. <Title4> ; <Title 5> . . . / <Composer2> - - [etc.]

The copy we are using has for v. 8 just

8. Duos / <composer9> ; <composer10> ; <composer11> ; <composer12>

Volume 8, however, consists of 8 titled pieces, and we'd like to include all 8, linked with their proper composers. If there were no overall volume title, we could do

8. <Title12> ; <Title13> / <Composer9>. <Title14> ; <Title15> ; <Title16> / <Composer 10> - - [etc.]

But we can't figure out a way to include the overall title. None of the composers titled his works *Duos*—the editor did that—so it doesn't work to use a <Whole. Part> pattern. We thought of using parentheses somehow, maybe:

8. Duos (<Title12> ; <Title13> / <Composer9. <Title 14> [etc.] . . .).

But we can't find any hint of parentheses being used for anything but performers or durations. Any ideas? We are editing this one, not making a new record, so we've just picked a method and gone with it for local purposes. But we'd like to know how we really should have done it. Thanks for any advice.

Answer: Given that we have only a limited number of punctuation marks at our disposal and an often large number of distinctions we are trying to make with some degree of clarity in a contents note, there are no perfect solutions. Parentheses are not the way to go in this context, since the convention of their use is pretty much limited to performers, durations, and the like, as you've pointed out. Perhaps the cleanest way to cut this particular Gordian knot is to simply continue the same pattern for the final volume and to omit that collective title from the contents note. Then, since this volume is a special case within this set, you could simply add a 500 note that says something like: "Vol. 8 has title: Duos" (or whatever the circumstances happen to be). Since it's such a generic title, you probably don't need a title tracing for it, but that's up to you. *Newsletter 81 (September 2002)*

6.11 QUESTION: I've tried to find a rule I remember from my student days, which I believe was a Music Cataloging Decision about "don't make a contents note if a complete work is presented, and don't provide descriptive information (e.g., song titles)." I'm thinking along the lines of a symphony, string quartet, and so forth, when you only have movements. I've checked Cataloger's Desktop, and am encountering an error when I go to search the MCDs, so while I try and figure out what that problem is, could you help me with finding if this is a real decision that I can reference?

Answer: Going through both the first and second editions of the LCRIs (into which I have MCDs interfiled), and the various separate print versions of the MCDs that I have, I find no such rule under 5.7B18 or 6.7B18. There is a fairly new MCD printed in CSB no. 90 (Fall 2000) pp. 14–15 that says in part, "Use judgment in deciding whether to include in a contents note titles of parts, titles proper of individual works within each part, parallel titles, other title information, statements of responsibility, performers, etc. Take into account the type of music or other recorded sound, the emphasis of the set, the amount of data to be transcribed, and the length, complexity, and readability of the resulting note." For sound recordings at least, that would give you the choice of including or not including the sorts of notes you refer to. *Newsletter 80 (May 2002)*

6.12 QUESTION: One of our paraprofessionals just came up with an interesting dilemma. She is cataloging a multivolume set that includes pieces by various composers. In this instance it is logical to include a contents note (at least for now; we may change our mind if many more volumes come out). It's going something like this:

505 1   V. 1. Aria / Telemann ; Song / Gluck ; Piece / Handel -- V. 2. Another
         song / Vivaldi ; Second aria / Lully ; <and so forth>

Now, in this format, how should she input two pieces in a row by the same composer? If we were using <dash-dash> between titles ordinarily, we could use <space> ; <space> to separate the titles and then follow the second title with / <statement of responsibility>. But since we're already using the <space> ; <space> technique to separate titles (the *volumes* are separated with <dash-dash>), that won't work. We need something to indicate one more step down in the hierarchy, to make the grouping clear.

Answer: There are only so many marks of punctuation, and even fewer that may be used if we are to follow AACR2 and ISBD. You may recall that LC's Deta Davis presented a workshop on contents notes several years ago, and I have incorporated her suggestions (as well as the relatively sparse guidance from AACR2, the LCRIs, and the MCDs) into the section on field 505 in the upcoming second edition of *Music Coding and Tagging*. Here is an excerpt with a related example. This isn't an exact science, of course, and our goal is to emphasize clarity over strict adherence to any vague rules of ISBD punctuation.

For multipart works and multivolume items, separate the larger designation (collective title, act of an opera, volume, etc.) from the individual titles with a period-space; volumes are set apart with a space-hyphen-hyphen-space.

505 0   v. 1. Aria, gavotte and variations, gigue / Elisabetta de Gambarini. Sonata in F major / Maria Hester Park. Lesson VI in D major / a lady -- v. 2. Sonata in A major / Marianne Martinez. Sonata in C major / Maria Hester Park.

Using your example, I've added two works by the same composer to show what that would look like.

505 1   V. 1. Aria / Telemann. Song / Gluck. Piece / Handel -- V. 2. Another song / Vivaldi. Second aria / Lully -- V. 3. First work ; Second work / Bach. First work ; Second work / Quantz.

That makes the hierarchy fairly clear without being too cluttered. *Newsletter 78 (May 2001)*

6.13 QUESTION: I have some CDs with blues music. Here is one that I have in our save file:

511 0   Various artists.
500   Compact disc.
505 0   Why are people like that? / Junior Wells (3:52) -- Credit card blues / Terry Evans (4:45) -- Misery and the blues / Maria Muldaur (4:22) -- Life will be better / Sugar Ray Norcia, Charlie Musselwhite (5:19) -- So mean to me / Luther "Guitar Junior" Johnson (5:09) -- Money / Debbie Davies, Kenny Neal (4:45) -- Love had a breakdown / Son Seals (5:21) -- Killed the goose that laid the golden egg / Kenny Neal (4:17) -- How do I tell my little sister / Lady Bianca (5:01) -- Somebody gotta do it / Sam Lay (3:09) -- If the sea was whiskey / Willie Dixon Tribute (4:21) -- Brutal hearted woman / John Primer (5:00) -- Hen house / Marty Grebb (3:43).

The question I pose is the following: I have listed the 511 as "various artists". I could list them on each piece in the 505. That follows 6.7B18 and 6.7B10 (LCRI) for duration. But the problem is that each piece has four or more performers different from the other. It seems to be a compilation recording or promotional recording. So, your opinion—what would you do? Leave it as is or extend the 505 information out further yet?

Answer: You'll have to judge how important the information is and weigh that against record and field size limitations. You are certainly allowed to delineate the performers for each individual cut parenthetically (usually after the composer's name and before the separately parenthetical duration). But if this leads to an unbearably long 505 or one that becomes so complex that it's no longer clear, you might want to stick with the "Various performers" 511 field. You also have the option of being selective, listing only the featured performer(s) on each track, if that's appropriate. *Newsletter 77 (November 2000)*

6.14 QUESTION: The Art Section of a large public library wants over 450 titles (about 20 screens of 505s) keyed into an existing record so that every title in this set will be indexed in the online catalog. Is this sort of thing done? Occasionally we enter song titles in 505s, but this request is for every title in every songbook and CD set to be put into the MARC records. I'm at a bit of a loss to explain why this is a distorted use of the MARC record, poor cataloging practice, and a possible cause of carpal tunnel syndrome among our Library Technicians. Just because it can be done to provide keyword access to titles is not the best reason for doing it. Suppose we could scan the titles from the packaging? There's also the consideration of impact on current cataloging production and limits to field length. I've suggested alternatives to such extensive indexing in the MARC record (conversion of the local card file to a separate database, or a separate song index on a locally maintained database, or a partial listing of contents), to no avail. We've also pointed out that, since the set says it includes "all known recordings," there's no reason to particularize. Might this be the direction in which MARC records are going?

Answer: In trying to add such a contents note to the OCLC record, one would quickly run up against one or another of the system limits for the number of characters per field (1,230 maximum), the number of variable fields per record (approximately 50), and the number of characters per record (4,096 maximum). Additionally, the Library of Congress Rule Interpretation for AACR2 2.7B18 (covering contents notes, generally) gives some guidelines about formulating notes that are much more restrictive than is being suggested in your message. One legitimate possibility that might help would be to enter a separate bibliographic record for each of the 24 volumes (or some other sensible breakdown of the volumes), with a complete contents note for each (if it does not exceed system limitations). OCLC allows such "analytic" records. *Newsletter 74 (November 1999)*

6.15 QUESTION: I have noticed that when viewing an OCLC record for a CD with a collection of songs on it, I have seen it recorded in the 505 field in two ways: title / performer and title (performer). Which is the correct way?

Answer: As you can imagine, the permutations of recording titles, composers, performers, and other information in contents notes are vast. Deta Davis of the Library of Congress devoted an entire session to contents notes at the Music OCLC Users Group annual meeting in Boston, February 1998. You can find a summary of the session in the *MOUG Newsletter* no. 70 (September 1998) pp. 20–21. The short answer to your question, though, is that performers are placed in parentheses. Schematically, it looks like this:

505 0   Title / Composer (Performer) -- Title / Composer (Performer ; Performer
        ; Performer).
505 0   Title (Performer) -- Title (Performer ; Performer ; Performer).

Newsletter 72 (May 1999)

6.16 QUESTION: I have a question about transcribing asterisks used in expletives when contributing records to OCLC. On a compact disc in hand, a song title includes the word BULLSH—TIN'. On the program notes the word is transcribed as I just wrote. On the compact disc itself, dots replace the dashes. Should I use dashes, asterisks, blank spaces, or something else?

Answer: Since the disc (label) itself is generally the preferred source for contents note information, I'd suggest transcribing the title exactly as it appears there. *Newsletter 70 (September 1998)*

6.17 QUESTION: Is it OK to add the word "medley" in parenthesis in the 505 field after each of the two medleys (three songs each, two occurrences) in the 505 for a CD? Also, the two medleys (out of 15 songs) contain songs by different composers, and we would like to add statement of responsibility information. Is it common to list individual medley titles together in the 505 like this: Song/Song/Song without spaces between the slashes? If we did that, we couldn't do the statement of responsibility until the end of the three songs, and they each have different authors. This particular CD is a religious singing group doing religious/gospel songs, and our problem here is creating the 505 with these little medleys and different composers.

Answer: As far as I'm aware, there is no standard convention for medleys such as these. So let's make things up as we go along, shall we? If there is a collective title for the medley, which doesn't sound like the case here (or if you can formulate some sensible and useful one, which may or may not be the case), you could do something like this:

505 0   Medley one. Title A / Statement of Responsibility ; Title B / Statement of
         Responsibility ; Title C / Statement of Responsibility -- [Supplied medley
         title]. Title X / Statement of Responsibility ; Title Y / Statement of Re-
         sponsibility ; Title Z / Statement of Responsibility -- Non-medley title W
         / Statement of Responsibility.

Come to think of it, even if there is no logical medley title to supply, you
could do the same thing with just the pseudo-collective title of "[Medley]"
prefacing the string of individual titles. Alternatively, you could simply list
the titles and statements of responsibility without the fake collective title. The
parenthetical "(medley)" bothers me a little, but mostly aesthetically. I'm not
sure where you might put it that it would clearly convey the fact that it's
modifying a string rather than simply the title it follows.

505 0   Title A / Statement of Responsibility ; Title B / Statement of Responsibil-
         ity ; Title C / Statement of Responsibility -- Non-medley title D / State-
         ment of Responsibility -- Title X / Statement of Responsibility ; Title Y /
         Statement of Responsibility ; Title Z / Statement of Responsibility -- Non-
         medley title W / Statement of Responsibility.

In this version, the punctuation would serve to differentiate the medleys from
the non-medleys, with space-semicolon-space between titles in the same
medley and space-hyphen-hyphen-space between the medleys and separate
titles. I'd say the parenthetical "(medley)" isn't really necessary. *Newsletter
70 (September 1998)*

6.18 QUESTION: AACR2R 5.7B18 reads, "If the works in a collection
are all in the same musical form and that form is named in the title proper
of the item, do not repeat the musical form in the titles in the contents note."
Rule 6.7B18 doesn't refer to this. Can we apply 5.7B18 in cataloging sound
recordings? I understand that the rules proceed from the general to the specific in AACR2 and that we have to consult Chapter 1 as well as Chapter 6
in cataloging sound recordings. Generally speaking, can we consult Chapter 5 (Music) in cataloging sound recordings and the other way round?

   Answer: Borrowing concepts from one chapter of AACR2 to use in another is a time-honored and often useful practice. It is also in keeping with
one of the cardinal principles of the rules, that of trying to treat all types of
materials alike as much as possible. This borrowing is supported by a passage in Rule 0.23: "Use the chapters in part I alone or in combination as
the specific problem demands." Why this particular (and common) circumstance was brought up in reference to scores but not sound recordings is
anyone's guess, but you can safely apply the idea to contents notes in both
formats. *Newsletter 69 (April 1998)*

6.19 QUESTION: It seems a particular idiosyncrasy of recordings (and specifically for those of popular music) to have on the label something like: *People will say we're in love* (Rodgers-Hammerstein) and I have been dutifully transcribing the 505 as:

People will say we're in love / Rodgers ; Hammerstein.

with a semicolon separating the two names because I happen to know Rodgers has the role of composer and Hammerstein the lyricist on this particular song. Isn't this what we do in 245? Are we not to do this in the 505? Have I been leading our patrons astray all these years? If I do not know what function the various people have, whether both/all folks named are in effect a composing and writing team without separate roles in the process (and if I do not have my administration's blessing to take the time to find out), I have been fudging and simply separating the names by a comma (e.g., "You must have been a beautiful baby / Mercer, Goodman."). I am loathe to keep the thing "Mercer-Goodman" or "Mercer/Goodman" because that is an honor I think reserved for the Mendelssohn-Bartholdys of the world. Then of course, we see animals like "Tilton-Field-Jones." It certainly does not affect access or anything. In short, do you recommend keeping the hyphens between names as they appear on the label or container? And/or do you separate roles of responsibility by a semicolon?

Answer: The rules for statements of responsibility (composers and lyricists, primarily) in contents notes are pretty much the same as those for statements of responsibility in the title field. Rule 1.7A3 says in part, "If data in a note correspond to data found in the title and statement of responsibility . . . give the elements of the data in the order in which they appear in those areas. In such a case, use prescribed punctuation. . . ." LCRI 2.7B18 also gives some details on creating formal contents notes. We may also refer back to the rules on statements of responsibility (6.1F, 1.1F) for guidance on how to formulate such statements. If the item says only "Rodgers-Hammerstein" or "Tilton-Field-Jones", you would transcribe them with space-semicolon-space, just as you would in the 245 field. This prescribed punctuation would properly be substituted for the hyphens or slashes. The relationship(s) between the name(s) and the title may be further clarified if you wish (and if you have the information, room, time, and patience) by bracketed explanations, but that's probably going beyond the call of duty.

505 0   Do-re-mi / Rodgers ; Hammerstein -- Blues in the night / Mercer ; Arlen. . . .

or (for the ambitious or obsessive)

505 0   Do-re-mi / [music by] Rodgers ; [lyrics by] Hammerstein -- Blues in the
        night / [lyrics by] Mercer ; [music by] Arlen. . . .

Of course with keyword indexing, access could be affected by how 505s are
transcribed. *Newsletter 69 (April 1998)*

6.20 QUESTION: According to MCD 5.7B10, we are now to indicate durations in nautical time in 500 notes. How does this square with transcribing information as it appears on the item (spelled out, etc., as appropriate)
in the 505 note? Seems a bit inconsistent, no?

   Answer: Music Cataloging Decision 6.7B10 (and MCD 6.7B18, which
says "For the forms of durations recorded in a formal contents note, see
MCD 6.7B10") is pretty clear: "In a statement of duration in the note area,
separate the digits representing hours, minutes, and seconds by colons. If a
duration is expressed in seconds only, precede it by a colon." Durations are
represented in the form "HH:MM:SS" in both 500 and 505 notes. *Newsletter 69 (April 1998)*

6.21 QUESTION: I'd like to suggest music sound recordings contents
notes conventions as a topic for an upcoming *Newsletter*. I've always pro-
ceeded on the assumption that performers included in contents notes were
given in parentheses and that the "/ [name]" configuration was reserved for
composers. I've noticed that quite a few OCLC records for popular music
titles that are collections featuring a number of different performers (511
note usually reads "Various performers") cite the performers as if they were
composers. It is tedious to change these to the correct format, and it would
be nice if this erroneous style of input could be eliminated altogether through
a little friendly education.

   Answer: Back in *MOUG Newsletter* no. 40 (August 1989, p. 7), we had
a mini-lesson on contents notes. As I noted all those years ago, there is not
much guidance beyond the example in AACR2 rule 6.7B18 about exactly
how to construct these notes. But you have captured the essence in your
question. The schematic construction would be:

505 0   First title / First Composer (Performer, instrument ; Performer, instrument)
        -- Second title / Second Composer (Performer, instrument).

   Where titles and performers are noted without mention of the composer,
performers are still set off in parentheses following the title; slashes are not
used.

505 0   First title (Performer, instrument ; Performer, instrument) -- Second title
        (Performer, instrument).

With popular musics especially, performers may be mentioned without instrumentation, of course (see OCLC #35177019). That's also part of the problem and why people may get confused: differentiating composers from performers with popular musics. Performers (even ensembles) may actually *be* the composers; generally though, it's preferable to treat performers as performers. Two good examples of the "serious" idiom are OCLC #30516770 (though the punctuation within the performers' statements is open to dispute) and #15859320. *Newsletter 65 (November 1996)*

6.22 QUESTION: When a cataloger chooses a source other than the disc or cassette label as the chief source, perhaps because it offers a collective title, does that mean that any other information taken from that source does not need the source indicated because it is now the chief source? What I mean is: Suppose you have decided that the chief source will be the container. If there is information on the container that you want to quote in a 500 note, do you then not need to indicate the source as container, because it has become the chief source?

Answer: When you are making a quoted note, I think you always need to indicate its source unless it is the chief source (according to Rule 1.7A3). Saying that the title comes from somewhere other than the chief source doesn't make that place the chief source, any more than calling a tail a leg makes a horse a "quintraped." *Newsletter 64 (August 1996)*

6.23 QUESTION: Is it correct to place musical performers' names in the 505 rather than in a separate 511, for a multi-performer collection with a collective title? This does increase the length of the record, especially with all the analytics.

Answer: You have various options on performers' names. If it's all too complicated, you can use a general 511 to mention the principal performers. If you feel the need to outline exactly who performs what work, the names can be scattered throughout the 505, as appropriate. If you hit up against system limits, you might need to reconsider the method chosen. *Newsletter 63 (May 1996)*

6.24 QUESTION: Is there ever a time when titles in the 505 are traced in 740s, at least according to national standards? My understanding is that is not done with any format, and I have found nothing in any of the various manuals that recommend using 740s for titles in the 505. I am also, however, seeing lots of records online that do that. I realize that libraries may choose to do it for various good local reasons, but I just wanted to nail down what the national standard may be.

Answer: There is no explicit national standard on tracing titles in contents notes, as far as I am aware. RI 21.30J, however, in the midst of its guidelines about title added entries, does state, "When in doubt, it is best to be liberal in assigning additional title added entries." We permit our members to trace titles from 505s, though we would prefer that only distinctive titles be so traced (that is, tracing titles such as *Symphony no. 3* would be meaningless). In fact, many users object when LC records come along and wipe out such entries.

As long as only distinctive titles are traced and system limits are not exceeded, there is no objection to titles from contents notes being traced. *Newsletter 60 (April 1995)*

6.25 QUESTION: My question concerns a contents note to be added to a master record as a "database enrichment." The record is pre-AACR2 cataloging. I understand that the contents note has the individual titles separated by "period-dash-dash." What about cases where durations are readily available: Can they be included in the format "(MM:SS)"?

505 0   Elegy (9:07). -- Memory (10.23). -- . . . <etc.>

Is there any rule precluding this practice?

Answer: In AACR1 252F7 and 252F10, the only provision for durations in Sound Recordings is in a separate note, in the form:

Durations: 9 min., 7 sec.; 10 min., 23 sec.; <etc.>

It's a bit unwieldy, to be sure, but those were the rules, pre-AACR2. Of course, you can't add a 500 note as a database enrichment. The format you've suggested mixes pre-AACR2 and AACR2, a practice I don't generally advocate. With the automatic transfer of certain fields during merges, however, such mixing can occur, so it isn't exactly unheard of. Let your Anglo-American Conscience Regulator (AACR) be your guide. *Newsletter 60 (April 1995)*

6.26 QUESTION: In a contents note, when you have several pieces by the same author and then durations, does one put " -- " between the individual pieces:

The magic flute -- Birds -- Wings / Stravinsky.

or

The magic flute / Stravinsky -- Birds / Stravinsky -- Wings / Stravinsky.

or

The magic flute / Stravinsky (2:03) -- Birds / Stravinsky (1:02) -- Wings / Stravinsky (5:03).

or

The magic flute (2:03) ; Birds (1:02) ; Wings (5:03) / Stravinsky.

Obviously, the examples are just made up, but do I have to repeat "Stravinsky" for each of the works? Is the punctuation " -- " between each work or ";"?

Answer: The details of contents note punctuation are not enumerated in AACR2, any Rule Interpretations, or Music Cataloging Decisions, but they correspond roughly to the rules for the title and statement of responsibility area. This is one of those cases where, for specific details, you have to resort to "cataloging by example." Jerry D. Saye and Sherry L. Vellucci's *Notes in the Catalog Record* (Chicago: ALA, 1989) yields a relevant example, 18.450, which is from LCCN 83-750380/R/r91 (#13147307). Your own final example would be the way to go. A space-semicolon-space separates titles sharing the same statement of responsibility; a space-hyphen-hyphen-space separates titles and statements of responsibility from others with different statements of responsibility.

505 0   Title (X:XX) ; Title (X:XX) / Composer One -- Title (XX:XX) ; Title (X:XX) / Composer Two -- Title / Composer Three (X:XX).

If, as in your own fictional example, *all* the works are by the same composer and that composer is the main entry of the record, you need not repeat the name in the contents note. In that case, the titles (none of which would have statements of responsibility) would be separated by space-hyphen-hyphen-space.

100 1   Composer, Only.
245 10 Collective title / $c Only Composer.
505 0   Title one (X:XX) -- Title two (X:XX) -- Title three (X:XX) -- Title four (X:XX).

LC has not been consistent in its formulation of contents notes, so when things get convoluted, the object is to be as clear as possible. *Newsletter 55 (August 1993)*

ENHANCED CONTENTS NOTES

6.27 QUESTION: What are our responsibilities in regard to "enhanced" contents notes? For the record in question, we have several more volumes to add. We would like to update the 505 field, but creating "enhanced" contents has not yet been our practice. Are we obliged to add subfielded contents information or can we add the new volumes in "basic style" and change the second indicator in 505? Or is a mixed practice not allowed, so that we should remove the formatting from volume 1 as well?

Answer: What we would prefer is for you to remove the "enhanced" subfielding from the existing text, add the remaining contents information in the "basic" style, and change the second indicator, so that the resulting note is entirely in the "basic" style. *Newsletter 80 (May 2002)*

6.28 QUESTION: This question is about using the "enhanced" contents notes for 505 where there is a title and part-title. Would the proper form for this case be "$t Title. $t Part-title / $r Composer" with each title in a separate subfield t. Or would it be proper to put both into a single subfield t: "$t Title. Part-title / $r Composer." The question came up when I used record #40393358. "Live in Italy" [sound recording].

Answer: As I understand it, each adjacent title element would be in its own subfield $t, so your first schematic version would be correct. *Newsletter 72 (May 1999)*

6.29 QUESTION: When the second indicator in the 505 field is coded "0" (for "enhanced" contents note), how does the field display in WorldCat? For example in BF&S p. 5:13, would "$t Blue like an orange / $r Michael Daugherty" display "Blue like an orange" as an additional title on WorldCat? Could Michael Daugherty, similarly, be searchable as an additional author? (This doesn't seem plausible, with his last name last.)

Answer: In OCLC, the 505 field displays just as it is input, with or without the "enhanced" subfielding. The titles are not included in the derived title index (that is, "3,2,2,1"), nor are the names included in the derived personal name index ("4,3,1"). Right now, only the subfield $a in the 505 is included in the Notes (nt) and Subject/Title/Contents (st) keyword indexes, but keyword indexing is currently under revision and will be expanded to include subfields $t and $r in the near future. Local systems can (theoretically) manipulate and index the "enhanced" 505s to their heart's content (if local systems can be said to have hearts). There's much more detail on all of this in OCLC's *Searching for Bibliographic Records* both in print and online (http://www.oclc.org/worldcat/searching/guide/). *Newsletter 72 (May 1999)*

6.30 QUESTION: Because of time and money pressures, I don't often have time to do complete tracings for composers and uniform titles for sound recordings. Instead, we rely on the 505, often using the "enhanced" contents note subfielding. What's your reaction to that? Do those subfields $t automatically disregard the articles?

Answer: As far as "enhanced" contents notes are concerned, different systems could be designed to do different things with all of that subfielding. There may be systems that can ignore initial articles in the 505, but I'm not aware of any. As a matter of fact, in OCLC, only 505 subfield $a is indexed for keyword searches at the present time (see the recent *Searching for Bibliographic Records* document). Because the 505 subfields $t, $r, and $g are fairly recent additions to the format, you should make sure that your own local system knows what to do with them. Under no circumstances should you think of the "enhanced" contents note as a substitute for title or name/ title added entries where they are appropriate. *Newsletter 69 (April 1998)*

6.31 QUESTION: About the 505, if either the basic or enhanced option is acceptable, why would one choose the latter? It takes a lot more time.

Answer: With the (theoretically) growing sophistication of local systems, the enhanced 505 was designed to allow improved access and greater differentiation among titles, names, and miscellaneous information in the future. The names and titles are uncontrolled, of course, and so don't benefit from any authority control. Unless your local system can now (or in the future might be able to) access such information and tell the difference by subfield coding, you will probably not want to bother with the enhanced 505. *Newsletter 62 (November 1995)*

COPY BEING DESCRIBED

6.32 QUESTION: Many of the items in question are signed by Sousa at the end. If I make a 500 note to indicate that the work is signed, do I use quotation marks? For instance:

500   Signed at end: "J. P. Sousa, Washington D.C., March 14th 1905."

or are the quotation marks superfluous?

Answer: As I read the rule 1.7A3 on "Quotations," if you are formulating a note as you have with an introductory phrase, you would not use quotation marks. *Newsletter 74 (November 1999)*

IN ANALYTICS

6.33 QUESTION: Are "In-Analytics" still acceptable? I have a collection of sixteenth- through nineteenth-century songs, most of which appear in no other source, for which I need to provide direct access to each item. We have expanded NOTIS so that I could add the 71 added entries, but, of course, OCLC could not accept such a record. The only alternative I can think of is the "In-Analytic". As I was searching the OCLC manual, however, I could find nothing about this practice (especially since I expected to find a special 5XX field for the "in" note). Is this still acceptable, and, if so, are there any special considerations, other than AACR2 rules, that I need to know?

Answer: In-Analytics are still acceptable when appropriate, but as LCRI 13.5 suggests, they should be used only in special cases. There is a brief section in the introductory part of *Bibliographic Formats and Standards*, 2nd ed., p. 36, that deals with them. You'll also need to look at field 773 and review AACR2R Chapter 13. A few things to remember about In-Analytics: If there is no record for the host item, you should create one along with the Analytics (and cite it in the analytical 773s). It isn't necessary to analyze every element in the host item; you may be selective, if you wish. You should omit the 260 unless the information would differ from that found in the 773 subfield $d. Since you will be creating a large number of records that will have at least some common information (the fixed field, some of the notes and subject headings, and the 773), I'd suggest using the constant data capability (described in *Cataloging User Guide*, 2nd ed., Chapter 7). It'll save you lots of typing. Depending on the host item you're cataloging, there may be another alternative to Analytics. If the item has some sort of logical subdivisions (volumes, chapters, etc.), you might be able to catalog each of those subdivisions separately and link them with "With" notes (as we commonly did with sound recordings, pre-AACR2). That is a sort of funky way to do it, but sometimes, desperate scores call for desperate measures. *Newsletter 69 (November 1997)*

6.34 QUESTION: In cataloging a volume of two different scores bound together, I noticed that AACR2, 1988 rev. 5.7B21 has an example with only the titles proper and statement of responsibility. Referring back to 2.7B21, the examples also have the publication information. Should I include the publication information in a score "With" note?

Answer: Remember that (as 0.14 in the introduction to AACR2 says) the examples "are illustrative and not prescriptive. That is, they illuminate the provisions of the rule to which they are attached, rather than extend those provisions. Do not take the examples or the form in which they are presented as instructions unless specifically told to do so by the accompanying text." Instead, go back to 1.7B21, specifically to its Rule Interpretation, which says, "For each item listed in a 'With' note, give the title proper (or uniform title if one has been assigned), the statement of responsibility, and the entire publication, distribution, etc. area. . . . Use ISBD punctuation, except omit the period-space-dash-space between areas." The RI itself no longer says it explicitly, but also add information that the works were bound together subsequent to publication. *Newsletter 40 (August 1989)*

CHAPTER 7

Subject Access

INTRODUCTION

Questions about subject access generally get us away from AACR2 and into the intricacies of the *Library of Congress Subject Headings*, the *Subject Cataloging Manual*, and the various classification schemes. (Because I consider many such questions to be matters of local policy, however, I have tended to avoid addressing those about classification schemes.) Geographic, chronological, form/genre, and other types of subject heading subdivisions are often matters of contention for scores and sound recordings.

SUBJECT HEADINGS

7.1 QUESTION: When I use the "pp" in "Comp" is it necessary to use the 650 Popular music or is the 650 Rap (Music) enough? And a source would help.

Answer: Remember that the Composition codes are optional. Even more important, many local systems cannot do anything very useful with them, as opposed to formal subject headings, which most systems *can* do something with. One of the main tenets of subject cataloging is to "Assign headings that are as specific as the topics they cover." (The definitive word on assigning subject headings is in LC's *Subject Cataloging Manual* [the current 5th edition, with updates], "Assigning and Constructing Subject Headings" SCM H 180. Generally, when you have an LC subject heading, such as "Rap (Music)," that specifically covers the genre, you don't need to have a more general heading such as "Popular music" as well (since this relationship is dealt with through reference to the LC Subject Headings list, the subject authority file, or whatever local means you may have). You needn't worry about any one-to-one correspondence between a more specific subject heading and a more general Composition code. Think of the subject headings and the Composition codes as related but separate means of expressing musical forms, genres, and other categories. Given that there are only a few dozen Composition codes but countless existing (and possible) musical subject headings, it's no surprise that the latter can be much more specific than the former. *Newsletter 81 (September 2002)*

7.2 QUESTION: We're having a bit of trouble interpreting AACR2. Who should get the main entry on a tribute album, the original performer or the person performing on the tribute album? AACR2 (21.23B1) gives the example of Woody Guthrie, performed by Arlo Guthrie, and gives Woody as main entry. But, he also wrote the songs. What about when the original performer did not write the songs? A lot of popular music is not actually written by the performer. Any tips you can provide would be appreciated.

Answer: As I interpret the rules, LCRIs, and MCDs for 21.23, I don't see how the object of a tribute album, who is neither a performer on the present recording nor the composer of the works (or most of the works) performed, can possibly be the main entry. To quote LCRI 21.23C in part, ". . . understand 'performer' in 21.23C1 to mean a person or corporate body whose performance is heard on the sound recording." If there *were* a principal performer (or two or three), as defined by LCRI 21.23C, that performer (or the first) could be the main entry. If there were four or more principal performers, as is often the case with tribute albums, one would go with a title main entry. An added entry for the object of the tribute would certainly be appropriate, in the spirit of 21.30F1. And a subject entry would also make sense. *Newsletter 80 (May 2002)*

7.3 QUESTION: The subdivisions for popular music, jazz, rock music, and similar headings include both geographic and chronological subdivisions. Geographic subdivisions can be assigned to these headings except for those listed under LC *Subject Heading Manual* H 1916.5 and the authority records for those headings that indicate this in the geographic subdivision byte of the fixed fields. The authority records established for the subject heading subdivided by decade (e.g., Popular music -- 1911–1920) indicate that these headings are not to be subdivided geographically, that is, this byte is blank. However, general practice seems to be that the place is included (e.g., Popular music -- France -- 1911–1920). LC's *Subject Heading Manual* H 1916.5 gives instructions for geographic and chronological subdivision, but does not specifically indicate that the two are to be combined, nor are the decade subdivisions considered free-floating or pattern subdivisions, as far as I can tell. It makes sense that subject headings of the pattern, Popular music --

1911–1920, would not be geographically subdivided, because that would violate the [Topic]--[Place]--[Date] order established for subject headings by placing the place after the date (e.g., Popular music--1911–1920--France). If the instructions in H 1916.5 were followed precisely, it would appear that two subject headings should be applied (Popular music--France and Popular music--1911–1920) to express the concept, Popular music--France--1911–1920. Is there any rule or policy that confirms the use of headings such as Popular music--France--1911–1920? There are clearly advantages for users both ways. I guess what confuses me about these headings is that the authority records for the Popular music--1911–1920 type headings do prohibit geographic subdivision.

Answer: When it comes to subject heading subdivisions, the philosophy that seems to work is: That which is not forbidden is permitted. As far as I can find, there's nothing in SCM H 1916.5 that says not to combine geographic and chronological subdivisions in these instances (except, by implication, those that cannot be subdivided by "United States"). In fact, Section 3 of H 1916.5—which reads in part "Use geographic and period subdivisions for all items to which the subdivisions apply, collections and separate works"—seems to say it's OK. If we probe further and more generally, we find in H 1916.3, Section 3.j, "In general, geographic subdivisions are added to music subject headings according to the provisions of H 690 through H 1055." That leads me to H 860 and H 870, both of which refer to the "[topic]--[place]--[chronology]--[form]" pattern that has been adopted as widely as possible since 1992. There are numerous recent LC music bibliographic records that reflect the "[topic]--[place]--[chronology]" pattern for popular, jazz, and rock musics.

Popular music $z Hawaii $y 1991–2000. (OCLC #44702386; LCCN 00-528037)
Popular instrumental music $z Norway $y 1991–2000. (OCLC #45486874; LCCN 00-726236)
Popular music $z Colombia $y 1991–2000. (OCLC #45487587; LCCN 99-490651)
Jazz $z Germany $y 1991–2000. (OCLC #38496386; LCCN 97-708782)
Rock music $z Mexico $y 1991–2000. (OCLC #36982793; LCCN 97-751261)
Rock music $z Czech Republic $y 1991–2000. (OCLC #34115461; LCCN 96-70048)

Although the popular/jazz/rock headings subdivided chronologically prohibit further subdivision by geographic area (that is, geographic subdivisions *following* the chronological subdivision), the root headings (Popular music [sh85088865], Jazz [sh85069833], and Rock music [sh85114675]) all allow geographic subdivision directly following the heading proper but *before* any chronological subdivision. So, I think the rules do, in fact, allow these formulations. *Newsletter 78 (May 2001)*

7.4 QUESTION: Which subject heading would be more appropriate for a CD of, say, a jazz saxophonist with rhythm section: "Saxophone music (Jazz)" or "Saxophone with jazz ensemble"?

Answer: According to LC's *Subject Cataloging Manual* (H 1916.5), such headings as "[Instrument] music (Jazz)" may be used for solo instrumental jazz or "to bring out featured instruments in ensembles on recordings, either real (in the recording itself) or advertised (on the record jacket for promotional purposes." "[Instrument] with jazz ensemble" and "Concertos ([Instrument] with jazz ensemble)" are used when "a solo instrument is accompanied by a jazz ensemble." It sounds like either heading or both headings would be perfectly appropriate. *Newsletter 75 (May 2000)*

7.5 QUESTION: When is a song not a song? I have a couple of collections of instrumental versions of Hebrew and Yiddish songs. Do I still use the subjects "Songs, Hebrew" and "Songs, Yiddish"? If not, what would I use?

Answer: Check out the subject heading subdivision "Instrumental settings" (sh99001570, sh85066779, and in the LC *Subject Cataloging Manual*). *Newsletter 74 (November 1999)*

7.6 QUESTION: I'm a little confused about geographical subdivisions. I've seen on some records that "$z United States" is added when the music is sung/produced in the United States regardless of the origin of the music. My instinct would be that if people in the United States were singing European songs to either indicate the European country/region or leave off the geographic subdivision altogether. Any words of wisdom on this?

Answer: The best guidance on this is LC's *Subject Cataloging Manual*, especially H 1916.3, H 1916.5, and H 1917. SCM H 1916.3 Section 3j specifically addresses geographic subdivisions, referring to other parts of the manual. Usually if the item itself calls attention to a national, ethnic, or religious aspect of the music (in the title, series, etc.), subject headings to bring that out are appropriate. Subdividing everything by "United States" is neither helpful nor appropriate. *Newsletter 74 (November 1999)*

7.7 QUESTION: If a musical sound recording was originally released in 1965 on LP, then rereleased in 1992 on CD, what dates go in subfield $y of the 650: Jazz $y 1961–1970, or Jazz $y 1991–2000?

Answer: The chronological subdivision for a music heading (650 subfield $y) should be based on the date of the original recording (the original capture), if that can be determined or estimated. That may not necessarily be the same as the date of original release, remember. *Newsletter 67 (August 1997)*

7.8 QUESTION: Should the heading "Rock music" be coded as a 650 subject heading or as a 655 genre heading?

Answer: The Library of Congress Subject Heading "Rock music" (and its various subdivisions) should be coded as 650, second indicator "0". Genre headings should also come from similarly controlled lists. If you don't have a copy of the *USMARC Code List for Relators, Sources, Description Conventions* (LC, 1997), you should. You can get more information about it on the MARC Home Page, http://lcweb.loc.gov/marc/ and there is an online version available at gopher://marvel.loc.gov:70/00/.listarch/usmarc/ relators.txt. It lists the legitimate sources for genre terms; LCSH happens to be one of them. The definition of "genre" in terms of cataloging is much more narrow, however, than it is in everyday speech. So not every LC heading will be a valid genre term. You might take a look at how USMARC defines the 655 field. The music thesaurus currently being compiled will likely have legitimate genre terms, but that's in the future. *Newsletter 67 (August 1997)*

7.9 QUESTION: How should I code the second indicator for a subject heading that I have created following both the patterns in LCSH and the rules in the *Subject Cataloging Manual*, but does not appear in the subject authority file? Furthermore, how do I contact LC or a SACO library to try to get the heading established?

Answer: If you formulate a heading in accordance with LCSH and the *Subject Cataloging Manual* (including any of the millions of music heading permutations that could fill another four red books), you can regard it as LCSH form and code the second indicator as "0". Here's an excerpt from the LC Cataloging Directorate Home Page (http://lcweb.loc.gov/catdir) about where to address questions:

For MARC tagging and inputting, descriptive and subject cataloging (serials and monographs), LC Subject Headings, or LC classification matters, contact:

Barbara Tillett
Chief, Cataloging Policy and Support Office (CPSO)
Library of Congress
Washington, D.C. 20540-5017
cpso@mail.loc.gov<address>

The Program for Cooperative Cataloging Home Page (http:// www.loc.gov/catdir/pcc/) has a SACO section that includes forms for

LCSH Subject Authority proposals and heading change proposals. *Newsletter 66 (May 1997)*

7.10 QUESTION: There are thousands of bib records in the OLUC for music sound recordings with the 650: "Compact discs." Although this is an LC subject heading, the use of it in this situation is incorrect. The scope note in the LC authority record says the heading only applies to works about compact discs. What is most interesting is that in some cases the heading has been added to DLC/DLC records. Can anything be done to stop this practice, at least as far as DLC/DLC records are concerned?

Answer: You're absolutely correct about this being an incorrect application of the LC subject heading "Compact discs." The actual authority record scope note reads, "Here are entered works on small optical disks in general as well as audio compact discs." In other words, the heading is properly used for works *about* audio and optical compact discs, not on records for the discs themselves. Libraries that choose to apply the heading incorrectly should edit the records for their own use and *not* add the heading to the master record in the OLUC. If you happen to be "enhancing" or otherwise upgrading a record that has the heading incorrectly applied, please feel free to remove the heading. *Newsletter 65 (November 1996)*

7.11 QUESTION: When there is a subject heading such as "Guitar music, Arranged", does it mean it is music written for the guitar but arranged for some other form, or does it mean music written for some other instrument which has been arranged for the guitar? I have studied some records I have access to, and can't be sure if I understand how they are using them, or even if they are correct themselves.

Answer: LC Subject Headings formulated in this manner refer to the medium arranged *for*. In this case, it would be music originally composed for some other medium, arranged for guitar. *Newsletter 65 (November 1996)*

7.12 QUESTION: I have seen several records here and there that have as a 650 "Audiocassettes" or "Videocassettes" (not in the same record, of course). Is that correct?

Answer: Unless the audiocassette or video is *about* audiocassettes or videos, those are not correct uses of the subject headings, assuming that we're talking about 650s with second indicator "0" for LCSH. *Newsletter 64 (August 1996)*

7.13 QUESTION: While I understand that "$x Scores" is inappropriate for subject analysis of a piece for a single instrument, is it correct to assign this subdivision to headings of the form "Songs (High voice) with piano"?

Answer: The subdivision "Scores" (and most of the other such musical format subdivisions) are not to be used under categories of works that are generally published in only one format, such as hymns, solo instrumental works, songs, vocal ensembles, and the like (*Subject Cataloging Manual* H 1160). It should not be used under the heading you've mentioned. *Newsletter 60 (April 1995)*

7.14 QUESTION: Another question about musical format subdivisions: The musical format subdivisions cannot be doubled up, right? For example, "Concertos (Violin) $x Solo with piano" cannot further be subdivided using "$x Scores and parts"?

Answer: "Doubling up" the format subdivisions is generally not done. Looking at a bunch of LC records, I find that they use the subdivision "Solo with piano" both when the item is a score alone (with the ensemble arranged for piano) (87-751358) and when the item is a score with part(s) (89-750066). *Newsletter 60 (April 1995)*

7.15 QUESTION: Am I correct in assuming that the term "Arranged" is used in a subject heading to qualify the current form rather than the original? For example, a Haydn trio for baritone, viola, and bass arranged for three guitars should have "Trios (Guitars (3)), Arranged" rather than "String trios (Baryton, viola, double bass), Arranged"?

Answer: Yes, "Arranged" is used to qualify the medium arranged *to* (the current instrumentation), not the medium arranged *from* (the original instrumentation). *Newsletter 60 (April 1995)*

7.16 QUESTION: I am in the midst of cataloging lots of jazz recordings and am having a problem with subject headings. Could you explain to me when to use headings of the type "[Instrument] music (Jazz)" vs. the heading "[Instrument] with jazz ensemble"? The call number given in the record for the former heading would indicate that it should be used only with solo instrumental music; however, I am finding numerous records where the heading is used for recordings of jazz ensembles (i.e., quartets, quintets, etc.). Can you set me straight on this?

Answer: According to the *Subject Cataloging Manual* (H 1916.5), such headings as "[Instrument] music (Jazz)" may be used for solo instrumental jazz or "to bring out featured instruments in ensembles on recordings, either real (in the recording itself) or advertised (on the record jacket for promotional purposes." "[Instrument] with jazz ensemble" and "Concertos ([Instrument] with jazz ensemble)" are used "where there is a solo instrument accompanied by a jazz ensemble." *Newsletter 58 (August 1994)*

7.17 QUESTION: Could you please clarify how users are supposed to tag subject headings that follow LC's form and policy, but are locally created?

Answer (courtesy of OCLC's Linda Gabel): There are several types of headings that LC does not establish routinely, but can still be considered as LC headings. These headings should be coded as 650 with the second indicator of "0".

The headings fall into distinct categories:

- Headings for instrumental chamber music not entered under musical form, for example, **Sextets (Piano, clarinet, flute, percussion, violin, violoncello)**; headings for musical forms that take qualifiers for instrumental medium, for example, **Choruses, Sacred (Mixed voices, 4 parts) with orchestra**
- Headings where LC has indicated a pattern for subdivisions, for example, **Postage stamps $x Topics $x Birds, [Canada, Elizabeth II, Queen of Great Britain, 1926– , Sports, etc.]**
- Free-floating phrase headings showing a geographical coverage, for example, **Columbus Metropolitan Area (Ohio)** (coded 651 with a second indicator of "0")
- Free-floating phrase headings including -- **in fiction, drama, poetry, etc.**, and -- **in literature**, and -- **in art**

Instructions for constructing these headings can be found in the LCSH (red book) 15th ed., v. 1, pp. xvi–xvii, and in *Subject Cataloging Manual: Subject Headings*, 4th ed. (H198, H362, H910, H1090, H1110, etc.).

A second group of headings that can be considered compatible and coded as LC are those where LC has given instructions that a heading can be qualified or subdivided. For example, "Depressions" may be "subdivided by date and, if world wide, may be further subdivided by country, city, etc.; e.g., Depressions -- 1929 -- United States; Depressions -- 1929 -- Illinois -- Chicago." The instructions under "Folk songs" say, "Here are entered collections of folk songs in various unrelated languages. Works in a single language or group of languages are entered under this heading with language qualifier, e.g., Folk songs, English; Folk songs, Slavic. . . ." In this latter case, users may construct headings using newly established languages, as long as they follow LC spelling for the language. LC will establish these headings as they are needed.

City and other jurisdictional names that do not yet appear in the Name Authority File can be coded as 651 second indicator of "0". Libraries can consult the same reference works that LC uses, and be fairly confident that their headings will match LC's final form. If there is a question as to the preferred spelling or Romanization, the headings should be coded as locally defined.

Chemical and biological names represent a more ambiguous case. OCLC's recommendation has been to tag these as 650, second indicator of "0" when there is no authority record for the term, and there are no authority records for the higher class or broader category. However, if there is doubt about the predominant form or spelling, the term should be coded as locally defined.

New concepts and topics, and headings with new subdivisions or non-standard chronological subdivisions should be tagged and coded as locally defined. Until there is consensus on the form or concept, it is very likely that users will fragment their efforts, entering similar but not identical headings. The result would be headings that do not collocate the necessary information, and run the risk of future conflicts with LC headings.

The choice between tagging nonstandard headings as 650 second indicator "4", and 690 can be left to the inputting library. If they feel that having the term remain on the master record (650 4) will assist other libraries and patrons they may do so. If the nonstandard headings are appropriate and meaningful only to the inputting library, the second option (690) may be best. All libraries using the records should know the implications for their own use of both options, such as retention in a local system or printing on cards. *Newsletter 54 (May 1993)*

7.18 QUESTION: What can you tell me about the use of "Arranged" in subject headings for songs and for choruses?

Answer (the quotation is from an unidentified LC source): ". . . I quote from the *Subject Cataloging Manual*, H1160, p. 1: 'Add the qualifier Arranged following a comma to medium and form headings for instrumental music to form free-floating phrase headings, e.g. Piano music, Arranged. . . .' It is therefore not used in any vocal music subject headings."

However, the subdivision "Excerpts, Arranged" is legitimate with such subject headings as "Cantatas, Sacred" (sh85019784), "Cantatas, Secular" (sh85019793), and "Oratorios" (sh85095293). Some forms such as "Operas, Arranged" (sh85094970), "Oratorios, Arranged" (sh85095296), and "Requiems, Arranged" (sh85112998) are also OK. *Newsletter 48 (August 1991)*

7.19 QUESTION: Where does "celesta" go in subject heading instrumental qualifiers, at the beginning with the keyboards, or later on with the percussion?

Answer (the quotation is from an unidentified LC source): "... I quote a policy statement we came up with back in 1976, which serves as our guideline in the positioning of celesta within subject heading instrumental qualifiers: 'The celesta will be considered a percussion, not a keyboard instrument. But because it is chordal it will be named last in duet headings with a melody instrument: Violin and celesta music.'"

Hence, such subject headings as:

Variations (Harpsichord, reed-organ, celesta, vibraphone, violins (2), viola, violoncello) sh85142174
Concertos (Clarinet, harp, celesta, violin with string orchestra) sh85029799
Octets (Clarinet, flute, saxophone, guitar, harp, celesta, percussion) $x Scores. on 85-752362/M/r87

It is interesting to note that this treatment of celesta as percussion in subject headings (which echoes the LC Classification placement of it among the percussion instruments, in ML1040) contradicts LC's coding of celesta as a keyboard instrument in the 048 field (code "kf"). But then, you know what they say about consistency. *Newsletter 48 (August 1991)*

7.20 QUESTION: Please expand on the difference between "vocal score" and "chorus score."

Answer: ACCR2's glossary defines each, but Music Cataloging Decision 5.5B1 (MCB 12:6 [June 1981] pp. 2–3) goes into considerably more detail. The principal distinction between the two is that a chorus score omits any solo voice(s) found in the original work (at least where the chorus itself does not also sing), whereas a vocal score must include any solo voice(s). Neither term should be used to describe a work that is unaccompanied in its original form or any manifestation of an accompanied work with its original accompaniment. *Newsletter 48 (August 1991)*

7.21 QUESTION: The following are appropriate subject headings for items that I am cataloging, but they do not appear in the *Library of Congress Subject Headings*:

Shinobue music.
Flute and sitar music.
Saxophone and piano music, Arranged.
Woodwind quartets (Saxophones (4)), Arranged -- Scores and parts.

I interpret the Sound Recordings Format section for the 650 ("The second indicator identifies the subject authority on which the subject entry is based") to suggest that second indictor "0" is to be used only for headings actually found in LCSH. Yet these are the appropriate headings, patterned after LC. Should I use 690 instead?

Answer: Headings that are "based on" LCSH—that is, based on the patterns established by LC and understood to include all the instruments and combinations that would double the size of LCSH if they were included—may be tagged as 650s, as the format documents say. OCLC's documentation is based on the real official word, the USMARC Format, of course. There, the pertinent passage reads: ". . . the formulation of the subject added entry conforms to . . . LCSH." It goes on to list certain types of headings, including "headings not printed in LCSH in the past" and "headings based on patterns given in multiples in LCSH or authorized by instruction in LCSH." This clearly allows the use of 650 second indicator "0" for such LCSH-based headings as yours. For more details on the types of headings LCSH includes and excludes, check the LCSH 13th ed. (1990) introduction, pp. xvi–xvii, "Categories of headings included in the list," "Categories of headings omitted from the list," and, especially, "Establishing and printing certain music headings." *Newsletter 47 (April 1991)*

7.22 QUESTION: When can I use the subject heading subdivisions "Excerpts" and "Excerpts, Arranged"?

Answer: These are to be used mostly under musical form headings, such as Suites, Symphonies, Cantatas, Concertos, Sonatas, Operas, Overtures, Requiems, Musicals, and so on. They may also be found under more general headings as Motion picture music and Incidental music. These subdivisions may be further subdivided by musical format subdivisions such as Vocal scores with piano, Piano scores, Scores and parts, and so forth. *Newsletter 46 (November 1990)*

CLASSIFICATION NUMBERS

7.23 QUESTION: Although LC and many other music libraries no longer use LC classification for sound recordings, our institution does. I am confused as to how we should record the LC class number for original bibliographic records that we create for sound recordings. Should we use the 099 field, since our LC class numbers are not what LC currently uses for sound recordings? Should we use the 090 field, since we do use LC's music classification schedule? Should we use the 090 for labels, producing, and exporting, but then delete the number right away, before anyone else might, perchance, see the LC class number assigned outside the scope of LC policy?

Answer: Since you are using LC's Music classification, you can justifiably put the numbers in the 090 field. LC itself may not use them, but other institutions do and may well find them useful. I hope you are also aware that you may add an LC call number to records that do not already have one, via Database Enrichment, and earn a credit in the process. The *Cataloging User Guide*, 2nd edition, p. 6:6–6:8, provides details. *Newsletter 67 (August 1997)*

7.24 FOLLOW-UP QUESTION: To follow up, when doing original bibliographic records, I can add LC class numbers in the 090 field and leave them there. And I can also enhance sound recording records that I am editing by adding LC class numbers to them. I am really surprised! Since I hardly ever find LC class numbers in sound recording records, I have always thought it was "bad form" or something to add them. I thought that that was something that all "real" music catalogers just knew not to do, and I had missed out on the news somewhere along the line. I enhance other bibliographic records with some regularity—when I am certain that my choice of LC class number is correct. If it is OK to do so, I will begin to add class numbers to sound recordings as well.

Answer: One finds LC (or other) classification numbers on Sound Recordings so infrequently because LC no longer routinely assigns them (as they used to assign broad LC class numbers in the days of cards) and because relatively few libraries classify their recordings. As far as I am aware, though, there is nothing inherently incorrect about using LC or Dewey (or ANSCR or any other appropriate system) to classify recordings. Please feel free to include them on original records. When you are using existing records, you may do a Database Enrichment (on a Full Level record) or a Minimal Level Upgrade, locking the record, adding the call number or what have you (details are in the *Cataloging User Guide*, as I noted), and replacing the record. This is optional, of course. *Newsletter 67 (August 1997)*

7.25 QUESTION: An entire session and much discussion at MLA were devoted to the Dewey Decimal Classification 20th Edition's 780 phoenix schedule. How can we tell, or let others know, which edition has been used to assign the classification number?

Answer: Both the 082 field (for LC-assigned Dewey numbers) and the 092 field (for locally assigned Dewey numbers) have the required (if applicable) subfield $2 that explicitly identifies the DDC edition from which the number was derived. If you are using the 20th edition, just input "20" into subfield $2 (without the quotation marks, of course). When using subfield $2, also remember to code the first indicator according to the version and edition used. An example:

092 0 786.219366 $2 20

Newsletter 39 (May 1989)

CHAPTER 8
Numbers

INTRODUCTION

The number of numbers—Library of Congress Control Numbers, Universal Product Codes, International Standard Music Numbers, plate numbers, Music Publisher Numbers, International Standard Book Numbers, International Standard Recording Codes, International Article Numbers, matrix numbers—could be considered out of control. And if they didn't sometimes help bring a little bit of bibliographic control out of the chaos, we might not be so concerned about them.

LC CARD NUMBERS

8.1 QUESTION: How do you tag the LC card numbers when you combine pre-AACR2 LC cataloging containing "With" notes into one record? I've seen LCCNs in 010 $z and in 011, but can't find anything in the MARC format that addresses this particular issue.

Answer: ODQCS prefers that LCCNs in situations such as this be put in separate subfields $z in the 010 field. Field 010 has an added advantage of being indexed in the OCLC system; 011 is not indexed. LC does not use the 011 field and the USMARC format has never adequately defined its use. This issue is addressed briefly in my book *Music Coding and Tagging* on the middle of p. 62. *Newsletter 44 (August 1990)*

STANDARD IDENTIFIERS

8.2 QUESTION: Will UPCs ever be indexed?

Answer: UPCs and all other standard numbers found in field 024 *are* indexed, and have been since the September 2000 enhancements to keyword searching. Technical Bulletin 235 Rev, Keyword Searching Changes in WorldCat (httphttp://www.oclc.org/oclc/tb/tb235/tb235.htm) has the details. The new "standard number" (nn) index is where they are to be found. *Newsletter 78 (May 2001)*

8.3 QUESTION: I was cataloging this morning and wondered about input standards for UPCs for sound recordings that are issued in multiple containers. The item is a Centaur issue of the "Complete organ works" of Pachelbel. I am cataloging as a set without analytics (at least at this point), and wondered whether or not it would be kosher or appropriate to add volume information after the individual 024 fields.

Answer: MARC 21 is silent on the issue of parenthetical information in the 024, but LC's internal *Music and Sound Recordings Online Manual* (1999, with updates) says to basically do the same in 024 as you do in the 020 with ISBN parenthetical information. Under field 024 subfield $a, it says: "Parenthetical qualifying information, such as the publisher/distributor, binding-format, and volume numbers, is included in subfield $a when subfield $c is not present. It is not separately subfielded." By extension, if there is a subfield $c present containing price, availability, or other information, the parenthetical volume number would follow it within subfield $c, again like the 020. *Newsletter 77 (November 2000)*

8.4 QUESTION: How do you search OCLC by ISMN Number?

Answer: At the moment, 024 is not indexed, but as part of the revamping of the FirstSearch indexing associated with the New FirstSearch, it will soon be. You may be able to find a small selection of ISMNs that appear in 500 fields by searching the number in a keyword "nt" search. *Newsletter 75 (May 2000)*

8.5 QUESTION: The instructions in BF&S for field 024 state that 10 digits of the UPC should be recorded. Many users have been adding the other two digits on various records they have entered. Is there some sort of error in BF&S? Are the 10-digit examples in USMARC incorrect when the first indicator is "1"? Should all 12 digits be transcribed even if the numbers appear in different sizes?

Answer: The 10-digit Universal Product Code (UPC) examples are probably incorrect. In one of life's minor but interesting ironies, the standards for entering these "standard" numbers into USMARC records have changed over the years. For a long time, USMARC and BF&S called for omitting certain digits when transcribing some standard numbers. More recently, guidelines stipulate that all eye-readable digits be transcribed. As a result, 024 fields in some older records may contain less-than-complete standard numbers, many of which may appear to violate the very standard they are supposed to represent. Additionally, until the scope of the 024 field was expanded with Format Integration, some standard numbers (such as the European Article Number) were ignored all together. To complicate things further, some publishers have been careless about printing standard numbers in their entirety, sometimes omitting a first digit and/or a final check digit. There may also be other discrepancies between the number printed on an item and the scanned bar code that accompanies it. The second indicator has been defined to account for differences between eye-readable codes and the corresponding scanned bar codes. Being able to code the second indicator accurately presupposes that the cataloger has access to some sort of bar code reading apparatus. What you should do now is transcribe all 12 digits of the UPC, without any of the hyphens and spaces that appear in its printed version. *Newsletter 69 (April 1998)*

8.6 QUESTION: My new assistant goes crazy over calling numbers 028s, when they're repeats of 024s (as given below the zebra-striped bar code). But many publishers are, I feel, assigning the same number to their 028 as they do to their 024. I have no qualms about repeating the number in the 028 subfield $a. But should I be more leery about that? (I was raised in the day when there was a 028 on most recordings, but 024s came about much later. Maybe these days there could be a 024 and no 028?) Most of these 028s that we've seen vary slightly from the 024 (i.e., spaces, hyphen before the final "2" that indicates it's a CD format, etc.).

Answer: Some publishers do use UPCs (and variations) or other numbers that we may think of as "024s" as their Music Publisher Numbers, but each use must be considered as it is presented, in isolation. Remember that the numbers we put in field 024 are supposed to be "standard" numbers of one kind or another, devised according to certain rules, and should be coded accordingly. MPNs are merely control numbers assigned by music publishers and may sometimes be the same as, or based on, some standard number, but only coincidentally. There are probably cases where some standard number is the only one on the item. In those cases, we probably have to consider it to be the MPN as well. There are also a few other considerations. Field 024 does not print and is not currently indexed (although indexing of 024 is on a list of possible future enhancements). Field 028 was designed to accommodate both printing of the proper AACR2 note for Sound Recordings (6.7B19), when that is possible, and to provide indexing. In short, even when the same number serves both as UPC, etc. and MPN, each use should be entered in its proper field. *Newsletter 68 (November 1997)*

8.7 QUESTION: A question for you concerning inputting of the 024 field. But, first some background to get us to the question. On p. 0:66 of BF&S, there is an explanation of the UPC and its basic parts. The last sentence in the first paragraph states: "Enter all digits found on the piece." I interpret this to mean that the 12 digits (10 digits below the bar code and the digits on either side of the code) are to be input in the 024 field. The three paragraphs following the first one discuss audio and video products, serials, and paperback books. The last paragraph on UPCs says: "Enter the UPC without spaces, hyphens, Numbers Systems Designator, or check digit. Use first indicator value 1." That is followed by an example with 10 digits. Does this last paragraph mean that audio, video, serials, and paperback books use the 10 digits and the other formats (maps, computer files, hardback books, etc.) use the 12 digits? You may have answered this question elsewhere and I apologize for revisiting it. However, I need some clarification as the question has come up with map cataloging.

Answer: That final paragraph and example in the UPC section on p. 0:66 (and the ten-digit UPC example on p. 0:68) simply are incorrect and should have been edited. The paragraph should read: "Enter the UPC without spaces or hyphens. Use first indicator value 1." We'll need to find correct UPC examples with 12 digits. The confusion arises because USMARC changed its policy, first not recording, then deciding to transcribe the Numbers Systems Designator and check digit. Sorry for the confusion. Corrections will be made in the next round of BF&S revisions. *Newsletter 68 (November 1997)*

8.8 FOLLOW-UP QUESTION: In reading your response to the question about how many digits to use in the UPC code for field 024, I have come up with another question. You said the change was made to accommodate users who would like to scan the UPC instead of typing. I tried this and every time I get an extra zero at the beginning of the numbers. So that makes 13 instead of 12. Is this acceptable, or should I delete the extra zero? It really does make it easier to wand in. I have come across a couple of titles that have 13 digits already, so when wanding it, it is correct. One example is Kenny G.'s *The Moment*, which has the UPC 0078221893527. Can you shed any more light on this?

Answer: It should come as no surprise that these so-called "standard" numbers turn out to be a lot less standardized than we might want to think. I couldn't really be sure from your question whether you are finding that the eye-readable (12-character) code differs from the (13-character) scanned version of the code or if both have 13 characters. Or perhaps you are finding both circumstances. When the UPCs are both the same and both have 13 characters, I can only conclude that they are invalid codes and should be input in 024 subfield $z (with a second indicator of "0" since both the eye-readable and scanned versions are the wrong number of characters). In cases where the eye-readable code differs from the scanned code but both are 12-character codes, you may enter both in separate 024 fields, each the second indicator "1", which says that they differ. They can be put in the same 024 if one is a valid code (12 characters, in subfield $a) and the other is invalid (13 characters, in subfield $z). There is also the possibility that the code in question is not a UPC at all, but an EAN instead. Standard EANs are 13 digits. In my experience, eye-readable UPCs tend to be printed with hyphens and EANs without hyphens, but that might not be 100 percent reliable. USMARC suggests that you may find hyphens in printed EANs. Another hint for differentiating them is that EANs are not usually found on U.S. imprints, but that might not be universally true, either. *Newsletter 67 (August 1997)*

8.9 QUESTION: I have always wondered about the numbers that often show up on foreign CDs that have 10 digits below the barcodes, but which are not formatted in the xxxx-xxxxx-x pattern shown in *Music Coding and Tagging*. They are usually formatted "xxxxx xxxxx". The example that you give of a number *not* to record (EAN) has 12 digits under the barcode. Since these 10-digit numbers occasionally show up only on labels that have been added by distributors such as Allegro, I have been unsure of their status; yet I see cataloging from institutions whose work I respect who record them, so I have followed suit in most cases—don't agonize, right? Still, it's a gray area that an example could help clear up.

Answer: The 024 section will be greatly expanded in the second edition of *Music Coding and Tagging* since the use of the field itself has exploded with the definition of new indicators. There seem to be more variations in these so-called "standard" numbers than are dreamed of in our bibliographic formats, Horatio. It's possible that some of these could be familiar numbers with the Number System Character and/or the check digit missing; but who knows? If these numbers are showing up on distributors' labels, I'd say they usually won't be candidates for 024 at all. These might be clear-cut distributor's stock numbers, which would currently go in 037. Field 024 is supposed to be reserved for widely recognized standard numbers, after all.

But I'd have to look at some examples before I could say anything definitive. *Newsletter 67 (August 1997)*

8.10 QUESTION: I'm cataloging a Barenreiter edition of Schubert Lieder, each of whose volumes carry ISMNs. According to the USMARC Format (1994 edition), an ISMN consists of eight numbers and one check digit. However, each of the Schubert ISMNs is 13 digits long, for example: 9 790201 805009 (Heft 1). Should I input the number in $z as an invalid number, or is there a way of determining which digits to ignore?

Answer: It sounds like your "ISMN" may not be one at all. A legitimate ISMN should be preceded by the designation "ISMN" on the piece and have the letter "M" as its first character. What you probably have is an International Article Number or a European Article Number (EAN), sort of a European UPC. It also goes in field 024, but with the first indicator "3". Look at the USMARC description of the EAN and see if that's not what you've got. *Newsletter 63 (May 1996)*

8.11 QUESTION: I'm cataloging a score with an ISMN, the first that I've personally seen. Please remind me how we're to code such things. To my knowledge, MARBI hasn't authorized a new field. Should it go into a 028 field with first indicator "3" or just into a 500 note?

Answer: The ISMN goes in field 024. If you have access to the *USMARC Format for Bibliographic Data*, 1994 edition, instructions can be found there. It's pretty simple, though: first indicator "2"; then the letter "M" followed by the eight digits of the ISMN with hyphens or spaces removed, in subfield $a. That's it. *Newsletter 62 (November 1995)*

8.12 QUESTION: I have noticed any number of scores coming through with International Standard Music Numbers on them. Has some provision been made for entering this data into a MARC record? Can it be placed in a $x of a 020 field, or a 500 note?

Answer: Check out the new elements of field 024 in the BF&S revision pages distributed earlier this year, p. 0:57. First indicator "2" now covers the ISMN. The ISMN consists of the letter "M" followed by eight numbers and a check digit. It usually appears on an item preceded by the "ISMN" designation and with hyphens or spaces between the publisher identifier, the item identifier, and the check digit. When inputting an ISMN in the 024 field, omit the "ISMN" initials and the hyphens or spaces. *Newsletter 61 (August 1995)*

8.13 QUESTION: Field 024 is presently valid for recording only the Universal Product Code (UPC) and the International Standard Recording Code (ISRC). Will this be expanded to include other standard numbers?

Answer: Once the International Standard Music Number (ISMN), for printed music, is approved (Lenore Coral reported that the draft had been completed in May 1990 and expected final approval within a year or so), we can expect it to be added to the list. Australia is reportedly reworking a proposal that includes adding the European Article Number (EAN) to the list, as well. All such changes to the MARC format need to go through MARBI. *Newsletter 47 (April 1991)*

8.14 QUESTION: On some imported compact discs, I find a bar-coded number that looks like a Universal Product Code but has 12 or more digits rather than the standard 10 digits of the UPC. What is this number and what should I do with it?

Answer: Most likely, this is a European Article Number (EAN), a standardized numbering system used by some European manufacturers. There is no provision for including the EAN in a MARC record at this time; it should *not* be input in field 024, as that presently is defined only for the UPC and the International Standard Recording Code (ISRC). An EAN could be put in a general 500 note under the provisions of AACR2R 6.8B2, I suppose. Speaking of ISRCs, if anyone has ever encountered either an ISRC or an International Standard Music Number (ISMN) in real life, I'd be interested in seeing it. *Newsletter 44 (August 1990)*

PUBLISHER NUMBERS

8.15 QUESTION: There is an OCLC record that seems to have a problem with the 028 fields. It indexes only the first 028 field (which has a set number and a double-dashed range for the individual numbers in the three-CD set) for a music number search. I "enhanced" the record and retyped the next 028 field, but it still does not index this line.

Answer: Only the first 028 is being indexed in this instance because it is a case where the range of music publisher numbers increases in increments not by the final number, but instead by the next-to-last number. Although there are only three discs and three individual numbers associated with them (5 56221 2, 5 56222 2, and 5 56223 2), when these are entered as a range (5 56221 2 -- 5 56223 2), every number in between (up to the system limit of 20 numbers) is also indexed (that is: 5562212, 5562213, 5562214, 5562215, etc.) As *Bibliographic Formats and Standards* says ("Ranges of consecutive numbers in increments of more than one," p. 0:74, http://

www.oclc.org/bibformats/en/0xx/028.shtm in the electronic version), such numbers must be entered separately in order to index correctly. I've revised the record, splitting the numbers into individual 028 fields, which all should now index correctly, and added an explicit 500 field for the whole range. *Newsletter 74 (November 1999)*

8.16 QUESTION: We have several cards for scores with imprints like this: "Wien, A. Diabelli & Comp., Graben No. 1133 [1846?] Pl. no. 8389." Does that "Graben No." mean anything to you? Should it be entered in the 260, or somewhere else, or not at all?

Answer: Though I've never seen that before, my guess is that here "Graben No." means "engraving no." I would have thought that meant "plate number," but since you also have a plate number in your example, you should treat it as another music publisher number. Put the notation in a 500 note and add a field 028/3 for the number, with the publisher in subfield $b. *Newsletter 71 (December 1998)*

Correction: A reader asked the question, "We have several cards for scores with imprints like this: 'Wien, A. Diabelli & Comp., Graben No. 1133 [1846?] Pl. no. 8389.' Does that 'Graben No.' mean anything to you? Should it be entered in the 260, or somewhere else, or not at all?" Employing a dictionary and my trusty (or is that rusty?) high school and college German, I extrapolated from the verb form of "graben," meaning "engrave," and figured it was a publisher number of some sort. Thank you to eagle-eyed (and much more German-competent) reader Stephen Luttmann, Music Librarian at the University of Northern Colorado (COV), who provided the following correction:

> With regard to "Graben No. 1133": This is an address. Graben is one of the major streets in the old city; the number refers to the house number. (Napoleon had all the houses in the city numbered during his occupation; the street name is fairly irrelevant, as there would be, in this system, only one house numbered 1133 in the entire city.) The same thing happened all over Europe. The most notable example is the original cologne (i.e., from Cologne) known as 4711 because the manufacturer was in house no. 4711. Sounds like neither a 500 nor an 028/3_ is warranted.

Leslie Troutman of the University of Illinois at Urbana-Champaign also pointed out my error. Thanks to all. *Newsletter 72 (May 1999)*

8.17 QUESTION: What is a matrix number and how do you distinguish one from other issue numbers?

Answer: A matrix number is the unique numeric or alphanumeric sequence assigned by the sound recording publisher or manufacturer to the matrix or mold used to stamp one side of a pre-CD recording. (Since CDs are single sided, there is no need to distinguish sides.) Matrix numbers usually appear etched into the sound recording surface between the inner grooves and the label, but they also sometimes are printed on the label itself. When printed on the label, they usually appear either in conjunction with the manufacturer's numbers (generally in parentheses—I recall many older Columbia discs like this) or as the only identification. It is in this latter instance when catalogers need to pay attention to matrix numbers. Richard Smiraglia's 1989 text *Music Cataloging* (p. 22) suggests that matrix numbers are distinguished from publisher's numbers in that matrix numbers usually differ for each side of the disc. In years past, matrix numbers often contained coded information about the recording session, the pressing plant, take numbers, and so on. In that respect, they can be valuable for archival and historical purposes. *Newsletter 69 (April 1998)*

8.18 QUESTION: I am puzzled why OCLC will not allow a non-numerical 028 publisher "number." I have a recording with "EKL BOX A—EKL BOX H" as the publisher number, and nothing else, yet I continually receive the dreaded error message telling me this $a is invalid. I suppose I can get around all this 028 nonsense and put the thing (as an unformatted publisher number) in a 500 note, but this won't allow for "mn:" searching. Anything else to be done?

Answer: The error validation routines built into OCLC's implementation of the 028 field expect all alphabetic characters to be identical on both sides of the double hyphen. That works great in preventing typos in the most common instances where there are ranges of alphabetic prefixes followed by numerals. But unfortunately, the same safeguards stymie the less common situation that you have, where a range is alphabetic instead of numeric. To get correct indexing, you can either input separate 028 fields for each "number" (EKL BOX A, EKL BOX B, etc.) if you don't exceed record or field restrictions, or you can alternatively string all of these together in a single 028 field, each "number" separated by a comma-space. In each case, you'll probably want to input an explicit 500 note with a simplified version of the range. *Newsletter 69 (April 1998)*

8.19 QUESTION: What do the letters "SR" stand for on an audiocassette? Does it stand for "stereo"? Could it be part of the music number?

Answer: Either of your suggestions looks plausible at first glance. The photocopies relating to your question show this mysterious "SR" designation in two different places on two cassette labels. In one, the music publisher number appears at the left, directly below the label logo, with the "SR" below that, right above the Dolby "double-D" symbol. In the other, the music publisher number appears on the left, directly below the label logo but the "SR" appears across the label on the right, above but removed from the Dolby symbol. In my own files, I happen to have two more photocopies of different label versions of what appear to be the same recording. Both of these resemble the first of your labels, but where one has that same "SR", the other reads "AR". That would seem to rule out the "stereo" theory. Because of the erratic placement of whichever alphabetics may be involved, I'm also reluctant to consider it part of the music publisher number. One possibly significant fact was that all the examples involved cassettes on a Warner conglomerate label (Atlantic, Reprise, and Warner Brothers). I suspect that these alphabetic designations are really some sort of Warner code having to do with pricing or distribution or pressings (for radio stations versus general consumption, who knows?). Given all of this evidence, and especially considering that these alphabetics don't always appear in direct conjunction with the music publisher number proper, my inclination is to ignore them. *Newsletter 65 (November 1996)*

8.20 QUESTION: Have you ever seen a fraction in a music number? How should it be entered? It appears as a fraction with a superscript 1, horizontal bar, and subscript 2 ("Edition Schott 01201½").

Answer: That's a new one on me. My best guess is that it should be entered as closely as possible to how it appears, substituting the slash for the horizontal bar.

028 30 01201 1/2 $b B. Schott's Sohne

It might even be appropriate to include a clarifying note to say that the publisher's number is fractional, to avoid further confusion. Wonder what it's supposed to mean. *Newsletter 64 (August 1996)*

8.21 QUESTION: According to the MCD for AACR2R rule 5.7B19, "When transcribing two or more distinct numbers, give each in a separate note. (Follow the rule as written for the transcription of numbers for an item in multiple volumes.)" Does this mean giving two separate notes (500s) for two or more different publisher's numbers? For example, I frequently catalog scores published by Associated Music Publishers and Hal Leonard. So, in that example, would the number assigned by Associated Music Publishers be in one note and the number assigned by Hal Leonard be in another note or would they be in one note and if so, how should/would the note appear? I have seen a lot of inconsistency in this area and the rules do not give clear examples.

Answer: That there is little consistency in the disposition of music publisher's numbers, even in Library of Congress cataloging, suggests that the rules are pretty vague on the issue. That, in turn, suggests that we probably shouldn't agonize over it, either. RI 5.7B19 seems clear in saying that "distinct numbers" are to be given in separate notes, but what exactly makes numbers "distinct" from each other is open to debate.

From looking at a bunch of LC cataloging, I conclude that expediency may be a factor, at least sometimes. If intelligible notes can be generated from multiple 028 fields and re-keying into 500 notes can be avoided, separate notes are allowed to stand (or be generated). This would be in line with cataloging simplification and most ideas of efficiency.

Because of the different capabilities of different systems, it's hard to generalize for every user's needs. LC's system can generate a note from all 028s, but every number must have its own 028. OCLC can generate a note only from the first 028, but can accommodate multiple numbers in the same 028 field. Local systems may differ in all sorts of ways.

With that in mind, I'd say that whenever you can avoid inputting the same data twice (thereby doubling the chance of errors), you should do so. Where you have to (or choose to) input explicit 500 notes:

Put numbers that identifiably belong to different publishers/distributors in separate notes.
Put numbers for scores and parts in the same note, in the form "XY-1234 (score); XYZ-1234 (part)."
Put a range of numbers or a series of individual numbers in a single note, following the second paragraph of Rule 5.7B19.

Above all, be flexible and be clear, both to users and other catalogers. The goal should be to present the information as usefully as possible. *Newsletter 59 (November 1994)*

8.22 QUESTION: We are in a quandary over the correct way to input subfield $b in the 028 field. The directions say to input the name of the publisher. In the case of Edition Peters items, the publisher is actually C.F. Peters, not Edition Peters, which is actually a form "series" or a special imprint of C.F. Peters. However, the examples given in the Scores Format show "Edition Peters" in $b. Complicating the issue is the fact that some of the Edition Peters issues also have different plate numbers that appear at the bottom of each page. These appear to be a different category entirely and are treated differently when recorded in the 028 field. Would it be correct to say that Edition Peters numbers are recorded as:

028 30 [number] $b Edition Peters
500   Publisher's no.: Edition Peters Nr. [xxxx].

while plate numbers for Edition Peters scores are entered as:

028 22 [number] $b C.F. Peters ?

   Answer: Over the years, there has been considerable confusion (not the least of which was my own) over this issue, compounded by the seemingly contradictory examples. Now, with more years of using AACR2 under our belts and tens of thousands of LC music records to examine (not that LC is always consistent, either), it is safe to say that the 028 $b should contain the name of the publisher itself. In most cases, that will be the name found in the 260 $b (exceptions include rereleased recordings where previous record labels and numbers are noted, and printed music where old plates are reissued and are identified with the original publisher). Hence, the correct forms of the examples shown in the question would be:

028 30   [number] $b C.F. Peters
500   Publisher's no.: Edition Peters Nr. [xxxx].

and for the plate number:

028 22   [number] $b C.F. Peters

Newsletter 51 (August 1992)

8.23 QUESTION: In a discussion with some AV catalogers about the use of the 028 field, they held that since it is called a "Publisher's Number for Music" it should not be used for spoken word (Type "i") recordings. I say that a recording is a recording and the 028 should be entered into the records whether it is musical or not. Who is right?

   Answer: "Publisher Number for Music" has long been an unfortunate misnomer. In the OCLC Sound Recordings Format, we explicitly state (p. REC 0:21): "This field may be used for both musical and nonmusical sound recordings." In the USMARC format, the definition reads, in part, "This field contains formatted publisher's numbers used for sound recordings and printed music." It does not limit use to musical recordings. The 028 field should, by all means, be used for both musical and nonmusical recordings. *Newsletter 51 (August 1992)*

8.24 QUESTION: LC seems to be considering Melodiia issue numbers that appear on the record labels to be matrix numbers. Are numbers on the labels considered matrix numbers because they appear directly on the disc as well?

Answer: Richard Smiraglia's *Music Cataloging* (p. 22) says that matrix numbers may appear on the label as well as etched in the vinyl; he suggests that the distinguishing feature is that they usually differ for each side of the disc. He also states that matrix numbers sometimes appear *with* manufacturer's numbers, usually in parentheses (I recall lots of older Columbia discs like this). In short, matrix numbers may also appear on the label. Perhaps some of the confusion stems from the term "label" meaning both the paper attached to the disc and the manufacturer itself (as in "a recording on the RCA label"). *Newsletter 49 (November 1991)*

8.25 QUESTION: Appearing at the bottom of the first page of music in a score is the publisher's number "Cat 009, 1983." Though I know that the "Cat" should be dropped from the 028 field, what should I do about the "1983"? It's clear from the item that this is the date of publication.

Answer: If it is positively identifiable as a date and not strictly as part of the publisher's number, it should be left out of the 028. In case of doubt, you might want to input two 028s, one with and the other without the date-like number. *Newsletter 48 (August 1991)*

8.26 QUESTION: On some musical compact discs, in addition to the usual music publisher number, one sometimes finds additional numbers, often with the prefix "DIDX." Should we put these additional numbers in 028 fields or ignore them?

Answer: It's hard to know just how bibliographically significant such additional numbers are, so I would tend to err on the side of more access by including them in notes and 028 fields. *Newsletter 47 (April 1991)*

8.27 QUESTION: Increasingly I find ranges of music publisher numbers where a digit other than the last one changes. How should I enter these numbers in 028 fields?

Answer: Because of the way OCLC indexes music publisher numbers, each of these numbers should be input in a separate 028 field, not in a single field with the range separated by double hyphens. Some record labels are standardizing their numbering systems so that the final digit of a music publisher number indicates the recording format (most often "1" for LPs, "2" for CDs, and "4" for cassettes). So, if you come across a range of MPNs such as 410 500-2 through 410 502-2, enter each number in its own 028.

028 00 410 500-2 $b Archiv Produktion
028 00 410 501-2 $b Archiv Produktion
028 00 410 502-2 $b Archiv Produktion

This will prevent the false indexing of all the numbers that the system would imagine (using that term loosely) filling in the increments between 4,105,002 and 4,105,022. Of course, an explicit 500 note should be input for the correct range.

500 Archiv Produktion: 410 500-2 -- 410 502-2.

Newsletter 46 (November 1990)

8.28 QUESTION: When a plate number ends with a dash and then a number that also happens to be the number of pages, do we include that as part of the plate number? An example would be "J.F.&B. 1234-35," where the item has 35 pages.

Answer: Music Cataloging Decision 5.7B19 (*Music Cataloging Bulletin* 13:1 [January 1982] p. 4) states, "If an additional number, corresponding to the total number of pages or plates, follows the plate number (often after a dash), do not consider it part of the plate number." By implication, if such a number does not correspond to the number of pages or plates, include it in the plate number. *Newsletter 43 (May 1990)*

8.29 QUESTION: In the Scores Format under field 028, it says to "omit such designations as *no.*, *Nr.*, *cat. no.*, and *Ed. no.*" With many Schirmer publications, there are publisher's numbers such as "Ed.1234." Does this example fall under this guideline? Should it be entered as "Ed.1234" or as "1234" with an explicit note for the full number?

Answer: Judging from LC practice, the intention of this guideline, which derives from Music Cataloging Decision 5.7B19 (MCB 16:12 [December 1985] p. 5) was to exclude only generic alphabetic prefaces that included abbreviations for the word "number." As such, the example cited would be entered as "Ed.1234." To be safe you *could* input another nonprinting 028 with the number alone ("1234"), but that would be optional. Where abbreviations for "number" or its equivalents in other languages are embedded in non-generic alphabetic prefixes (such as many M.P. Belaieff numbers: "Bel. Nr. 494"), input the entire number and prefix as they appear in subfield $a of the 028 field.

028 32 Bel. Nr. 494 $b M.P. Belaieff

Newsletter 43 (May 1990)

CHAPTER 9

Fixed Fields

INTRODUCTION

To the casual observer, the distinctions between musical and nonmusical sound recordings and between print music materials and print nonmusic materials probably seem fairly well defined. But questions about the proper Type Code for such things as music instructional materials or sound effects recordings can often be a source of debate. Other fixed field elements can cause their own headaches as well, most notably Type of Date/Publication Status.

FORM OF COMPOSITION

9.1 QUESTION: Could you give me some advice regarding the coding for the Composition field for rap music? I would also like a source if you have it. I have read *Music Coding and Tagging* but I am still confused a bit. I have rap music, which is a narrower term for popular music. So the rule says you should code for a given term rather than "zz" or "uu". So I would think that "pp" would be the correct code. Others in my department believe that the correct code would be "zz". I have checked several titles and it seems that a lot of people are using the "pp" code. So I'd appreciate some advice from you on this matter.

Answer: Not that *Music Coding and Tagging* is necessarily the final word on anything, but it does say at the top of p. 13 that code "pp" may be used "for both instrumental and vocal works not covered in . . . other 'popular' categories . . . use for . . . rap, salsa, world music." Here's one means by which you might be able to decide which broader code to use for more specific genres that don't have their own code, such as rap. Check the LC authority record for the specific genre and see what's listed as a "broader term" in the 550 fields. For "Rap (Music)" (sh85111437), there are three 550 fields, only one of which has a corresponding Form of Composition code, "Popular music." Since according to MARC 21, the Composition codes "are based on Library of Congress subject headings," this does have a certain logic to it. Of course, remember that this is an optional fixed field, and no one should agonize too much about it. *Newsletter 81 (September 2002)*

9.2 QUESTION: According to BF&S, the 028 and 048 fields are required. Our catalog librarian, however, has found a CSB (No. 55, Winter 1992) that states that the 045, 047, and 048 are being discontinued in LC music records. Could you please address the use of the 048 field. Since LC does not seem to be doing this, he would like to know whether he needs to implement the 048 field.

   Answer: The Library of Congress stopped using fields 045, 047, and 048 in music records on October 3, 1991, although many other libraries have continued inputting them when appropriate. Fields 045 and 048 are, and always have been, optional. You must be referring to the "Required if applicable" status of field 047. Remember that field 047 is used in conjunction with the Fixed Field "Comp" (Form of Composition), which is itself optional. The application for which field 047 becomes required is when "Comp" is coded "mu" (Multiple forms of composition) and the specific multiple forms must be listed in 047. If you code "Comp" with a single, specific composition code or leave it blank, you need not use 047. You also mentioned field 028, which continues to be "Required if applicable." *Newsletter 67 (August 1997)*

9.3 QUESTION: It came to my attention, while working on a related matter, that the 047 field, according to BF&S and the old MARC format documents, is "Required if applicable." I have always thought it was optional, even for Level I records. What really confuses me is that Comp is optional. Thus, if you have, say, a recording of a symphony, you don't have to put "sy" in Comp. But if your recording has a symphony and a concerto, then you are required to put "sy" and "co" in the 047 (but not "mu" in Comp, since Comp is optional?). That doesn't make any sense. Can you clarify this for me?

   Answer: You need to remember how "Required if applicable" differs from "Mandatory" and the connection between FF Comp and field 047. What it boils down to is that 047 is required when Comp has been coded "mu" but is optional otherwise. That's not really made very clear in BF&S. *Newsletter 63 (May 1996)*

9.4 QUESTION: Exactly what is meant by the value of two blanks in the Comp fixed field? BF&S says it means "no information supplied" and your *Music Coding and Tagging* book does not elaborate on that. Does the value of two blanks mean that the cataloger has chosen not to code the field (it is an optional field), or that the piece you're cataloging has not supplied any information (such as by having a nondescriptive title, e.g., *Pumpkins on the Plains*)?

    Answer: Regarding "Comp", "no information supplied" generally means that the area simply has not been coded (as you point out, it is optional); the blanks do not otherwise convey any information. The code "uu" would cover pieces with nondescriptive titles or that do not have a readily determined form or genre. The code "zz" would cover pieces in forms not on the code list. *Newsletter 57 (May 1994)*

9.5 QUESTION: The 047 fields of the Sound Recordings Format previously included the code "zz" for "other forms of composition not on list." The recent updates of the format have omitted the "zz" code. Since we used "zz" in the 047 so frequently in the past, we are now wondering if this is a mistake in the format or if there is something else we are supposed to do with our "other forms of composition."

    Answer: Code "zz" as well as all of the other nonspecific 047 codes found in the MARC format ("mu", "nn", "uu") were meant to be place holders in the Composition Fixed Field (Comp) and should only be used there, when appropriate. Only specific composition codes (all those other than "zz", "mu", "nn", and "uu") should be input in the 047 field. *Newsletter 43 (May 1990)*

COUNTRY OF PUBLICATION

9.6 QUESTION: I am cataloging an unpublished compact disc that was recorded locally. What we're wondering is whether it is appropriate to code the fixed field Ctry for the recording location? Another colleague here was under the impression that Ctry is generally not coded for unpublished works but we can't seem to find any explicit statements to that effect in the documentation. The field definition includes place of "production or execution" and indicates information may come from fields other that the 260. One could also extrapolate from the guidelines for visual materials, which favor place of production over publication. My inclination would be to go ahead and code Ctry for the recording location. Would you agree with this interpretation or are we missing something?

    Answer: This seems to be such a basic question that one would expect to find a definitive answer in MARC 21, but that appears not to be the case.

In the 008/15-17 "Place of publication, production, or execution," it says in part: "Choice of a MARC code is generally related to information in field 260 (Publication, Distribution, etc. (Imprint)). . . . For sound recordings, the code represents the place where the recording company is located. . . . When the place of publication/production/execution is totally unknown, code xx [blank] is used." There is no further guidance in the field 260 description, in the *MARC Code List for Countries,* or anywhere else I can find. Since the item in question is locally produced and otherwise unpublished, I like the analogy to locally produced and unpublished visual materials, where the place of capture is coded. Finding nothing to contradict this, and taking comfort in the implied license granted by that "generally" in MARC 21, I'd agree with you. *Newsletter 81 (September 2002)*

9.7 QUESTION: How should FF Ctry be coded for pre-AACR2 records that have Field 262 with no place?

Answer: Unless the name of the publisher implies a place (Deutsche Grammophon, Harmonia Mundi France), code "xx", especially when inputting from retrospective copy. If you have the item in hand, you might determine the place and code it, but don't go out of your way and don't bother changing existing records. *Newsletter 49 (November 1991)*

9.8 QUESTION: What will German reunification do to the USMARC geographic area and country codes?

Answer: The *USMARC Code List for Countries* (used mainly in Fixed Field Ctry and field 044) is maintained by LC's Office for Descriptive Cataloging Policy; the *USMARC Code List for Geographic Areas* (used in field 043), by LC's Office of the Principal Subject Cataloger. As of this writing (mid-October 1990), no word has come from either office on Germany or any of the other geopolitical questions now pending. When they let us know, we'll let you know. In the meantime, continue the Cold War coding for the Germanys and the Berlins (East and West, not Irving). *Newsletter 46 November 1990)*

[Note: Not long after that answer was published, the official words came down from LC concerning the codes for Germany. The geographic area codes are as follows: "e-gx -- " is used for Germany as a whole regardless of time period, including Germany (East) and Germany (West) as a whole between 1949 and 1990; "e-ge -- " is used for the eastern part of Germany before 1949 or after 1990 and for the German Democratic Republic between 1949 and 1990; "e-gw -- " is used for the western part of Germany before 1949 or after 1990 and for the Federal Republic of Germany between 1949 and 1990. For more details see the "MARC Code List for Geographic Areas" (http://www.loc.gov/marc/geoareas/gacshome.html). Things are simpler for the country codes (see the "MARC Code List for Countries," http://www.loc.gov/marc/countries/cntrhome.html). The country code "gw" is to be used for all parts of unified Germany, including reunified Berlin. Irving still does not have his own code.]

TYPE OF DATE/PUBLICATION STATUS

9.9 QUESTION: G. Ricordi publications often carry a copyright date (sometimes two or three) and a "Ristampa" date of 10, 20, or 30 years later. I've always ignored these dates and just recorded the latest copyright date (if there were more than one), figuring that the date more copies were run was bibliographically unimportant. However, maybe I'm misinterpreting 1.4F6 and the LCRI for it. Should the printing date be considered a date of manufacture as explained in LCRI 1.4F6, point 3? If so, then BF&S, under DtSt, would be "t" and the *printing* date would go in Date 1, with the copyright date in Date 2 (see BF&S p. FF:32). Or have I been a music cataloger too long and I'm getting myself mixed up?

  Answer: Those Ricordi "Ristampa" dates are problematical and people have treated them all sorts of different ways over the years. All other things being equal, my inclination is to disregard them all together (which one might take to be the implication of LCRI 1.4G4 when things are reprinted frequently over long periods) or include them only in the 260 subfield $g as a printing date (as shown in LCRI 1.4F6, point 3). If you transcribe the date in subfield $g, DtSt remains "s" and only the latest copyright date appears as Date 1, with Date 2 blank. (There's an example, complicated by other factors, at the top of BF&S p. FF:27.) If you can determine that there is some real bibliographic significance to the "reprinting" that would make the item, in essence, a new edition, regard the latest printing date to be an implied (and bracketed) date of publication with the latest copyright date following. In this case you would use DtSt "t" with the bracketed date in Date 1 and the copyright date in Date 2. Such instances might be full score versus miniature score, new front matter, and so forth. *Newsletter 69 (April 1998)*

9.10 QUESTION: With Format Integration Phase 2, we use the "u" character in the Dates fixed field for any digits missing from a date in all materials, not just serials. What impact does this have on searching with a date qualifier and on displays of search results?

  Answer: The system treats the "u" character both with date qualifiers and in the display of search results the same as it always has. But with Format Integration, what *has* changed is that those of us who never cataloged a serial and had previously never used the "u" character in a Date fixed field, suddenly see what the system's been doing all along. The brand-new manual *Searching for Bibliographic Records*, pp. 5:4–5:9, 7:7–7:9, and 10:3–10:4, and the "Format Integration Phase 2" Technical Bulletin no. 212, p. 43, deal with the dates qualifier. For search key searches, when there is no date of publication or Date 1 contains at least one "u", the only date qualifier that will retrieve the record is "????". You cannot use this qualifier for keyword searches. In Group Displays, records that have no date of publication or that have a Date 1 with at least one "u" will be listed under the "No Date" category. *Newsletter 66 (May 1997)*

9.11 QUESTION: When is one allowed to infer the millennium and use "1uuu" in one or the other of the Dates fields, and when is it not allowed and "uuuu" must be used? For example, in BF&S, p. FF:21, the fourth example has a "1uuu" in Date 1 with the explanation that if a date is completely missing, you may infer the millennium. The next example is a 1966 reprint of *Green Howard's Gazette*. Why is Date 2 "uuuu"? Can't we assume that whatever was reprinted first appeared in the *Gazette* sometime after A.D. 1000? Similarly, on p. FF:29, first example: depending on the nature of the multipart item, we may be able to infer "19uu", or almost certainly "1uuu". Why is it "uuuu"? Related question #1: can we use knowledge of technology, personal expertise, or local knowledge to infer dates? If we're cataloging a subtitled version of a Japanese animation video and the item says "Original Japanese language version first released on VHS" (i.e., this thing started out as a video, not a film or TV program), can we use "19uu"? If my paraprofessional who catalogs this stuff happens to be a Japanese animation buff and knows this item came out in the mid-1980s, can we use "198u"? Also, look at BF&S FF:33, third example. If we know the English Victorian costume was donated from the local theater and they tell us it was made for a performance of X in the late 1970s, can we use "197u"? Related question #2: Do all dates in the Dates field have to be justified somewhere in the record? I've always thought that a really good idea. And can the date come from any one of several fields? All the examples in BF&S seem to be using only the 260 date(s) when deciding when to use a "u" in the Dates field. As mentioned in the paragraph above, we may be using "u" in the Dates field when the date appears only in a note; or perhaps not at all.

Answer: Many of the Format Integration changes for dates remain pretty confusing, especially those related to practices that were formerly limited to serials. So I consulted Robert Bremer, our serials specialist, as he has had much more experience with those pesky little "u" codes. He really couldn't make much more sense of it than you or I could. He thought (mainly in desperation) that the key might be in the word "may," both in BF&S and in USMARC. In serials cataloging, there are apparently certain circumstances when you might actually infer a millennium if you lacked all other information. That's not generally the practice for monographic publications. In neither case does it seem particularly helpful. You'll notice that AACR2 rule 1.4F7 doesn't go down to the millennium level (though examples are "illustrative and not prescriptive" according to rule 0.14). I'm guessing that the authors of AACR2 might not consider "[1 --]" to be "an approximate date of publication." One would almost certainly be pre-AACR2 cataloging, since DtSt code "n" was used. For current cataloging, it is certainly legitimate to use personal knowledge of technology and so forth (as well as any supplementary research) to infer an approximate date. We know, for instance, that Beta videos cannot predate 1975, VHS videos cannot predate 1977, and prerecorded audiocassettes cannot predate 1965. That might help us infer dates for some items. As far as justifying dates in a record, my policy is the more information supplied (within reason, of course), the better. We don't need to reiterate the history of videocassettes in every record for a video with unknown dates. But in the costume example, a note (500, 518, 520, 545, etc., depending on how it is presented and what it concerns) about when the piece was created would certainly be helpful. Dates information can derive from many places in a record, including any number of 5XX fields. For sound recordings, we often get a Date 2 from the 518, for instance. *Newsletter 65 (November 1996)*

9.12 FOLLOW-UP QUESTION: To follow up, when I heard that most zeros and nines in the Dates field were going to be replaced by "u"s, I thought it was a great idea. We could say exactly how much we knew for sure and not make it look like something that was probably published in the 1970s was published in 1970, period, end of sentence. I agree, "1uuu" is not very helpful, and "19uu" is becoming almost as useless. But doesn't the matching algorithm for one format or another have to match on Date 1? If we have one person using "uuuu" and another "1uuu" and still another "19uu", we're gonna have a lot of dups.

   Answer: We did some minor tweaking on parts of the matching algorithms so that uncertain dates of various sorts coupled with particular DtSt codes would be looked upon as equivalent. Between those tweaks and the many FI conversions we have done, we hope that many, if not most, of those instances would be taken care of. It's hardly perfect, though. *Newsletter 65 (November 1996)*

ENCODING LEVEL

9.13 QUESTION: We have recently come across what appear to be full-level (Encoding Level blank) cataloging records for scores in OCLC that have the OCLC symbols of participating institutions—not necessarily Enhance participants—in the subfields $d of the 040 field. This seems anomalous since, if Encoding Level is blank, we suppose that to mean that this entered the OCLC database as full-level LC cataloging, not minimal-level and not upgradable even by Enhance libraries. Libraries upgrading Level "7" cataloging are supposed to upgrade the Encoding Level; we had assumed that we *had* to do that or the system would not let us replace the record. Is this not so? How can we tell what's *really* full-level DLC cataloging for scores and not something upgraded by a non-Enhance, OCLC member institution if the Encoding Level is misleading?

Answer: OCLC has been creating these Encoding Level blank records with other symbols in the 040 subfields $d for about as long as we've been able to merge duplicates. Whenever records merge, either manually, automatically via the Duplicate Detection and Resolution (DDR) software, or during tapeloading of national library records (DLC, NLM), there is the potential for certain fields to transfer. When information transfers, the three-letter codes from the deleted record's 040 also transfer. As far as music records are concerned (scores and sound recordings are currently merged manually only), the transferred fields are usually in the 0XX range (033, 041, 043, 045, 047, 048), many of which LC no longer inputs. Generally, no field will automatically transfer if the retained record already has a field with that tag number. Upgraded minimal-level DLC cataloging (originally Encoding Level 2, 5, or 7) can be identified by 040 "DLC $c DLC" and a member-input Encoding Level of K or I or an unchanged Encoding Level. Actually, PRISM will allow you to lock and replace a minimal-level record without upgrading the Encoding Level, but will not award you a minimal-level upgrade credit for your efforts. *Newsletter 53 (November 1992)*

FORMAT OF MUSIC

9.14 QUESTION: I just discovered a contradiction in online and printed documentation for OCLC. Did something change and I didn't notice? The issue is the coding of FMus (previously Format) in the fixed fields, specifically for unaccompanied choral works. From the online OCLC help accessed through CatME (which goes to the OCLC Web site):

"d"   Voice Score. Editions of a work for voices and instruments in which the voice parts are notated and the instrumental parts omitted completely. Use for unaccompanied or a capella choral works.

An earlier print version of the Scores Format says as the last sentence under Voice score, "For unaccompanied or a capella choral works, use code a." Which code is correct, "a" or "d"?

Answer: Looks like you've caught an error that appears in both the second and third editions of *Bibliographic Formats and Standards*. Code "d" is used for choral and vocal works that were composed with accompaniment, but for which the accompaniment has been omitted. Choral and vocal works that were composed without accompaniment should be assigned other codes, depending upon the format of the score in hand (code "a" for full scores, code "b" for miniature scores, etc.). *Newsletter 81 (September 2002)*

9.15 QUESTION: Is it possible to tell from any particular field or fixed field code if a score is in modern or original medieval notation?

Answer: The "Format" fixed field may occasionally be a hint of out-of-the-ordinary notation, but not usually. The only place where such information may be found is in a 500 note formulated according to AACR2R 5.7B8. Most of the time, one can assume modern notation unless otherwise noted or if the item is a facsimile, but aside from an explicit note, there is no other surefire way to tell. *Newsletter 50 (May 1992)*

LITERARY TEXT FOR SOUND RECORDINGS

9.16 QUESTION: How does one choose the LTxt Fixed Field codes when more than two could apply?

Answer: Both the list in the *USMARC Format for Bibliographic Data* and that in the OCLC *Sound Recordings Format* are in order of priority. If you cannot choose two codes on the basis of predominance on the recording, choose the two that come first in the priority list. *Newsletter 40 (August 1989)*

TYPE OF RECORD

9.17 QUESTION: I'm having one of those nagging moments of self-doubt. We just received four of those CD-ROMs containing huge amounts of public domain music as PDF files (there goes our paper budget). I thought I might have to do original cataloging for them; I would do them as format "c" with field 006: "m" for the computer aspect of them. I found OCLC records for all four of them (#48155485, #48212724, #46802200, #48155309) and the inputting library has done just the opposite, input them as computer files with field 006 for scores. Am I losing my mind?

Answer: Doubt no more. You are correct, and I have done Type Code changes on these four (as well as several others). CD-ROM publications of scores should be cataloged as scores, with 006 and 007 for the computer file aspects. *Newsletter 80 (May 2002)*

9.18 QUESTION: For the first time in several years, I have to input a new record for a book of hymns without music. My instincts are telling me to use the Scores format, even though there is no music, and I think I've read about this in the past (when all the manuals were separate before Format Integration), but I can't find anything in the documentation. Should I use Books or Scores format?

Answer: The treatment of hymnals without music has, indeed, changed since Format Integration. Current practice is to treat hymnals without music as books (Type "a"). *Newsletter 76 (September 2000)*

9.19 QUESTION: I'm cataloging a children's sound recording that has five musical numbers and four narrated stories. What type would you use, an "i" or a "j"? Also if you used a "j", what would you place in the "Comp" field, "sg" or "mu"?

Answer: You should choose the Type Code for the predominant format. I'm guessing that it's musical ("j"), but the actual timings of the five songs versus the four stories may be the determining factor. Whichever choice you make, you can add a field 006 for the other, allowing you to code the Composition fixed field for the songs and the "LTxt" fixed field for the stories. Even a single item can exhibit aspects of different bibliographic formats: those "enhanced" CDs that have both sound recording and computer file aspects are a prime example. The 006 field would be optional in the case of your item, of course, but would allow you to code for both the songs and the stories. Only if the musical numbers were not all songs might you code "Comp" anything other than "sg". Since the stories are not musical, they would not have a Composition Code. *Newsletter 71 (December 1998)*

9.20 QUESTION: I'm cataloging a score with an accompanying computer disc containing MIDI files. How is the MARC coding handled for this situation? A 006 field could be coded to show there is an accompanying sound recording. Are you also supposed to indicate that this particular recording consists of computer files? Is there a way to do this?

Answer: Catalog the item as a score (Type "c") with the computer file described in the 300 subfield $e. You may further describe the computer file's contents in notes, as may be appropriate. I'd probably just use a 500 to identify or describe the accompanying material as MIDI files (with any degree of detail you want). Using a 516, which limits the terminology you can use, won't work, I think, as it would imply a description of the whole item and not just the accompanying material. A CF 006 field would be useful (Code

File as "h" for "Sound"). A CF 007 could also be added for the accompanying material (I'm guessing that it's a 3½ inch floppy):

007   c $b j $d n $e a $f a

Newsletter 70 (September 1998)

9.21 FOLLOW-UP QUESTION: To follow up, perhaps you can clear up
some of my confusion. In the *USMARC Bibliographic Formats* under Leader/
06 (p. 3) it says: "Computer files are identified by a distinctive Type of record
code only if they belong to certain categories of electronic resources as speci-
fied below; in all other cases the type of material characteristics described by
the codes take precedence over the computer file characteristics of the item."
Turning the page (Leader/06 p. 4), the definition of code "m" suggests to
me that since this computer disc is essentially music recordings in the form of
MIDI files that code "j" should be used as the type code. (Similarly, a disc of
word processing files would be coded "a" rather than "m", right?) So, if the
006 is coded for music recording, what 007 do I choose, computer files?

Answer: My head was just beginning to hurt from the implications of
your question, the potential of an infinitely reflecting set of facing mirrors.
But as I was beginning to formulate an answer to your question, an e-mail
message arrived announcing the availability of LC's *Use of Fixed Fields 006/
007/008 and Leader Codes in CONSER Records* (http://lcweb.loc.gov/acq/
conser/ffuse.html). Although it addresses serials specifically, the principles
hold with other formats, too, I think. Here is the whole pertinent passage,
but the main point is the difference between the Leader/06 definition of
"computer file" and the 006 definition.

> The mandatory use of field 006 for computer file characteristics is a temporary
> means of identifying the carrier of the item. With the redefinition of leader/
> 06 code "m", the presence of field 006 with code "m" in the first byte ("form
> of material" 006/00) allows OCLC and other systems to identify records for
> electronic resources for purposes of searching and duplicate detection. Note that
> the definitions for the two "m" codes differ. The definition of code "m" in the
> leader is very specific to the content, as noted above. The definition of code
> "m" in 006/00 reads: "Code m is used to identify field 006 as containing coded
> data elements relating to a computer file." For current purposes, interpret this
> statement as applying to any resource whose carrier is electronic, regardless of
> the nature of the content.

In other words, I think that the mandatory 006 should be a computer
file 006. Optionally, you may also add a second 006 for the musical sound
recording aspects of the accompanying material. Regarding the 007, I don't

think there's any question but that it should be a CF 007. Remember that the 007 field is defined as "Physical Description Fixed Field." Besides, you'll notice that if you try to code a sound recording 007, almost every value will be "other", "not applicable", or "unknown". Not very useful, even by 007 standards. *Newsletter 70 (September 1998)*

9.22 QUESTION: I'm trying to be sure I understand the right thing to do for cataloging a reproduction of a composer's manuscript. I have such a critter on my desk. It does not appear to have been commercially produced, but is, rather, the score that was used to conduct the work's premiere performances. When I read the scope notes under the Type fixed field, it appears to say that a reproduction (even a published facsimile) is to be coded "d" if the original is a manuscript. In the scope note for code "d", it isn't quite so clear that this is the case. I did a search in MUMS on the note words "Photocopy" and "holograph" and did a browse through about 10 records, of which a slight majority coded Type "c" (Box 41 of the MUMS fixed fields). I've also been confused as to why photocopies of manuscript scores don't seem to be treated under the principles of LCRI 1.11A; most LC records for photocopies eliminate "ms." from the 300, even if the Type field has been coded "d". Any clarification you can offer would be welcome.

Answer: There is some garbled text in the "Type" section of the paper BF&S. On p. FF:75 under "Manuscript music": only the first sentence should be there. The remaining two sentences ("Use Scores format . . .) should be deleted. Similarly in the "Manuscripts" box on p. FF:73, the sentence beginning "For Scores format . . . " should instead say something like: "Use Type: d for manuscript music, microforms of manuscript music, and score theses." The final sentence ("Adjust . . . ") should be deleted. (This was pointed out in my *MOUG Newsletter* Q&A column in issue 67, August 1997, p. 11 [9.27]; and issue 68, November 1997, pp. 10–11 [9.25].) As it happens, LC's Deta Davis answered a similar question for us back in *MOUG Newsletter* no. 60 (April 1995, pp. 9–10). Here's that Q&A:

9.23 QUESTION: Under what circumstances is it appropriate to use Type "d" for the cataloging of photocopied holographs, copies produced and distributed (hence published?) only by the composer? I have always treated these as Type "c", with "[S.l. : J.Q.Public, 198–?]", a "Reproduced from holograph." note, and the appropriate subject headings for manuscript facsimiles. Should Type "d" be used if the only available date is a date of composition *and* the score lacks a publishing statement? Is this not worth agonizing about, since format integration will be with us soon enough?

Answer: After searching for and finding a number of LC records for photocopies of manuscripts and holographs, I was just as confused, as I found about as many entered as "d" as I did those entered as "c". So I asked LC directly.

Here was the reply of LC's Deta Davis: "Our policy is to use code 'd' only if it is an actual, original ms. Any photocopy or published reproduction is code 'c.'" Any inconsistencies are errors and should be reported. *Newsletter 60 (April 1995)*

As to why LC doesn't follow LCRI 1.11A for photocopies, that question more properly belongs to LC. *Newsletter 70 (September 1998)*

9.24 QUESTION: Some time ago, I had sent in a type code change request for OCLC #11193392, which is entitled *Mel Bay's dulcimer chord encyclopedia*. I wanted it changed from "c" to "a". It seems to me that chord diagrams are generally treated as books by LC, not as scores. For example, see #31520339, Neal Hellman's *Dulcimer chord book*. I can find other examples, especially of guitar chord books, if need be, to support this argument. You said something in the latest *MOUG Newsletter* (no. 68) about this very issue, where you leaned toward scores format for such items. The item in question really is not in musical notation. It has a representation of the fret board of a dulcimer with dots where the fingers are to be placed to give the chord, represented as a letter symbol at the top of the diagram. Do you really think that is a type of score?

Answer: In various Q&As over the years, I have said to consider such items as scores even when they do not have traditional staff notation. To my mind, this seemed in line with other things that do not have staff notation but are still considered scores (scores that consist entirely of performance notes, all sorts of graphic notation, etc.). As backup evidence, I found numerous LC records that seem to treat such guitar chord collections as scores, but there were as many where they were treated as books. As I so often do when it comes to the *really* difficult questions, I deferred to the Library of Congress. Deta Davis was kind enough to provide the following definitive answer:

You might not like my answer since it contradicts your position. We do not consider chord diagram books to be scores if they are exclusively chord diagram books. We even have a policy statement to that effect at the beginning of the *Music-File Input-Update Manual* under "Scope of the Music File." [The relevant passage in that internal LC document is quite explicit, had I thought to refer to it: "Records for books and book-like materials relating to music but whose primary content is not music notation, such as librettos, songbooks without music, books of chord diagrams, etc., reside in the BOOKSM file." That is, they are coded as Type "a."] We treat them as books. If a piece of music is written in chord diagrams or a chord diagram book had enough music in it to be considered music, then we would consider it a score. Another way of looking at it is, since the chord diagram books generally are not musical compositions but information on playing an instrument, then they should not be treated as music. As a result of [this] query I examined our practice and discovered some recent chord diagram books cataloged in the Music File as scores. We will be correcting those records and sending a reminder to the catalogers of what the appropriate treatment should be.

Newsletter 69 (April 1998)

9.25 QUESTION: We have a two-page score of sheet music that appears to have been produced by (1) a printer printing some lines of staff, with a nice Wyoming scene at the top; (2) someone handwriting in the music notation and typewriting in the text; (3) a printer reproducing the publication. Would this be coded Type "c" or Type "d"? Type "d" includes published facsimiles; this would not be a facsimile in the sense of a reproduction of, say, Beethoven's handwritten scores, and I wouldn't put a 600 with $x Manuscripts $x Facsimiles on the item in hand. But is it used in cases like this? I just accessed MLA's *Sheet Music Cataloging Guidelines*, but they don't address MARC tagging.

Answer: When you say "a printer reproducing the publication," I'm not sure exactly what you mean. Published facsimiles of music manuscripts would be Type "c", as they have always been, BF&S to the contrary. Some text got garbled and put in the wrong place and will be corrected in the next revisions. In BF&S p. FF:75 in the section entitled "Manuscript music," only the first sentence should be part of this passage. The second and third sentences (starting with "Use Scores format . . . ") should be removed. A very similar passage appears in the "Manuscripts" box on p. FF:73. That next-to-last sentence that begins "For Scores format . . . " should probably read something like: "Use Type: d for manuscript music, microforms of manuscript music, and score theses." The last sentence ("Adjust . . . ") should be deleted. The first edition of *Music Coding and Tagging* is correct (and I expect the second will be too, if I have anything to say about it). If this is the original or a photocopy of the original, it would be Type "d" (with a 533, if appropriate). *Newsletter 68 (November 1997)*
    [Note: A photocopy should be coded Type "c".]

9.26 QUESTION: A question arose in our Fine Arts Department concerning the difference between using the Scores format or Books format for musical instruction. Our understanding is that musical instruction is put on Scores format if the item is predominantly music and features standard musical notation (i.e., staves). If it features musical notation like chord diagrams or some other formation unique to an instrument (like how to beat a drum or pluck a dulcimer), then it goes on Books format. Is our interpretation correct? We have checked several sources including BF&S and back issues of the *MOUG Newsletter*, which usually take us back to AACR2 and LC classification. LC classification doesn't help us because we use Dewey. The question of which format to use for nonstandard musical notation has bothered us for quite some time. Illumination on this question would be greatly appreciated.

Answer: Although the AACR2 definition of "score" limits itself to the traditional "series of staves," we include on the Scores format some things that don't fit this narrow stricture, among them all sorts of graphic notations and works that consist entirely of performance instructions. You should consider to be Scores items that use other types of musical notation unique to certain types of instruments or musical genres (chord diagrams, tablature, etc.) as well as any non-Western notational systems. Back in the *MOUG Newsletter* no. 62 (November 1995) p. 9, for instance, there was a question about a handbell "score" that consisted of the text with words circled when that particular bell was to be sounded. I judged this to be a Score, also. A note indicating what kind of notation is involved (see AACR2 Rule 5.7B8) would be advisable in such instances. *Newsletter 68 (November 1997)*

[Note: Do not consider chord diagram collections as scores.]

9.27 QUESTION: Has there indeed been a change in the coding of the Type for published facsimiles of music manuscripts? *Bibliographic Formats and Standards*, p. FF:75 says to use Type "d" for published facsimiles of music manuscripts (I just noticed). *USMARC Format for Bibliographic Records* doesn't specify so clearly. Your *Music Coding and Tagging*, 1st ed., indicates that published facsimiles were Type "c". That surely reflects coding when the book was written. So I wanted to verify whether OCLC coding practice, as on FF:75, indicates a genuine change in practice.

Answer: There has been no change in policy, just some garbling of text that we must have missed in the proofreading process. I conferred with Glenn Patton just to make sure I wasn't forgetting something, but we both agree that published facsimiles of music manuscripts should be Type "c" as they have always been. In BF&S p. FF:75 in the section entitled "Manuscript music," only the first sentence should be part of this passage. The second and third sentences (starting with "Use Scores format . . . ") should be removed. A very similar passage appears in the "Manuscripts" box on p. FF:73. That next-to-last sentence that begins "For Scores format . . . " should probably read something like: "Use Type 'd' for manuscript music, microforms of manuscript music, and score theses." The last sentence ("Adjust . . . ") should be deleted. We'll try to get it fixed during the next round of BF&S revisions. I've also made sure that I have it right in the second edition of *Music Coding and Tagging*, which is in (slow) progress. *Newsletter 67 (August 1997)*

9.28 QUESTION: One of my libraries wants to catalog a series as sound recordings and OCLC is split in whether this is a recording or a score. Approximate vote online: Score: 225, Recording: 150. Who do you think is right? The series is: A new approach to jazz improvisation. It is a score with a sound recording. Or is it a sound recording with a score? How do we tell? Check out LC on #22980660, #7106251. Others are #28304166, #20844964, #20844964. The whole mess can be seen with the search: "new,ap,to,j".

Answer: Your approximate count is backwards, I think, with 233 Sound Recordings and 162 Scores. It is a toss-up, though, especially not having any of the items in hand for examination. My inclination would be to follow the lead of read-along book/recording sets; we recommend cataloging those as recordings with accompanying book. All else being equal here, I'd lean toward treating them as sound recordings with accompanying scores. But reasonable catalogers will differ. Sorry if that doesn't help much, but I don't think there's a definitive answer. Don't forget that by adding a 006 for the other format's aspects, the item will be retrieved when the search is qualified by either format. *Newsletter 67 (August 1997)*

9.29 QUESTION: I'm presently cataloging a number of works for handbells. One of them contains no musical notes, only the texts with the word circled on which the bell-holder rings. There are 8 v., one volume for each different pitch of bell. My gut reaction is to treat this as type "a" rather than "c", with the rest of the record (especially 300) treated accordingly. I have a 500 note: "Texts only, with circled words for ringing." What do you think?

Answer: My inclination would be to treat it as a score. (One wonders if this is the standard "notational" system for handbell scores.) Other types of scores lack actual music (instructions for performance, for instance). You would certainly want to describe in a note the peculiarities of this "score", as you have said. You could describe it in the 300 as "8 v." and avoid calling it "of music", but I don't know enough details to offer any more help than that. *Newsletter 62 (November 1995)*

9.30 QUESTION: I have three CDs, each of which is one of Karl Haas's *Adventures in Good Music* radio programs. Each is Type "i", and I find that odd. The programs are mostly music interspersed with Haas's commentary; the timings show that the music content far outweighs the commentary as far as sheer duration. Seems to me they should be Type "j". If there's a good reason they should be "i" instead of "j", I'd love to hear it!

Answer: It's been a long time since I listened to Karl Haas, but as I recall, the musical excerpts tended to be fragmentary and illustrative of whatever his topic happened to be that day. The catalogers of the three items in question thought of the excerpts as musical examples embedded in a spoken text, much like printed musical examples might appear in a printed text. I would lean toward regarding these as properly Type "i" with the spoken commentary being the focus and the musical excerpts being the illustrations. Of course, if you want them in your local system as Type "j", remember that you can change the Type Code within the same format (j/i, c/d, g/k/r/o) for your own use. *Newsletter 61* (*August 1995*)

9.31 QUESTION: A colleague of mine has just encountered the following item as part of her artists' book backlog:

Musical book / by Lionello Gennero ; in collaboration with Michael Goodman. — Atlanta : Nexus Press, 1979. (see OCLC #11336265)

We're trying to decide if this is a score or a book. The "Directions for use" state: "This book contains 15 leaves of different materials including the printed leaves. These leaves, plus the covers, can be played in different ways by: striking, scraping, rubbing, engraving, crumpling, tearing, breaking, snapping, etc. All this can be done by or with hands, using sticks, drum brush and each and every kind of instrument/tool normally used for percussion or any kind of utensils such as hammers, scissors, whatever. . . ." The directions go on to describe the chance nature of the performance. The leaves include corrugated cardboard, aluminum foil, wire mesh, sandpaper, bubble wrap, and the like. Given my background, I'm inclined to treat this as a score, even though there is no musical notation. However, I could be talked into calling this a book. If we catalog this as a book, is it appropriate to use musical score subject headings, such as "Percussion music" or "Chance compositions"?

Answer: This is probably one of those items that could go either way. Since its intention is clearly score-like, though, my inclination aligns with yours to treat it as a score. Many scores consist entirely of performance instructions without a note of traditional notation or even a jot of graphic notation. This one happens to be both the score and the instrument.

On the other hand, a strong argument can be made for treating it as an artist's book. Because of their nature however, I tend to think of these more as sculptures (Type "r", Type Material "a", "c", or "r", depending upon that nature) than as books, per se. Even that could be argued. We have here a case where seeming duplicates may have to be tolerated because the ambiguity of actual things does not always fit neatly into the categories we've devised.

You may use the existing book record, create a score record, or create an AV record. Where's format integration when you need it? That doesn't really clarify anything, but I hope it helps. *Newsletter 56* (*December 1993*)

9.32 QUESTION: I'm cataloging an LP called *Shakespeare's people*, an original cast recording that consists of scenes from his plays with some Morley/Arne and other settings of his songs thrown in. How do I code the Type in the fixed field? Is it a musical recording because it contains some songs, no matter how few, or is it a nonmusical recording, because it's mostly dialogue?

Answer: By various analogies, I would lean toward considering this a nonmusical recording. Recordings of plays with incidental music are considered nonmusical; though this is a collection of scenes, the bibliographic point is similar. And when we look at music instructional materials, we consider the proportion of music to nonmusic, so it also seems appropriate here. *Newsletter 54 (May 1993)*

9.33 QUESTION: If you have a book and a floppy disk, should they be cataloged as a book with accompanying computer file or as a computer file with accompanying book?

Answer: That would depend upon which item is predominant. In many cases the choice is obvious. Catalog a disk with an accompanying manual (one that explains how to use the software and is clearly dependent on the software for its very existence) as a computer file with accompanying matter. If the disk merely contains illustrations or examples, for instance, consider it subordinate to the book and catalog it as a book with accompanying disk. For cases in between, try to determine which is the more important element and use your judgment. *Newsletter 47 (April 1991)*

CHAPTER 10
OCLC Services

INTRODUCTION

Over the decades at OCLC, technology has evolved, services have come and gone, access methods have changed, indexes have expanded, displays have improved. Questions abound concerning searching, the input of certain characters, what is indexed and what is not. Cooperative programs such as OCLC's Enhance, record-editing capabilities such as Database Enrichment and Minimal-Level Upgrade, and the reporting of duplicates and other errors raise perennial questions.

CATALOGING SERVICES

10.1 QUESTION: I'm cataloging a CD of the Faroese band Spaelimenninir; it will be a new record in OCLC. The title is one word and contains an "eth," a special character that I think occurs only in Faroese and Icelandic. We can input it OK, but are wondering about searching for others who may want to find this record by title. A derived-title search will work since the "eth" is the seventh letter, but the search will be "3,,," since the title is only one word. No one will find it by keyword or title browse since the special character cannot be input in the search. We've looked in the *Diacritics and Special Characters* manual and in the LCRIs to find if there is an equivalent character(s) that we could put in a 246, but found no help. My gut says make a 246 substituting a "d" (since the "eth" kind of looks like a "d") and another 246 substituting a "th" (since I think the "eth" became a "th" in English). But that's just my gut. Any ideas?

Answer: According to OCLC's *Searching for Bibliographic Records* (http://www.oclc.org/worldcat/searching/guide/), here's how the "eth" should be treated in various search situations. In derived searches, substitute "d" (Section 4.2, p. 4:5); in title phrases scan searches, substitute "d" (Section 6, p. 6:6); in keyword searches, substitute "d" (Section 7, p. 7:11). Guidance for alternative title treatments in field 246 is provided in LCRI 21.30J, but there appears to be no specific provision for characters such as the "eth" that can be represented by the ALA Character Set. That suggests to me that no alternative 246 fields are needed when such characters are present. *Newsletter 78 (May 2001)*

10.2 QUESTION: It's often difficult to find OCLC documentation on the OCLC Web site. Can you help?

Answer: The central place to bookmark for online versions of OCLC documentation is http://www2.oclc.org/connexion/documentation/. It has links to *Bibliographic Formats and Standards*, *Searching for Bibliographic Records*, *OCLC Cataloging Service Users Guide*, *Authorities User Guide*, all the recent Technical Bulletins, all of the online Enhance documentation, and many of the other most useful items. *Newsletter 75 (May 2000)*

10.3 QUESTION: Are there any plans to add more searching modifiers to represent new material formats? For example:

/dvd DVD videos
/cdr CD-ROM
/vhs VHS video
/cds Sound CD
/cas Sound cassette

I work with Special Format acquisitions, and an expanded set of search modifiers would help my work greatly.

Answer: As far as I am aware, there are no plans to expand the list of search modifiers. The format modifiers are at the bibliographic format level (BKS, REC, COM, VIS, SCO, MIX, SER, MAP), a level at which they are always coded and fairly reliable. Any sort of more specific qualifier would tend to be considerably less reliable, especially in excluding items that one would want to be included in a search. In most of the cases suggested, a theoretical qualifier would have to rely on coded information in the 007 field, a field that is optional in K-Level records and not always accurate even when coded. There are large numbers of records that were created before specific codes were validated for particular formats or sizes (for instance, there is no valid code that currently differentiates DVDs from other videodiscs). What might be just as useful to the questioner in many cases is to simply use key-word searching to act as a pseudo-qualifier, although even this would not be completely reliable. Adding a keyword search element for the Notes fields (for instance, "nt dvd" or "nt vhs") would catch records in which the speci-fied designation appears in a 5XX field. Again, this won't be foolproof (for instance, many videorecording records have the video format incorrectly in the 300 field rather than in the notes) and isn't terribly useful for things such as audiocassettes that don't have any distinctive indication in notes. *Newsletter 72 (May 1999)*

10.4 QUESTION: Sorry that I haven't attempted to look up the search documentation on this, but I've been noticing that the presence of a "u" anywhere in the fixed field date seems to require that a search qualified by date must be qualified with "????". Take 97-703945 (#37491825), one ex-ample of gazillions. The fixed field date is "195u", but when I try to retrieve that record with a search key qualified by "195?", the search is unsuccess-ful. Now consider #3030895, the same (?) recording on Columbia, done with the old practice (DtSt:q; Dates 1950, 1959), which is retrievable with date qualifiers "1950" or "195?", of course. Isn't this a giant step backwards? Needless to say, I've been using "u" for as long as it's been authorized, but why hasn't the search program been reconfigured to accommodate this change in coding practice? Am I missing something here, or is this a real problem?

Answer: Yes, a "u" in the Fixed Field Date 1 will mean that the system will not index any date at all as a qualifier for that item. (There are further details and special circumstances in *Searching for Bibliographic Records* p. 7:8 and p. 10:3–10:4; the document is also online at http://www.oclc.org/oclc/man/9798sbr/frtoc.htm.) When you qualify a derived or keyword search by a date with a question mark (for instance, "/195?"), you will retrieve the full range of numerals from 0 to 9 substituting for the question mark, but not records coded "195u". This is hardly an ideal situation, as we all recog-nize, but really, it's just an extension of the "No Date" dichotomy that ex-isted long before we could use the "u" character. All pre-AACR2 records that had no date ("[n.d.]") have always been gathered into the "No Date" category in group displays. Ever since AACR2 required that some guess be made on at least the century, the divergent practices have made for split search results. The change in USMARC coding practice (going from "1950, 1959" to "195u" for the designation "[195–?]") has meant that more records go into the "No Date" category. Before we were generally able to use the "u" in all formats, the Serials format had it and the qualifier worked the same way. I'm honestly not sure if this quirk is a legacy of its serials cata-loging heritage (my colleague Robert Bremer doesn't think so), some sort of technical limitation, or what. As long as one is aware of this particular trouble spot, one should (usually) be able to fashion searches that take it into consideration. *Newsletter 72 (May 1999)*

10.5 QUESTION: I seem to recall an instruction, somewhere in OCLC documentation, not to input the special characters "æ" and "œ" (and their uppercase equivalents) as they occur in many European languages, collapsed into a single character to show that they're a diphthong. I know that one must *search* those characters as separate "oe", and so forth, but I also thought that we were not supposed to input the characters, despite their presence in the MARC character set and the capability of OCLC terminals of doing so for years now. Am I mistaken on this? The presence of a large number of bibliographic records input by Enhance libraries where the special characters were avoided (perhaps only out of local systems considerations) is another factor making me think that I did actually see this instruction somewhere, but the existence of LC Name Authority Records *with* the characters in both names and uniform titles militates against it. Thanks for anything you can tell me about this

Answer: The ligatures "æ", "Æ", "œ", and "Œ" are legitimate characters in the OCLC character set (see *Diacritics and Special Characters*, 2nd ed., pp. 21–22). AACR2 chimes in on the issue, though, in LCRI 1.0E under "Pre-Modern Forms of Letters":

> In general transcribe letters as they appear in the source. However, convert earlier forms of letters and earlier forms of diacritical marks into their modern form, as specified herein. Separate ligatures that are occasional stylistic usages (Œdipus, alumnæ, etc.) rather than standard usages in the modern orthography of the language, e.g., œ in French (as in œuvre) or æ in Danish (as in særtryk). If there is any doubt as to the correct conversion of elements to modern forms, transcribe them from the source as exactly as possible.

So it sounds like you use the ligatures when the modern language calls for it and separate them when it's just a matter of style. *Newsletter 66 (May 1997)*

10.6 QUESTION: My recollection was that you couldn't qualify Music Publisher Number searches by format. Is that still true?

Answer: We've both been laboring under an illusion, or at least some outdated information. Looking at the old First System searching guide, I find that search qualifiers could then be used only with title, name/title, personal name, and corporate name searches. Now, however, all searches except the OCLC Number search may be qualified. For search key searches (including the "mn:" search), you can qualify by format, dates, microform, and/or cataloging source. For keyword searches, only the format and dates qualifiers apply. More details can be found in *Searching for Bibliographic Records*,

p. 3:10–3:12 and in Chapter 5 on qualifying searches. *Newsletter 66* (*May 1997*)

10.7 QUESTION: The new manual *Searching for Bibliographic Records* looks good, with some minor problems that I've found so far. In the section "Numeric Searching," p. 3:10–3:12 on the "mn:" search, you keep referring to it as the MPN, Music Publisher Number; but since Format Integration Phase 1, the 028 field (and so also the "mn:" search) index contains both Music Publisher Numbers *and* videorecording numbers. So it is a little misleading to continue to refer to the "mn:" search as a "Music Publisher Number" search, and also to say, as the manual does on p. 3:10, that it covers only numbers for scores and sound recordings. One more quibble on MPN: You've included the standard, up to two letters, up to 10 numbers search key formula, but in reality, "mn:" searches can be input with all letters and all numbers, no spaces even without using the "exact form" structure. This isn't in the manual anywhere and should be.

Answer: Right you are. The 028 field was renamed "Publisher Number" during Format Integration. The field (and the "mn:" search) now includes videorecording numbers for visual materials as well as plate and publisher numbers for printed music, and serial and matrix numbers for sound recordings. The "mn:" search continues to index only 028 $a and 262 $c. You are also correct about the ability to input complete publisher numbers without regard to the two-alphabetic and 10-numeric indexing limits. Putting in the complete number won't change your search results, though. Corrections and clarifications will be made in the next revision of the new manual. *Newsletter 66* (*May 1997*)

10.8 QUESTION: Although I like the new display format of individual authority records in PRISM, I find the undifferentiated listings produced by some subject authority search keys to be frustrating. As one example, I was looking for the heading "Dance-orchestra music" and had to page through more than four screens to find it. When I got to it, there were eight identical-looking entries for the heading. Is there a way around this?

Answer: Development is even now underway to solve this authority searching glitch as well as a number of other longer-standing authority search problems. In a future authority search enhancement, you will be able to search for headings in the authority file as exact phrases, with the addition of right truncation of phrases. For example, the derived search key for "Dance-orchestra music" is "[dance,mus" but the future capability will allow you to search:

scan su dance orchestra music

The new indexes will allow users to find a desired heading with precision and efficiency and will allow the scanning of headings in alphabetical proximity, much as PRISM's title scan index now allows. As an additional feature, the future indexing will also group together headings that are used as related terms in other records, thus isolating "Dance-orchestra music" as an authorized heading from the same heading used as a related/broader term.

These new authority searching capabilities, which will effectively eliminate the 600-record limit that now plagues a number of composer searches, are among the Post-Release I PRISM features currently being developed. Though it's too early to talk about a specific timetable, this will be one of the first PRISM enhancements to be rolled out.

In the meantime, some hints about these blindingly unhelpful displays are in order. The authorized heading usually sorts first in a list of look-alike truncated entries, with the remaining headings as the broader/related references in alphabetical order. However, what you might want to do is set up a function key (see Chapter 11 of the *Passport Software User Guide*, 2nd ed.) "dis all br". When you get one of these displays, enter this command and PRISM will display all those entries in brief form, which is much more useful (see *Authorities User Guide*, pp. 51–53 for details on brief and truncated authority displays). *Newsletter 48 (August 1991)*

10.9 QUESTION: Getting around in truncated displays in the PRISM Service doesn't seem to be as easy as it was in the First System. Do you have to go linearly through such a display, screen by screen, or are there other options?

Answer: Pages 51–52 of the Prism Service *Guide to Searching the Online Union Catalog* outline the options. Instead of "paging" through a truncated list, you could use the forward or backward commands with numbers to specify how far forward or backward in a list you need to go. Using the search heading to determine how many records have been retrieved, enter *for [n]* or *bac [n]* to move "n" entries up or down from the middle entry in the current display. The commands "home" or "hom" will take you to the start of your currently displayed truncated list; "end" will take you to the end. *Newsletter 47 (April 1991)*

PASSPORT

10.10 QUESTION: In Passport for Windows, cut-and-paste doesn't seem to work the way it used to in Passport for DOS. What happened?

Answer: The cut-and-paste capabilities of Passport for Windows really are comparable to those in Passport for DOS, but they are a bit different. In

DOS, one could use function keys to cut (F6) and paste (F7), and a whole series of ALT sequences for copying and pasting blocks. The function keys no longer work in Windows. You can still use the "ctx" and "pst" commands in Windows, however. Replacing the old DOS function keys are the Windows toolbar buttons for cutting (the scissors), copying (the two overlapping sheets of paper), and pasting (the sheet of paper on the clipboard). You can still use ALT sequences to copy (ALT-B) and paste (ALT-G) text you've high-lighted with your mouse. The toolbar buttons and ALT sequences also work in combination with each other. Although things are a bit different under Passport for Windows, these new methods are at least as efficient as the old capabilities. Try experimenting with various combinations to determine what works best for you in different situations. *Newsletter 65 (November 1996)*

10.11 QUESTION: We are using Passport for Windows and have some questions about the ALA character set. There are four diacritics in the ALA set that appear twice, once with a space and once without a space [grave, tilde, circumflex and underscore]. I cannot find anything in the PRISM Service *Diacritics and Special Characters*, 2nd ed. about a difference and we are wondering which ones we should be using. Can you tell us what the difference is?

   Answer (courtesy of OCLC's Rich Greene): You must use only the non-spacing diacritics. The spacing diacritics, while valid in Passport for Windows, are not valid in PRISM. If you input one of them, you will receive an error message. The non-spacing diacritics, as well as a few other characters such as musical sharp, have been approved for addition to the character set used in USMARC records but have not yet been implemented by LC, OCLC, and RLIN. The characters were added to align the USMARC character set with ASCII and ANSEL, the two predominant characters sets used in the United States by most software and hardware. They were added to Passport for Windows in anticipation of the future capability. As of now, there are no immediate plans to implement the characters. The differences are primarily in appearance in printed products and display. The non-spacing character prints in the same space as the character it precedes; so, if you have a non-spacing tilde, it prints over the character it precedes, such as an "ñ" in Spanish. The spacing tilde, on the other hand, gets its own space and prints as a separate item, so you'd have the printed sequence "~n" instead. There is little use in bibliographic records for the spacing characters, with the ex-ception of the spacing underscore. If it were implemented, it could be used for electronic addresses in field 856. For example, one of my email addresses is "richard_greene@oclc.org"; this is a spacing underscore and is a separate character. If I were to use a non-spacing underscore instead, the email sys-tem would not recognize the address. *Newsletter 64 (August 1996)*

10.12 QUESTION: Passport for Windows was loaded on my machine while I was away in Seattle, and in my recent explorations of it, I noticed that the ALA character set now includes the musical sharp symbol, distinct from the old pound sign (<shift>3) that we have been using for years. May we assume from its presence in the character set that it is valid for use in bibliographic and authority records now in the OLUC? If so, is OCLC planning a batch job to convert all occurrences of the pound sign in music uniform titles (and possibly other fields, such as call number tags) to the musical sharp symbol?

Answer: Although the musical sharp sign does appear in the ALA character set of Passport for Windows, if you inserted it into a record, you would find it was not valid. The character has not been validated by anyone yet, as far as we know, and there are no current plans to do so. As you can easily imagine, there is no foolproof way to distinguish every existing use of the pound sign that should be a musical sharp. Any future effort to do some sort of conversion would be far from trivial. We recommend that you continue using the pound sign until we let you know that the sharp has been validated. *Newsletter 63 (May 1996)*

AUTHORITY FILE

10.13 QUESTION: We all know, I guess, that the omission of initial articles from German titles produces odd results, but is it correct to omit "Des" or "Der" when it means "of"? For instance, in *Des Knaben Wunderhorn*, I believe the title literally translates as: *The magic horn OF the youth*, right? In nr94021148, *Rose Pilgerfahrt* is given a reference from *Der Rose Pilgerfahrt*, and I have found other examples of this, which seems to be having it both ways. By scanning "Der" and especially "Des" in the NAF, there are numerous cases in which these articles are filing elements. (I won't list any—you can see for yourself.) Despite all too many years of German in college, I still have a lot of trouble with it. This question has probably been asked before, but perhaps the issue needs to be raised again.

Answer: The dropping of initial articles in titles where those articles may be grammatically meaningful has been a source of irritation for many of us. It happens not only in German, but also in Hebrew and several other languages (arguably even in English, where the article "a" can sometimes be read as "one"). The practice is dictated, of course, by AACR2 (25.2C1, in particular) and by the MARC 21 Appendix F list of "Initial Definite and Indefinite Articles." Although I've not checked every authority record that comes up in a title search beginning with "der" or "des", I think that you'll find a good many of them to be cross-references from unauthorized forms of the heading or uniform title (no95046879, for example), or titles in a language other than German (the French title in n93097334, for instance). In some cases (*Knaben Wunderhorn* n81078991 being the most obvious example), the heading cross-reference *with* the article is coded as an "earlier established form." Of course, some of the authority records may simply be incorrect under current practice. MARC 21 does offer one way around the troublesome dilemma. Include an entry in field 246 or 740 (depending on the circumstance) that files on the article, as an alternative. Not perfect, but it will give that grammatically correct access. As far as I'm concerned, these English-centric violations of non-English grammar rank up there with the authority file's "living dead" (such as "Bernstein, Leonard, $d 1918–" n50007704 as an open entry even though we know he died in 1990) as catalogers' embarrassing crosses to bear. They make us look ignorant. But them's the rules, sad as they may be. *Newsletter 79 (November 2001)*

10.14 QUESTION: Looking in a recent *Music Cataloging Bulletin*, I noticed a new pair of subject headings for "Cristal" and "Cristal music." Since I had never heard of such an instrument, I decided to look it up in the Marcuse and *New Grove* dictionaries of musical instruments, but couldn't find anything. The 670 field in the authority record for "Cristal" in OCLC (sh92004693) listed the work cataloged as K. Smith's *Concerto for cristal four-hands and orchestra*, c1992. The text of the 675 field is as follows: "Marcuse; $a New Grove dict. of mus. inst." So I went back to Marcuse and NGDMI Still nothing. What's the point of listing Marcuse and NGDMI in the authority record if nothing appears in them? Or if something does, why not a page reference in the authority record?

Answer: Field 675 in authority records is for "Source data *not* found" (emphasis mine), that is, reference sources that provided *no* information about the heading. That doesn't help you identify what "cristal" is, but it does tell you where others have already looked and failed to find anything, theoretically saving you the trouble of doing the same. *Newsletter 55 (August 1993)*

10.15 QUESTION: How would you search Bo Diddley in the OCLC authority file? I tried "bo,did," "bo,," "bo d,," "bod,," without success.

Answer: Mr. Diddley's name can be searched in a number of ways especially if you happen to know his real name(s). But knowing only "Bo Diddley" and not knowing if the name is entered directly or in inverted form, I'd try "didd,bo," first; that search would access no91015859. The other key would be "bodi,," which considers the name in direct order as a "forename only" name to be searched as a single word. See the middle of page 43 in the PRISM *Authorities User Guide* for further details. *Newsletter 50 (May 1992)*

10.16 QUESTION: Why does the search "[walt,wil,]" *not* bring up the William Walton name-only authority record?

Answer: That search should bring up the record in question. Remember that entries in authority truncated displays sort kind of funny: Names in the form of "Surname, Forename, date" (Walton, William, $d 1902–) file at the end of any list that includes entries with the same name plus middle names or initials. If you are searching on the First System, depending upon the type of monitor you have, that final line of text may appear below the ordinary display. Try the search again, then go down to the bottom of the screen plus another line and see if the entry you're looking for isn't there. *Newsletter 47 (April 1991)*

ENHANCE AND DATABASE ENRICHMENT

10.17 QUESTION: Shouldn't we encourage the NACO-Music Project members to apply for OCLC Enhance?

Answer: Taking the list of NACO-Music Project participants from the *MOUG Newsletter* no. 72 (current through March 31, 1999), I found that of the 50 institutions listed, 28 were already Enhance participants in at least one bibliographic format. In a few cases, subdivisions of institutions that have different NUC symbols but the same OCLC symbol, can also be counted among Enhance participants, bringing the total to an even 30, which is 3/5ths. Because NMP extends beyond just OCLC, of course, some of those NMP libraries are not OCLC members or don't do cataloging online with OCLC, so they would have no use for Enhance capabilities. The doors are always open for new Enhance applications. *Newsletter 75 (May 2000)*

10.18 QUESTION: Is there such a thing as PCC Full records (not Core) for Scores, Sound Recordings, and AV? Can one have National Enhance status for PCC without OCLC Enhance status?

Answer: There theoretically exist both PCC Core and PCC Full records for Books, Scores, Sound Recordings, and Computer Files, but there are currently no National Level Enhance authorizations for Visual Materials format. OCLC grants National Level Enhance authorizations only to institutions that have had BIBCO training from LC or its PCC representatives *and* who have passed the Enhance evaluation process, either as part of a previous Regular Enhance application or (if the institution was not currently a Regular Enhance participant) specifically as part of the National Level Enhance application. *Newsletter 75 (May 2000)*

10.19 QUESTION: We are contemplating a digital library project that will involve digitizing about 70 published items of various formats (sheet music, books, government documents) that relate to the assassination, funeral, and burial of Abraham Lincoln. We are wondering if for those items that already have records in OCLC if we can add an 856 field that indicates an electronic address for an online version of the item. Our serials department says that they do that for serials.

Answer: Sounds like a wonderful idea to me. The current version of LC's *Guidelines for the Use of Field 856* (revised August 1997) is available at http://www.loc.gov/marc/856guide.html. OCLC's own *Cataloging Electronic Resources: OCLC-MARC Coding Guidelines* (http://www.oclc.org/connexion/documentation/type.htm) should also be consulted. OCLC has also recently implemented the latest changes to the 856 field that are outlined in the introductory paragraphs of the LC *Guidelines* (the first indicator values blank and "4" and the second indicator), although LC and others may not have. Revisions have been made to OCLC's electronic documentation and the changes are outlined in both OCLC System News and in the March 1998 issue of *Bits & Pieces* available on the OCLC Web site (for which I do not have an address at this writing). The second edition of Nancy Olson's *Cataloging Internet Resources* (http://www.oclc.org/oclc/man/9256cat/toc.htm or http://www.purl.org/oclc/cataloging-internet) is now available and should also be consulted. *Newsletter 69 (April 1998)*

10.20 QUESTION: Can Full-level libraries lock and replace to enrich CIP records with call numbers and/or subject headings (e.g., for fiction) at the same time that we fill in the 300 field, or is filling in the 300 the only thing we can do with CIP if we're not an Enhance library? I find there is a lot of confusion over CIP issues in general in the cataloging world.

Answer: Any Full-mode or higher authorization can lock and replace a CIP record to add a 300 field, a 505 contents note, and/or call numbers and subject headings in authorized schemes not already present on the record. This information and more details may be found in *Cataloging User Guide*, 2nd edition, p. 6:6–6:8. Regular Enhance authorizations may additionally make changes or additions to most other parts of the CIP record except the Encoding Level 8 itself. A National Level Enhance authorization can also change the Encoding Level. *Newsletter 67 (August 1997)*

10.21 QUESTION: I've been replacing OCLC master records by using the lock command, adding an LC-type call number of my own devising (class portion from the LC schedules) and then sending the replace command. It just occurred to me that maybe I don't really know what I'm doing. Am I on the right track or should I desist?

Answer: If the record to which you are adding a call number does not already have one in that scheme, what you are doing is called a Database

Enrichment and your library is getting a credit for it (see the PRISM *Cataloging User Guide*, p. 6:6–6:7). Your network can tell you how much the credit is worth. *Newsletter 58 (August 1994)*

DUPLICATE RECORDS

10.22 QUESTION: When duplicate records are reported to OCLC, how does OCLC determine the "preferred" record? We've been doing a lot of cataloging of standard repertoire on CDs lately and have run into a lot of duplicates, which we have duly reported. We always state a preferred record and list the others as dups; but sometimes it's hard to decide: I like this part of record #1, but record #2 has contents note. Or, record #1 is really great except the cataloger forgot to put in a 007, while the others all have a 007. I know that when records are merged, access points from each are kept, but how about other parts of the record? I guess my behind-the-scenes question really is: Does it matter which record we give as the "preferred" one? Or will OCLC decide and we can stop thinking about it?

  Answer: Although I cannot speak for everyone who does merges here at OCLC, the general policy is to retain the most complete record, the one to which we have to do or add the least. I always try to transfer manually any important unique information that will not automatically transfer, and I hope I have trained others doing music duplicates to do the same. There is a list of more than two dozen fields that will transfer from a deleted record if not present on the retained record (007, 010, 020, 024, 028, 033, 037, 041, 043, 045, 047, 048, 050/090, 082/092, 300/305, 306, 505, 520, 538, among others). Some users will also write little notes about what they want transferred, and I certainly consider those suggestions. OCLC has always said that records will be merged at our discretion, so you really needn't worry too much about telling us which record you prefer; in most cases, we tend to agree with users' suggestions, anyway. *Newsletter 62 (November 1995)*

INTER-LIBRARY LOAN

10.23 QUESTION: Lately, I've noticed that our OCLC symbol has been displaying on holdings screens of OCLC records in lowercase. Why is that?

  Answer: Check out Technical Bulletin no. 198. In PRISM, location records now distinguish between ILL suppliers (UPPERCASE SYMBOLS) and nonsuppliers (lowercase symbols). Your institution is profiled as an ILL nonsupplier. *Newsletter 54 (May 1993)*

Bibliography

Although in many cases, earlier editions of works are cited in the text, only the most current versions are listed in this bibliography. See the list of Acronyms, Abbreviations, and Other Cryptic Designations for references from superseded documents.

Anglo-American Cataloguing Rules: Prepared under the Direction of the Joint Steering Committee for the Revision of AACR. 2nd ed., 2002 revision. Ottawa: Canadian Library Association; Chicago: American Library Association, 2002 (with updates).

Hartsock, Ralph. *Notes for Music Catalogers: Examples Illustrating AACR2 in the Online Bibliographic Record.* Lake Crystal, Minn.: Soldier Creek Press, 1994.

Hemmasi, Harriette. *Music Subject Headings: Compiled from Library of Congress Subject Headings.* 2nd ed. Lake Crystal, Minn.: Soldier Creek Press, 1998.

Library of Congress. Automated Systems Office. *Descriptive Tabulation: Library of Congress MUMS Format Data: MUMS Music Records.* Washington, D.C.: Library of Congress, 1987.

———. Cataloging Distribution Service. *Library of Congress Rule Interpretations.* 2nd ed. Washington, D.C.: Cataloging Distribution Service, Library of Congress, 1989 (with updates).

———. Cataloging Policy and Support Office. *Subject Cataloging Manual: Subject Headings.* 5th ed. Washington, D.C.: Cataloging Distribution Service, Library of Congress, 1996 (with updates).

———. *Music Cataloging Decisions.* Washington, D.C.: Library of Congress, 1981 (with updates).

———. Network Development and MARC Standards Office. *MARC 21 Format for Bibliographic Data: Including Guidelines for Content Designation.* Washington, D.C.: Library of Congress, 1999 (with updates).

———. Processing Services. *Cataloging Service Bulletin.* 1978–.

————. Special Materials Cataloging Division. *Music and Sound Recordings Online Manual.* Compiled by Richard H. Hunter. Washington, D.C.: Library of Congress, 1999 (with updates).

Music Cataloging Bulletin. 1970–.

Music Library Association. Working Group on Bibliographic Control of Music Video Material. *Cataloging Musical Moving Image Material: A Guide to the Bibliographic Control of Videorecordings and Films of Musical Performances and Other Music-Related Moving Image Material with Examples in MARC Format.* Edited by Lowell E. Ashley. Canton, Mass.: Music Library Association, 1996.

————. Working Group on Types of Compositions. *Types of Compositions for Use in Music Uniform Titles: A Manual for Use with AACR2 Chapter 25.* 2nd, updated ed. [S.l.: s.n.], 1997. Available: http://www.library.yale.edu/cataloging/music/types.htm. (Accessed July 21, 2003.)

Music OCLC Users Group. *MOUG Newsletter.* 1977–.

The New Grove Dictionary of Jazz. 2nd ed. Edited by Barry Kernfeld. London: Macmillan, 2001.

The New Grove Dictionary of Music and Musicians. 2nd ed. Edited by Stanley Sadie and John Tyrrell. London: Macmillan, 2001.

The New Harvard Dictionary of Music. Edited by Don Michael Randel. Cambridge, Mass.: Belknap Press of Harvard University Press, 1986.

OCLC. *Bibliographic Formats and Standards.* 3rd ed. Dublin, Ohio: OCLC, 2002 (with updates). Available: http://www.oclc.org/bibformats/en/. (Accessed July 21, 2003.)

————. *OCLC Cataloging Service User Guide.* 3rd ed. Dublin, Ohio: OCLC, 2000. Available: http://www.oclc.org/connexion/documentation/guide/. (Accessed July 21, 2003.)

————. *Searching WorldCat User Guide.* Dublin, Ohio: OCLC, 2003 (with updates). Available: http://www.oclc.org/worldcat/searching/guide/. (Accessed July 21, 2003.)

Olson, Nancy B. *Audiovisual Material Glossary.* Dublin, Ohio: OCLC Online Computer Library Center, 1988.

Online Audiovisual Catalogers. *OLAC Newsletter.* 1981–.

Saye, Jerry D., and Sherry L. Vellucci. *Notes in the Catalog Record: Based on AACR2 and LC Rule Interpretations.* Chicago: American Library Association, 1989.

Smiraglia, Richard P. *Describing Music Materials: A Manual for Descriptive Cataloging of Printed and Recorded Music, Music Videos, and Archival Music Collections for Use with AACR2 and APPM.* 3rd ed., rev. and enl. with the assistance of Taras Pavlovsky. Lake Crystal, Minn.: Soldier Creek Press, 1997.

————. *Music Cataloging: The Bibliographic Control of Printed and Recorded Music in Libraries.* Englewood, Colo.: Libraries Unlimited, 1989.

Thorin, Suzanne E., and Carole Franklin Vidali. *The Acquisition and Cataloging of Music and Sound Recordings: A Glossary.* S.l.: Music Library Association, 1984.

Weitz, Jay. *Music Coding and Tagging: MARC 21 Content Designation for Scores and Sound Recordings.* 2nd ed. Belle Plaine, Minn.: Soldier Creek Press, 2001.

Indexes

TOPICAL INDEX BY QUESTION NUMBER

AACR2 RULE, LCRI, AND
MCD INDEX BY QUESTION NUMBER

OCLC-MARC FIELD INDEX BY QUESTION NUMBER

About the Author and Editor

JAY WEITZ is a consulting database specialist at OCLC, Online Computer Library Center, Dublin, Ohio. Formerly a music cataloger at Capital University, he received his B.A. in English from the University of Pennsylvania, M.L.S. from Rutgers University, and M.A. in Education from Ohio State University. He serves as OCLC Liaison to the Music OCLC Users group, and has participated in many other standards and professional cataloging committees. He compiles the Q & A column for the *MOUG Newsletter*. He is the author of *Music Codingand Tagging: MARC 21 Content Designation for Scores and Sound Recording,* Second Edition (2001).

MATTHEW SHEEHY is currently the Assistant Head of Access/Collection Services and the Performing Arts Bibliographer at Rutgers, The State University of New Jersey. He holds a B.M. in music composition from the University of Hartford/Hartt School of Music and an M.A. in music history and an M.L.S. from the University of Buffalo.